# SWAS..... IN THE ARCTIC

# SWASTIKAS
## IN THE
# ARCTIC

## U-BOAT ALLEY THROUGH
## THE FROZEN HELL

### JAK P. MALLMANN SHOWELL

FONTHILL

U44 in cold home waters.

*Frontispiece:* U457 (Korvkpt. Karl Brandenburg) with the partly extended attack periscope in the foreground. The man on the upper deck appears to be making his way to the external heads at the rear of the boat.

Fonthill Media Limited
Fonthill Media LLC
www.fonthillmedia.com
office@fonthillmedia.com

First published in the United Kingdom and the United States of America 2014

ISBN 978-1-78155-292-6

Typeset in 10.5/13 Sabon
Printed in England

# Contents

# Acknowledgements

There were so many diverse and abundant German military activities in the Arctic during the Second World War that it is difficult to include all in a single volume. So this book has become a potpourri to cover the wide variety of military operations with only one or two examples of each type. The Arctic was, and still is, a great enigma. Masses of unused documents occupy shelf space in various archives, meaning there is still ample room for more research. Some of the stories that emerged out of those desolate cold wastes are certainly fascinating beyond belief and people would label them as absurd and far-fetched if they had been written in a novel.

My interest in these Arctic happenings was aroused while still a child, when I was old enough to appreciate that my father, (Dieselobermaschinist of U377), had contributed to some major exploratory activities in those cold waters. The subject never became an obsession because early on during my first serious studies I met Franz Selinger, who has got to be 'the' leading authority on German military activities in the Arctic. He was kind enough to not only invite me to his home, but also to allow me access to his marvellous study filled with historic gems, and he more than satisfied my curiosity by providing already distilled information from his own research. This made it unnecessary to dive deep into the piles of raw documents. Franz Selinger was a good friend and a brilliant teacher who was always happy to share his discoveries, and he took great pains to explain aspects that were difficult to understand; the sort of special chap you don't meet very often.

Information for this book has also come from Kpt.z.S. a.D. Otto Köhler, the first commander of U377 and members of the crew who were not on board for the boat's last fateful voyage. Karl-Heinz Nitschke, Ernst-August Gerke, Hermann Patzke, 'Wilhelm' Böhm, Hans Staus, Josef Fürlinger, Werner Berns, Franz Albert, Fritz Beske and Siebrand Voss all supplied information and I am most grateful for their help. Eva Julius kindly helped with information about her husband Gerhard, who served aboard auxiliary cruiser *Komet* and I am also grateful for material from Hans Karl Hemmer, the youngest officer aboard auxiliary cruisers. He had originally set out with *Pinguin* and was in command of the captured whale hunter *Adjutant* when *Pinguin* was sunk. Following this he met up with *Komet*, to return home with her. Knut Sivertsen of Trondheim and Ivar Berntsen helped with information about the German Navy in Norway and I am also grateful to Michael and Brenda Lyons and Sharon Lyons-Pumfrey for their help.

During my early research I was also helped by Harry Hutson and Charles Walker; and Edward Rumpf from Bricktown in USA provided details from logs at a time when these were still classified in Great Britain. I am also grateful to the Scott Polar Research Institute in Cambridge for helping with reprints from various technical journals, for Christiana Ritter for help in finding her book and information about her husband, who served with my father in the Arctic, and Klaus Sommermeyer who served with the weather corps. These people made many early steps of long ago possible.

More recent research has been much easier inasmuch that there are vast piles of documents in the German U-boat Museum (www.dubm.de) and I am grateful to Horst Bredow for guiding me through his vast collection. The individual authors of these largely unpublished papers have been mentioned in the text and I am exceedingly grateful that so many people who have taken the time to illuminate what went on during those turbulent years of the Second World War. Much of the material compiled by Franz Selinger has now also found its way into the German U-boat Museum, and this has become a major source for information about military activities in the Arctic.

Nearer home, the Russian Arctic Convoys Museum at Aultbea on the shores of Loch Ewe (Scotland) has been exceedingly helpful. I am especially grateful to Jacky Brookes who did so much for so many to establish this project among the ranks of the juggernauts and I must thank all the veterans of the Arctic campaign who attended the reunions at Loch Ewe and talked so freely about their experiences. Much of what they said has been incorporated into this text. The people living around Loch Ewe who have helped to make the Arctic reunions such a success must also be thanked, for without their unflagging support it would be difficult to tackle projects like this book. (www.russianarcticconvoymuseum.co.uk)

# 1

# The Arctic Arena

Germany shared a frontier with Russia until the end of the First World War when the victorious Allies hived off large areas of the two nations and of the Austro-Hungarian Empire to create the new countries of Poland and Czechoslovakia. Despite their closeness as neighbours, the relationship between Germany and Russia had always been remote, with vast tracks of sparsely inhabited country separating the two. The barrier created by that vast emptiness was strengthened after the First World War when the newly created Poland and Czechoslovakia formed an additional insulation between Germany and Russia. The non-aggression pact, that was signed between Germany and Russia on 24 August 1939—just a few days before the outbreak of the war—did not bring the two countries closer together, instead it widened the gulf because the German government prohibited its intelligence services from spying on Russia. This prohibition was to such an extent that they were not allowed to eavesdrop on its military radio frequencies, and as a result, Germany was unaware of what was happening on other side of the frontier at the critical time, when the Russians started assembling a powerful force with its guns pointing to the west. The discovery of this military build-up then led to the invasion of the Soviet Union (Operation *Barbarossa*) on 22 June 1941, with the hope of nipping this powerful offensive in the bud before it was ready to strike. Later, during the initial stages of *Barbarossa*, Germany found that the arms being built up for an invasion of the west contained a fair proportion of recent British and American weapons.

Although Britain was further away from the Soviet Union than Germany, it would appear that diplomatic relations were closer. This can be illustrated by one of the biggest anomalies of the Second World War. We are told that Britain declared war on Germany because of its invasion of Poland, but we are less often reminded that the Soviet Union invaded Poland from the other side, and yet Britain did not declare war on Russia.

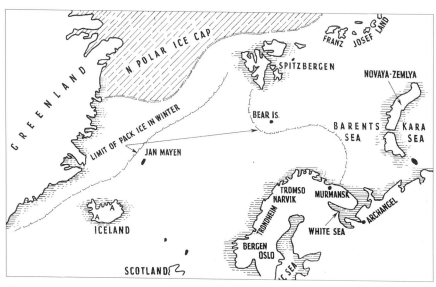

The Arctic Seas have two distinctly different characteristics. For several months of winter it never gets light during the day and the frozen ice cap creeps a long way south, preventing ships from crossing the waters. That ice recedes in summer, when the sun never sets for several months, the so-called midnight sun. Although the summer may be more hospitable for humans, there is no way that modern technology has ever managed to dominate any of the natural elements that rule the Arctic. Even the huge modern atomic-powered icebreakers have to work with, rather than against the natural elements. This map shows that while the Russian Arctic Convoys could sail under cover of constant darkness during the winter, they also had to come dangerously close to German bases in Norway. Unfortunately no map will ever show the power of the harsh Arctic weather that dominates and tortures all activities in the northern seas.

France and Britain had been negotiating an alliance with Russia right up to mid-August 1939. When the military talks began in mid-August, negotiations quickly stalled over the topic of Soviet troop passage through Poland if the Germans attacked, and the parties waited as British and French officials pressured Polish officials to agree to such terms. However, Polish officials refused to allow Soviet troops onto Polish territory because they believed that once the Red Army entered their territory it might never leave. The Soviets suggested that Poland's wishes be ignored and that the tripartite agreements be concluded despite its objections. The British refused to do so because they believed that such a move would push Poland into establishing stronger bilateral relations with Germany. The reaction of France and Britain to the Soviet invasion and annexation of Eastern Poland was muted, since neither country wanted a confrontation with the Soviet Union at that time. Under the terms of the Polish-British Common Defence Pact of 25 August 1939, the British had promised assistance if a European power attacked Poland. A secret protocol of the pact, however, specified that the European power referred to Germany. When Polish Ambassador Edward Raczyński reminded Foreign Secretary Edward Frederick Lindley Wood of the pact, he was bluntly told that it was Britain's business whether to declare war on the Soviet Union. Neville Chamberlain considered making a public commitment to restore the Polish state but in the end issued only general condemnations. This stance represented Britain's attempt to balance its security interests including trade with the Soviets which would support its war effort, and the possibility of a future Anglo-Soviet alliance against Germany. Public opinion in Britain was divided between expressions of outrage at the invasion and a perception that Soviet claims to the region were reasonable.

Throughout the 1930s there had been growing concern within the British Establishment about the Russian menace; not such much Soviet Union itself, but the influence of Soviet-styled communism among a disgruntled working class seeking to improve its lot. In the mid-1930s the concern about a potential revolution by lefties was a topic of much discussion in the fashionable Mayfair salons. Following Operation *Barbarossa*, Britain found a way to overcome the communist fears and embrace a new ally on the basis of 'my enemy's enemy is my friend', and Winston Churchill put himself at the forefront of embracing Russia, a complete *volte-face* of his stance just a few years earlier. Churchill now determined to help the Soviets as much as possible by the supply of war materials.

The outbreak of the Second World War on 3 September 1939 cut Britain's direct passage to the Soviet Union via the Baltic and left only two practical routes open. The shortest of these was the sea voyage to Murmansk or Archangel. The problem with the latter was that its location on the eastern side of the White Sea froze solid for five months during the winter. The other way of going to Russia, avoiding the dangerous Mediterranean, involved sailing around South Africa to the Persian Gulf and then continuing for more than a thousand miles by rail from Basra via Tehran to southern Russia. The first obvious problem with this route was that even when having the reached the relative safety of Russia, one still had to travel for more than another thousand miles before reaching Moscow. Yet, despite its length and many obstacles, it remained the safest route to make contact with Russia and was used right up to the end of the war. There was considerably more paperwork with necessary visas and permission to travel, but it did assure a relatively safe passage.

At the beginning of the war an embargo on food reaching Iran from India was lifted and every effort was made to improve relations so that the Iranian leadership would not only allow the free movement of goods along the railway line, but also assure its safe passage. This was vitally important; otherwise too many troops would have been required to

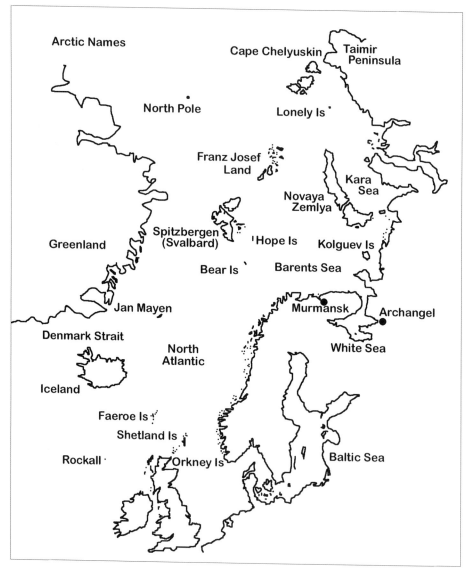

Arctic names are a mishmash from several languages, which has resulted in a wide variation of spellings and to make matters worse many of the places do not feature in the majority of atlases. So finding them can be quite some problem. However, it is necessary to know only a few of the main locations and this map will hopefully locate the basic names for navigating through this book.

protect the line and the trains running along it. Though Iran was officially neutral, its monarch Rezā Shāh was friendly toward Germany and was deposed and replaced with his young son Mohammad Reza Pahlavi. The Allied invasion of Iran was undertaken by Soviet, British and other Commonwealth armed forces from 25 August to 17 September 1941, and was codenamed Operation *Countenance*. The purpose was to secure Iranian oil fields and to consolidate Allied supply lines.

By the end of 1941, after both Russia and the United States had joined in the war against Germany, the British Government set itself three important objectives: 1: To prevent Japanese and German forces from meeting in the Indian Ocean, 2: to slow down and then stop the Japanese advance on Australia and India and 3: to keep the Soviet Union in the war at all cost.

The conflict between the USSR and Germany was so important to Britain that determined diplomatic advances were made to prevent Stalin from concluding a separate peace with Germany, should such an opportunity arise.

Notwithstanding these supply solutions with Iran, the Cape and Middle Eastern route was too long and much too strained to carry more than people and essential supplies, and the majority of war goods had to be transported along the northern seas to Murmansk or Archangel. As a consequence, this route became a most important link in the Allied war plan.

The commencement of the British shipping convoys rang alarm bells in Berlin, and Hitler had convinced himself that an Allied invasion of northern Europe was imminent.

Germany had invaded and occupied Denmark and Norway under Operation *Weserübung* which began on 9 April 1940. In response Britain and France had landed troops in the north of Norway at Narvik commencing on 15 April, but the force was too small and too late and finally withdrew on 31 May 1940. Notwithstanding the failed Franco-British action, by late 1941 Hitler had a hunch that a second attempt would be made in that region, and the seeds for this came from decrypted radio signals where Stalin was urging his western partners to start another front in the north. Britain kept rejecting such suggestions, saying an attack on Germany's west and the north could not mounted until 1943 at the earliest.

The outcome of this hunch was for Hitler to send the battleship *Tirpitz* to Trondheim during the middle of January 1942, and he ordered three other heavy units, the battleships *Gneisenau* and *Scharnhorst* and heavy cruiser *Prinz Eugen* to be moved from Brest in France, to be ready to repel an Allied attack on Norway. This resulted in the famous 'Channel Dash' of February 1942. Of course, these heavy units were supported by masses of smaller ships and Grand Admiral Erich Raeder, Supreme Commander-in-Chief of the Navy, succeeded in getting Hitler to also order a significant number of aircraft to the north. As a result torpedo bombers arrived in

Norway became a major hub of the Second World War, with both sides making a considerable effort to control its heavily incised coastline. Whilst German forces occupied the country in April 1940, there were some incredibly difficult areas that were fought over with a great loss of life. This shows U405 under Kptlt. Rolf-Heinrich Hopman touring one of the ships that was sunk earlier during the Battle of Narvik. The rod on the left is an extendible radio aerial and on the right is the attack periscope with the small head lens. The spiralling wires have been attached to help water wash past it without leaving too much of a wake.

When the Germans arrived in the Narvik area of Norway they found other foreign nationals already there manning the defences. These two crosses mark the graves of two soldiers from the French Foreign Legion. The one on the left states merely 'Jenesse' while the one on the right says Legionnaire Auxentiades, who was killed on 28 May 1940, more than a month after the start of the German occupation.

northern Norway at about the same time as Britain was starting to run the Arctic convoys. This mishmash of activity was made worse for the Allies because both of the main Russian ports were within range of the new German bases in northern Norway and the area became one of the most heavily contested of the whole war. When calculating the number of bombs dropped per head of population, these isolated Arctic outposts rank among the highest of the war.

The German heavy warships stationed in northern Norway became one of Britain's biggest problems, although, in the end, it was the dominant combination of aircraft and U-boats that decimated the convoys. Attacks by aircraft were a significant problem for Britain throughout 1942 when the Luftwaffe inflicted serious casualties. Yet despite these successes there were also long periods of inactivity with no shipping in the Arctic seas when the majority of the aircraft were moved to the Mediterranean by the end of the year. This gave Britain a substantial breathing space to strengthen its defences and to be ready for another onslaught if and when they returned. Anti-aircraft armament of both escorts and merchant ships was improved and escort carriers were later deployed to provide effective air cover for the convoys. What was more, after 1942 there were no further daylight convoys in the Arctic seas, making air attacks considerably more difficult.

From the British perspective, a number of dramatic events in other theatres of war made a significant impact on Arctic activities. First and most important was the sinking of the battleships *Prince of Wales* and *Repulse* in the South China Sea on 10 December 1941. This was the first time that two massive capital ships had been destroyed by air power alone without help from naval units, and that swift action made Admiral Sir John Tovey (Commander-in-Chief of the British Home Fleet) most unwilling to send his large ships to the Norwegian Seas, where there was high risk of suffering a similar fate. The other critical point was that High Frequency Direction Finders had made their first sea trials around the same time as Germany invaded the Soviet Union, and by that time radar sets had already become an operational tool for convoy escorts. U-boats maintained radio silence for much of the time they were searching for convoys, but sent of a large number of signals when they went in to attack one. By the time Russian Arctic convoys starting making their regular appearance, it was possible for both merchant ships and convoy escorts to determine the direction from which an attack was coming from and then dispatch an escort with radar to force the intruder under. Asdic was then used to locate the submerged U-boat for a depth charge attack. Radar alone was largely responsible for preventing many surface attacks at night by being able to 'see' submarines as they closed in.

Before the introduction of radar, each U-boat at sea was sinking up to about six ships per month, but with the benefit of radar this figure dropped to not more than two—and was often much less. As a result Britain was fairly confident that it could keep merchant ship losses from Arctic convoys in reasonable proportions and the losses would be no more in the Arctic than in other areas of operation.

According to British figures from 1954, and to put the Arctic convoys into perspective, 811 ships left for Russia and 720 of these completed their voyages; 33 turned back due to some problems and 58 were sunk. For the return leg, 717 ships left Russia and 29 of these were sunk. A total of 829 officers and men lost their lives. The Royal Navy (including the Polish submarine P511) lost 1,815 men protecting the merchant ships. In return the German battleship *Scharnhorst* and some 38 U-boats were sunk in the Arctic, making that theatre of war considerably more than a mere sideshow to the Atlantic. In addition to these heavy losses both sides had to endure extreme weather conditions that strained both men and machinery beyond imaginable limits. Gales of incredible violence often raged while men struggled to keep their ships from being sunk by the force of weather alone. This severity can perhaps be judged from the sinking of the converted whaler HMS *Shera*, a boat that had been built especially for the Arctic that capsized in the Barents Sea due to ice having collected on its superstructure.

The oldest of the Russian convoy destinations was Archangel which had already been known to the Vikings back in the Dark Ages, and which in its later history developed into a major port. The river Dvina, on which it stands, is about as big as the Rhine, and its rain catchment area is vast, yet despite this huge size, the rain that falls on the Russian capital is far enough away not to drain into this river system. Taking advantage of its remote situation, Archangel's inhabitants refused to recognise communist rule until several years after the Bolshevik revolution, when the churches of the city were destroyed on Stalin's orders. By that time the port was well beyond the end of its useful life as it was closed by thick ice for five months of the year. To overcome the problem of Archangel's winter closures during the First World War blockades, a new port was built in an ice free zone, and in consequence Murmansk became Russia's newest city.

The Russians were not the first to reach this rather practical spot some ten kilometres inland along the Kola River that changes its name to Tuloma further inland. The reason the settlement is so far from the open sea is that the coastal strip is dominated by glacier-formed bare rocks interlaced by masses of smaller lakes where there is insufficient land between the water for the building of any substantial towns. Those settlements that are there, such as Polyarny and Severomorsk, are naval bases that do not rely on natural features for their survival. In many ways this new city was even more detached from Russia's industrial centres than Archangel and a new railway spur had to be built for the Moscow–Leningrad–Archangel railway line of 1915.

A German grave photographed near
Narvik during the war. It reads, '3.5.40
Ltnt. Kordes, ObJäg. Bürger, MO Gefr.
Zende, MGefr. Arndt.'

Germany pitched highly qualified mountain troops into the Narvik area during the
invasion of Norway and these specialists returned for Operation *Barbarossa*, the
invasion of Russia with a view of heading east to capture the Arctic ports and the railway
line connecting them with the industrial centres further south. Bitter fighting ensued, but
the Germans never made much headway against the Russian Defences. The British side
brought several thousand mules with Indian keepers to the north of Scotland, where they
lived by the shores of Loch Ewe and trained in the Cairngorm Mountains. So, it would
seem likely that at one time Britain also had aspirations in northern Norway, where the
country is similar to where these mules and troops were stationed.

It is highly likely that this photo was taken in Narvik, early during the war and it acts as a reminder that much of the Arctic strip saw the bitterest of fighting with shelling from heavy guns and bombs from aircraft playing a major role.

The modern motorway running from Moscow, to the north with a poignant reminder that the distances are immense. The names on the road sign are: Yaroslavl 179, Vologda 394 and Archangel 1169 kilometres. During the Second World War this route would have been partly unsurfaced and progress along it would have been exceedingly slow.

The old core of Murmansk was made up largely of traditional wooden houses with ample insulation to make them comfortable during the cold winters and to keep out flying insects during the summer. The inside walls of these often did not reach all the way up to the ceiling so that a single oven in the centre, usually tiled and profusely decorated, could keep the entire building warm. With carpets on the walls, these were comfortable as well as practical. After the First World War, when expansion was accelerated by the central government, huge blocks of flats were built. These were destroyed by German bombing, and incendiaries burnt the old wooden houses. As a result, much of the town had been destroyed by the time the first of the Arctic Convoys reached it. The battles that raged in this area have hardly been described in English language books although they were more severe than other better-known actions. The Germans made a determined effort to capture Leningrad and the connections to the north coast, and it was only the constant and strong Soviet opposition that prevented them from achieving their objective.

Although the ports of Archangel and Murmansk feature strongly in the Arctic convoy war, one must not assume that their facilities were anywhere near what was found in Britain or other central European countries, and a report from the Senior British Naval Officer often referred to facilities having been dilapidated and the authorities not always helpful. Despite the Murmansk waters being free of ice throughout the winter, the land was still dominated by the severe Arctic climate and the railway line that served the port was often blocked by snow. The vastness of this problem can really only be appreciated by visiting it. One spends hour after hour travelling through thickly wooded but otherwise uninhabited country that is constantly at the mercy of incredible natural elements. This problem could also be seen in the port itself where loads of stores were unloaded and then covered by so much snow that they could not be reached again. There were incidents where ships arrived to find the goods they had delivered during the previous voyage were still lying near the berths.

The other Russian Arctic settlement that featured strongly in wartime records is Port Dikson, named after the Swedish explorer Oskar Dikson and guarded by an island with the same name. It was founded in 1915, at around the same time as Murmansk, and became a major base for Kara Sea Naval Activities after 1942, but it is not included in many atlases. It lies just over at 80 degrees east on the north coast and this longitude may be easier to find than the name. Although it is not necessary to mention many other towns, it is important to remember that there were a large number of isolated radio and weather stations along the north Russian coast and on many of the Arctic islands. In themselves they might not have been very significant, but they did help in providing important data to create the overall picture of what was happening with the natural elements—such as weather and ice—and without them it would have far more difficult to have run many of the convoys.

Russian motorways were not built until long after the war and roads of the 1940s were something to behold. In winter they were blocked by snow and once this thawed they turned into slushy mud tracks. This shows a road near Moscow that the local traffic did not have a great deal of trouble to negotiate. Yet the average driver from Western Europe would be horrified if he had to cope with such precarious terrain. Some of the people driving along here did not even have four-by-fours and were driving ordinary Russian cars.

The Russians do not seem to be blessed with the many health and safety issues that dominate the western world and there is plenty of evidence that they are geniuses at improvisation; as can be seen here with these temporary repairs over a bridge.

Old traditional Russian houses were made from timber with small windows for keeping out the cold in winter and masses of flying insects in summer. These logs had probably grown close-by and although the older houses might look primitive from the outside and lack paint, living in them can be rather comfortable. The problem that occurred in many of the Arctic settlements was that the resin rich pine logs burned exceedingly well once they were bombed with incendiaries, making it easy to wipe out entire settlements with little effort.

An old Russian house photographed recently. During the Second World War era it would also have had a wooden roof, showing how easy it was to set on fire with incendiaries.

The Barents Sea can be taken to be an extension of the North Atlantic, with its northern limits being defined most definitely by pack ice. This frozen desert creeps southwards to encase Bear Island during the winter and recedes further north and east during the summer. Knowing the exact limits of the ice was always an important part of the North Russian convoy operations and considerable efforts from both sides went into reconnaissance to gain this information. In summer the Barents Sea is bounded in the east by a massive set of islands, of which Novaya Zemlya is by far the biggest. Although largely uninhabited during the Second World War, this land chain blocks off the warm water from the south that helps to keep large parts of the Barents ice free during the winter. Therefore the conditions encountered in the Kara Sea, to the east, are notably different to the waters to the west of Novaya Zemlya and much of the Kara Sea remains frozen for nine months of each year. The coastal waters, especially sheltered bays without strong currents, tend to act as a backwater where ice collects even during the summer, making navigation through it unpredictable, difficult and dangerous. The other problem with many of the eastern coastal waters is that vast river systems empty into them, diluting the salty seawater. U-boats discovered this to their cost by diving and then finding that they had glided into a more saline area where the boat rose on its own accord, at times without the crew even being aware of the fact that they had surfaced. On the other hand, these stark differences in salinity and temperature were excellent at deceiving Asdic impulses by deflecting sound. This meant it was possible for a submarine to hide among the various layers without a hunter with an efficient Asdic (Sonar) set being able to locate it.

Anyone wanting to study the military activity in the Arctic will very quickly get lost in multitude of names, each with a variety of spellings and hardly any marked on a British atlas. In view of this, this book has avoided the vast majority names given in logbooks. U-boat commanders often had the use of large-scale charts which are difficult to find these days.

# 2

# *Komet*, the Siberian Marathon and the First Excursion into Arctic Waters

Auxiliary cruiser *Komet*'s voyage along the Siberian Sea Passage was not only a momentous event of the Second World War, but it is also one of the longest and almost forgotten milestones of modern marine exploration. The fact that the Northeast Passage exists was not proven until 1878–1879, when the Swedish explorer Nils Nordenskjöld sailed along it for the first time. This was such a hazardous undertaking that his ship, the *Vega*, remained locked in the ice for a complete winter and he needed two summer seasons to complete the voyage.

Sixty years later, in 1939, when Kapitän zur See Robert Eyssen first approached the Supreme Naval Command to suggest using this route to get an auxiliary cruiser into the Pacific Ocean, he was told in no uncertain terms that this was more than a ludicrous idea. Naval officers should concentrate on reality without coming up with harebrained schemes that were bound to end in disaster. The icebreaker *Sibiriakoff* may have been the first ship to travel the entire distance in one season during 1932, but despite Russian exploration of that area, there was no hard and fast evidence to suggest any other ship had ever attempted the feat. A non-Russian ship had certainly never travelled all the way along the Siberian Seaway and a German disguised freighter was likely to get stuck in the ice, be damaged beyond repair or just vanish into the vast Arctic emptiness. There was no way the admirals would agree to such an absurd suggestion.

Robert Eyssen was a complicated mixture of complexes that needed to keep enforcing his superiority on those around him. Men who worked with him described him as difficult and perhaps it was just this trait that prevented Eyssen from accepting the Naval High Command's decision. When he first made this suggestion, he was Head of the Military Department within the Supreme Naval Command and therefore came into frequent contact with the Supreme Commander-in-Chief, Grand Admiral Erich Raeder. Eyssen also had official reasons for calling on Raeder as

The raider *Komet* loading in Germany before starting its epic voyage along the Siberian Seaway. Raiders or disguised merchant ships with impressive guns were also called Ghost Cruisers or Auxiliary Cruisers. Their main objective was to tie up enemy forces to hunt them rather than to sink a lot of ships.

part of his daily duties and had no qualms about outlining his proposals personally to Raeder. The trick worked; Raeder was most enthusiastic, and two months after the start of the war Eyssen was given permission to prepare for his outlined mission. This presented no great problems towards the end of October 1939 because a large number of merchant ships were lying idle due to the war, and the building yards had not yet been geared to full war production. Therefore converting one more freighter into an auxiliary cruiser did not present too many significant sacrifices.

Eyssen had far more in him that might be imagined at first glance and his background was far from conventional. He spent much of his early life in Guatemala where his parents owned a coffee plantation, and after joining the navy he was dropped into a world where compromises and improvisation rather than official rules became part of everyday life. Eyssen joined the navy in 1911, one year after the U-boat Chief Karl Dönitz, and was aboard the legendary light cruiser *Karlsruhe*, based at the German East American Naval Station, when the First World War broke out. *Karlsruhe* then hunted some seventeen ships before she was finally sunk by HMS *Bristol* in West Indian waters not long after the outbreak of war. Eyssen escaped and returned to Germany aboard the blockade breaker *Rio Negro* to serve in torpedo boats and minesweepers before joining the new U-boat Arm. After the war he became first officer and then commander of the survey ship *Meteor*, with which he explored both the Atlantic and Arctic. This background gave him enough experience to appreciate the great contribution made by auxiliary cruisers and he had seen enough ice to know what was required to get through it.

Naval mobilisation plans for converting freighters into auxiliary cruisers demanded large ships of at least 4,000 GRT and as first choice bigger vessels of over 7,000 GRT should be used. These needed to sit comfortably deep in the water to remain stable in the wildest of weathers. Eyssen knew he wanted the exact opposite. His ship had to be small with the shallowest possible draught to twist through the most confined spaces between ice floes. He was fully aware that Russian shipping supplying the northern outposts was made up of sea-going river barges and freighters with flat bottoms and little draught. This was essential because the huge Siberian rivers carry vast quantities of alluvium to the Polar Seas and the main shipping routes there cross extremely shallow water. *Komet* actually found herself several times in positions where there was less than a metre of water below the keel. Enough information had also leaked out for the Germans to know that although Russia had been making concerted efforts to develop its Arctic coast, there had also been considerable drawbacks, some ending in tragic disasters. Despite several centuries of Polar exploration, it seemed as if no one knew exactly which were the best routes and no one could predict the movement of the ice. So, in many ways Eyssen was groping in the dark, without any firm convictions that this escapade could come off. Raeder was most impressed by the fact that Eyssen had not underestimated this difficulty and his plans included the possibility of remaining locked in the ice for a complete winter. Eyssen had even considered schemes for evacuating the entire crew if a dire emergency demanded it.

He found just the right characteristics in the dormant 3,287 GRT freighter *Ems* with a draught of only 3.5 metres. Belonging to the North German Lloyd of Bremen, she was quickly requisitioned and converted at Howaldtswerke in Hamburg, close to Deutsche Werft where she had originally been built. Besides having hidden guns installed, the hull was strengthened three times its original thickness. In addition to this, the frames of the bows were further braced by placing oak logs across the hull from one side to the other and an especially strong ice cutting propeller with a reinforced rudder were added for good measure. Just in case there were any problems with the screw, Eyssen ordered two so that he could take a spare if the ice proved too much of a challenge. The fact that *Komet* became the first non-Russian ship to sail along the Northeast or Siberian Sea Passage proves that this foresight and the preparations were correct.

Yet, when this conversion work was in progress there were no guarantees of success and the bureaucratic naval procedures were threatening to curtail the venture before it started. Whilst the normal breakout route through the Denmark Strait between Iceland and Greenland was open for much of the year, the Siberian Sea was blocked with so much ice that it was only possible to get through between July and September. This meant that the slow progress with *Komet* during the early summer of 1940 was threatening to prevent the ship from using his route until after the thaw of the following spring. 'Thaw' is really the wrong word. The Siberian Sea Passage remained covered in ice all the year round and even in summer there were huge areas of solid ice. Getting the ship ready in time meant

Raider *Komet* in the Pacific or Indian Ocean disguised as a Japanese freighter. Sailing around the ship and photographing it from every angle was an important part of checking that the disguise was perfect. Changes of identity had to be made by some raiders for half a dozen or more times.

everything had to take place at the double and Eyssen set about travelling to suppliers, to get deliveries of what he needed before he was defeated by the weather. This paid good dividends with independent suppliers but not with the Supreme Naval Command. Eyssen noted in his diary that not much was achieved by going to headquarters in Berlin. Despite not having had time for extensive trials, Eyssen knew that he had enough on board to deal with this before tackling enemy forces in Far Eastern waters. There was enough time to test the machinery in the Baltic but not enough to fully train the crew. Every day Eyssen saw the enthusiasm with which the men tackled their challenges and he felt confident that they would be fully operational by the time they have to face determined opposition.

The biggest stumbling block was not so much the crew but naval representatives in Moscow. The naval attaché there, Kpt.z.S. Norbert von Baumbach, had worked tirelessly to first get Russian approval for the scheme. Then he needed cooperation from local pilots and guarantees that the Soviet Union would supply the necessary icebreakers to get *Komet* to the Bering Strait. This in itself was a major achievement because the route was not only uncharted as far as visible obstacles were concerned, but there were also bound to be a vast number of submerged obstructions. Therefore local pilots were going to be an essential part of the equation. It

With ice being hard enough to destroy propellers *Komet* took a spare in case the Siberian Seaway proved too much of a challenge.

is interesting to note that *Komet* had been converted in such a manner that these guests never discovered the hidden guns and were not aware that they were aboard a heavily armed merchant raider.

Finally, at 22.30 hours of 4 July 1940, after everything that could be done had been done, *Komet* anchored at Point Red in the Baltic, to meet her escorts for the first stage of the voyage. These consisted of a Sperrbrecher, a converted merchant ship for detonating mines, and two of the new types of minesweepers (M17 and M18) to provide mainly anti-submarine support. Coincidentally, M18 was commanded by a Kptlt. Otto Köhler, who later became commander of U377, which installed both manned and unmanned weather stations on Spitzbergen. The following day, when *Komet* weighed anchor again, it was not long before Eyssen discovered that the essential Sperrbrecher sailing ahead could not reach speeds higher than nine knots. This was too slow for meeting the approved timetable, but there was nothing that could be done and the ships chugged on under close air cover until they received a warning that an enemy submarine had been sighted ahead of them.

A fresh but damp breeze, veering from SSW to NNW and blowing over a calm sea, assured that much of the water was covered with a distinct haze, making life rather uncomfortable for any large man-of-war. A small submarine and enemy aircraft on the horizon had the distinct advantage of being able to hide in this murk, while the considerably higher superstructure stood out like a blatantly rude advert. The eyes in the sky could easily have spotted *Komet*'s wake and passed those details on to the submerged menace. The officers on the bridge were still digesting this threat when another radio report came in of four enemy destroyers near the Norwegian coast. Not long after that came a third sighting of a British cruiser. This brought the undertaking to a halt and made *Komet* turn to head back into the comparative safety of the Baltic, but Eyssen could not find anywhere to hide. He was indeed in a most unenviable position, at the western end of a narrow channel through a German minefield. Deviating too far on either side could end in disaster. Luckily the navigation officer, very much against orders, had pencilled the German minefields onto his chart; otherwise such a move would have been more than suicidal. These defensive areas were considered to have been so secret that they were not to be marked on any chart that might be captured by the enemy. So the men were indeed in luck that they could avoid what looked like a very much superior force of enemy firepower.

Robert Eyssen, wrote in his diary that he and his men had come to a rude awakening. So far progress had been only hard work. Now, suddenly, a multitude of dangers around them made them vividly aware that there was also a war. The journey continued northwards, but not as it had been planned. The tanker *Esso*, that was due to have accompanied *Komet*, ran aground so hard in Norway that its tanks were seriously damaged. Not being able to delay the voyage due to having to negotiate the Siberian Sea Way between July and September, the Supreme Naval Command decided that *Komet* should go on alone and another Japan-based tanker would be made available once she reached the Pacific Ocean. Yet *Esso* was carrying 400 tons of fuel and 200 tons of fresh water for *Komet* and Eyssen was eager to get his hands on at least some of those valuable liquids. Going alongside in the safety of a fjord near Bergen, made it possible to transfer some of this cargo. The oil was pumped into large barrels and stored on the deck, helping to make *Komet* look like an overloaded merchant ship.

The problem with this entry in *Komet*'s log is that it has been impossible to find a ship with the name 'Esso.' The Esso fleet consisted of at least 31 ships, all with another name after 'Esso.' Two of these, *Esso Hamburg* and

*Above left:* Raiders like *Komet* had to remain at sea for as long as possible, to tie up enemy forces and therefore had to be topped up by provisions from their victims or from specially prepared supply ships. The canisters on the deck in the foreground look like metal tins for storing large calibre ammunition, so, at a guess this photo was taken when *Komet* met one of its supply ships on the high seas.

*Above right:* Escorting *Komet* though Norwegian waters. M17 photographed from M18 while making heavy going of rough seas as the three ships headed north, to get beyond the reach of British submarines.

*Esso Colon,* served as German supply tankers during the war, but so far it has not been possible to positively identify the ship which was due to have accompanied auxiliary cruiser *Komet.* Bearing in mind that it must have had its hull strengthened in a similar manner to *Komet,* one would have thought that it is relatively easy to trace, but so far the name has remained mysteriously illusive.

*Komet* was then disguised as the Russian freighter *Dejnew* and the men were told for the first time about their voyage through the Siberian Seaway. They knew from the conversion and from the stores that they were destined for cold areas, but thought they would break out into the Atlantic through the Denmark Strait between Iceland and Greenland and then head towards the South Pole.

The journey continued at neck-breaking speeds until Eyssen realised the engines were literally shaking his ship to pieces and he slowed down to somewhere in region of six knots. The old freighter *Ems* achieved a top speed of about sixteen knots, but the added weight of the ice protection belt had reduced this to no more than fourteen. Even then, the engines seemed to be struggling with the extra weight. The weather and the going were good and on 15 July 1940 Eyssen found himself so far east that he thought it unlikely for the opposition to come looking for him.

Yet, Eyssen was surprised to discover that these desolate Russian seas carried enough shipping to be worrying. Karl August Balser, the ship's Artillery Officer, explained that in addition to a multitude of fishing boats, they knew about colliers running between Spitzbergen and Russia and since it was essential to avoid being seen, *Komet* turned away from even slight traces of smoke, long before the ships themselves would have come into sight. Surprisingly, since this consumed considerable quantities of fuel, Eyssen decided it would be better to find a good anchorage while waiting for permission from the Russians to continue. Since time immemorial sailors had been using both the depth of water and the type of seabed as a means of navigating, and *Komet* even carried charts showing this type of information. So, it was easy to find locations over large beds of sharp rocks that would tear nets to shreds and were therefore avoided by fishermen. Despite this precaution, while at anchor in the Barents Sea, the lookouts kept reporting smoke and this together with the anchor not holding terribly well induced Eyssen to move still further east.

While *Komet* was waiting for instructions to meet a Russian icebreaker, the men were kept busy making a multitude of modifications, training with their weapons, trying out their seaplane and launching the small motor torpedo boat that they had stowed in one of their holds. They also changed the disguise to make the ship look like the German freighter *Donau.* In their spare time they were encouraged to fish. This was an ideal

Before the Siberian Sea Passage. *Komet*'s supply tanker was damaged by grounding in Norway and therefore the raider took on board a number of metal drums containing fuel oil. These were stored on the open deck until there was room in the bunkers. After leaving German waters the ship was disguised to look like a Russian freighter until it arrived in the Barents Sea, where *Komet* was made to look like a German merchant ship again. The star, hammer and sickle of the Russian disguise is visible in the foreground.

*Komet* in the Kara Sea after having negotiated the Matochkin Strait between the north and south islands of Novaya Zemlya. Since it was necessary to wait for a Russian icebreaker, the men were given permission to explore the hills of these desolate islands. Climbing down to a cutter for taking the men ashore.

activity to keep idle hands occupied and helped to add splendid fresh cod to the menu. The snag was that the season was known for not being good for fish in this area and pre-war deep-sea trawlers avoided going there during the summer months. The sea currents from the east were strong enough to bring a constant stream of timber past the ship and after a while the men took to also fishing this out of the water. *Komet* had not brought a great deal because the space had been so limited in Germany, but now where things had been sorted better; the officers thought this welcome gift might come in handy for shoring any damage in the future.

The annoying point about *Komet*'s hiding place was that those irritating smoke clouds continued to appear beyond the horizon. So far ship superstructures had not come into sight, but at the back of everybody's mind was the unsettling thought that a ship might accidentally burst upon *Komet*, perhaps during thick fog, and broadcast its discovery for the enemy to hear. Eyssen had no choice other than keep moving further away from the sporadic traffic. The news that the heavy cruiser *Admiral Hipper* was due to operate off the North Cape of Norway caused enough mild alarm for *Komet* to move still further east, to assure there was no way that she would become an accidental target for *Hipper*'s large guns. After all, these had a considerably longer range than lookouts could see and it could be mistaken for an Allied ship. At first everything that could be tested or drilled was worked to the

Robert Eyssen, the commander of the auxiliary cruiser *Komet*, having a close look at something during turbulent seas.

point where actions became automatic and then there followed a distinct lull after the storm, where the lack of progress was becoming most unsettling. Something had to be done to prevent the morale from sinking into an inactive ebb. This situation of finding work for idle hands was made worse by the radio news that *Komet* had been allocated a place in the second caravan of the season. This name had been adopted by the Russians because several merchant ships would sail in single file behind an icebreaker, a like a camel in the desert being tied to the rear of the one in front.

Not having that much to do, the engineer officer, Kptlt. (Ing.) of the Reserve, Ernst Alms, started experimenting with his machinery, hoping to find ways of using less fuel. This resulted in such a drastic drop of temperatures inside the ship that electric heaters had to be brought into service to prevent serious complaints. These trials were well worth it because by coupling machinery into combinations that had not been recommended before, it was eventually possible to maintain previous temperatures and, at the same time, save about one ton of fuel per day. The ship's medical officer, Dr Jürgen Hartmann passed some of the time by operating on his second acute appendicitis since leaving Germany.

*Komet* had dropped anchor in the Arctic for the first time during the middle of July and it was now going into the second week of August, without any news of that all-important rendezvous with the Russians. Despite the good results with the machinery the news from outside was not encouraging. On 8 August, when *Komet* anchored for the 12th time in the Barents Sea (this time at 69° 36′ N 57° 07′ E) there came the disappointing information that the ice conditions along the Siberian Seaway were considerably worse than in previous years and the departure of the second caravan would be delayed. Two days later came another demoralising whammy. The first caravan was stuck in the ice and the second one would therefore remain in port for the foreseeable future. The Russians living in the Arctic had got used to patience, something that was starting to wear exceedingly thin inside *Komet*. Three days later, on 13 August, while *Komet* was lying at anchor in her 13th location, at 02.30 in the morning came the instruction from the Supreme Naval Command in Berlin to make immediately for Matochkin Strait to meet icebreaker *Lenin*. The route through this 100 kilometre long channel had been considered before, but it still presented a considerable headache. It was known to be only 600 metres wide at its narrowest, with intimidatingly high mountains on both sides. Separating the north island of Novaya Zemlya from the south island, it connects the Barents Sea with the Kara Sea and provided *Komet* with a route far away from other commercial traffic.

The weather was nowhere near ideal when Eyssen ordered the anchor to be weighed immediately. So far everything the north could throw at the ship had come past; brilliant blue sky with an astonishing midnight sun and gales of Force 8 with almost nil visibility. Rain had fallen and snow had swept past the bridge. Now it was a case of keeping extra lookouts on the open decks for chugging through an unpleasant white pea soup. 330 nautical miles lay ahead and everybody breathed a deep sigh of relief when the visibility improved to a reasonable 10 to 20 miles. At first there was nothing but rocky desolation in sight and it was not until *Komet* had entered the strait that lookouts spotted signs of human habitation, with a few ships lying nearby. Sending over their Russian interpreter, Herr Kröpsch, the men in *Komet* discovered that the icebreaker *Lenin* had moved on a few days ago, but left two pilots to help them through the narrow channel.

The Germans quickly learned that ice pilots were of a special breed that was not the easiest to deal with. Instead of quietly obeying their orders, they spent a considerable time interrogating the officers, demanding to know a vast heap of highly technical information about the ship. At first Eyssen thought that this part of a putting-off manoeuvre by the Russians, but later he discovered that ice pilots do not like the idea of joining a ship that cannot physically get through. Having convinced themselves that their new charge had the necessary strength, they agreed to press on through the incredibly narrow channel to reach the open Kara Sea. As it happened the passage was so well marked that the Germans could easily have negotiated it without the pilots, and the four and a half hours of gliding past the most incredible mountainous scenery went without a hitch with the most brilliant weather. This continued for some time while *Komet* continued on into the Kara Sea.

So far there had been no sign of ice, but suddenly, not too far from Novaya Zemlya the men found themselves confronted with a solid barrier. Eyssen headed north, thinking that he might find a way through there, but no luck. *Komet* may have been strengthened to deal with heavy ice, but there was no way she could cut her own way through a thick solid sheet. Icebreakers had the advantage in having gently sloping bows that could ride up on top of the ice and then the weight of the ship would break through any solid mass. It was obvious that *Komet* could not continue on her own, so Eyssen ordered a return to a bay by the Matochkin Strait where he anchored to await the icebreaker. Since there were no indications of one arriving during the immediate future, he gave permission for the crew to go on land in two turns. The first party built a small pier so that men could step in and out of their cutters without getting their feet wet by landing on the small beach. This construction project was made possible by the presence of vast quantities of driftwood that had been washed up ashore. The majority of men took the opportunity of going on land to climb up the steepest and

*Above and below:* The Russia icebreaker *Kaganovich* seen from *Komet* with 8 Ball or eight tenths ice cover on the sea, enough to be worrying.

highest mountain. In the end the men's patience wore a little thin and they established their own radio contact with Russian stations, without waiting for instructions via the Supreme Naval Command in Berlin. This resulted in permission to proceed east through the Kara Sea.

Progress was possible because a southerly wind was blowing much of ice away from the land, but it was not long before *Komet* chugged through a tumbling sea of white blotches with three-to-six-tenth ice cover. It looked impressive more than terrifying and men at first stared at it in amazement rather than fear. Eyssen did not hesitate; the ship pressed on regardless. This at least proved that the protection belt worked exceedingly well and the engineers who had helped to convert *Ems* as auxiliary cruiser had done work their well. The noise made by shoving ice floes aside was something the majority of men had not experienced before; it was considerably more than terrifying and much louder than an orchestra warming up. It reached a pitch where men inside the hull complained of aching ears. Yet, despite the punishment, the ship could cope well and even winds of Force ten were still classed as tolerable because the ship had a predictable and almost comfortable pitch as it rode on through the real Arctic sea. The ice had got considerably thinner since the first attempt to cut through it and Eyssen discovered that he could make best progress by trimming his ship stern-heavy so that the bows were raised has high as possible while the back dropped down to more than six metres below the surface. The biggest problem was that the Germans did not have any reliable charts and were heading towards another narrow strait separating the north Russian mainland from the Severnaya Zemlya Island Group. The Russian icebreaker warned them to remain at least three miles from land, which made the Germans wonder whether this was genuine, or perhaps some excuse for keeping them away from some secret developments. The answer came quite quickly when the icebreaker commander asked whether they had any up-to-date charts? To the answer 'no,' he replied that this did not matter because all the charts of the area are inaccurate anyway and should not be used for approaching the coastal shallows.

Eventually, when *Komet* did meet the two icebreakers, *Stalin* and *Lenin*, they looked somewhat like dilapidated apparitions from a horror movie, although one of them was only two years old. Yet, despite their worn appearance, the Russian welcome was far warmer than the series of frustrating radio signals had led the Germans to believe. These meetings illustrated that the Russians had an ample supply of vodka and were not afraid to gulp it down in large mouthfuls, even when on duty. It became obvious that the two pilots they picked up some while ago had been under considerable pressure from higher authorities, but the Germans never discovered the reason for the official reticence. So far *Komet* had seen only the wildest desolation without the slightest hint of military or industrial secrets lurking in this forlorn part of the world.

As progress continued with *Komet* getting herself stuck in the ice, unable to move in any direction, it became obvious that at least one icebreaker was more than essential for negotiating the Siberian Sea. Eyssen had enough pre-war experience to judge the thickness of the ice, but it took him a while to realise how the icebreaker ahead of him found the best route through their rather solid barrier. Twisting and turning it cut a path through the thinnest sections, but spotting these from the bridge of a ship was not at all easy and almost impossible the way the Germans had been trying to do it. Even with double lookouts, one set focusing on the ice immediately in front of the bows and the other looking a little further ahead, did not produce good results until the men learned from the two Russian pilots that you do not look at the ice as much as the sky. The reflection on the clouds provided the best picture for determining whether the ice was white and thick or dark and thin. Following the icebreaker *Stalin* through this inhospitable desert was no easy matter, especially when fog cut visibility down to almost nothing, making it impossible for men on the bridge to see the bows of their own ship and the foghorn gave the only indication that there were others around. On the one hand the Germans were elated when it came for *Stalin* to return west, but on the other they felt somewhat apprehensive, wondering whether their next icebreaker was going to be at the rendezvous in the middle of nowhere.

The Russian icebreaker *Kaganovich* from Vladivostok close to auxiliary cruiser *Komet*.

There was a ship waiting at the remote meeting point, but the initial parley with its commander resulted in Eyssen going on alone. The *Malygin*, due to escort *Komet* from the Sannikow Strait had neither the speed nor the power to cut through thick ice. Taking the gamble, Eyssen moved on alone to meet the icebreaker *Kaganovich* and it did not take long to confirm that the help from this smoke-squelching giant was going to be essential. *Komet* ran into such hard ice on so many occasions that she would have been unable to move on her own; the ice was simply too thick. Progress, even with the icebreaker, was excruciatingly slow and on average often not much more than walking pace. To make matters worse, this insignificant headway was only achieved by Eyssen being on the bridge for twenty-two hours at a time. At one stage, when he dropped into his bunk for six hours or so, he woke up to find they were still in the same place where he had earlier gone to bed. This was nerve wracking and depressing and got even worse when they encountered a number of icebergs that had apparently run aground in the shallow seas. These presented such a dangerous hazard because they would not budge when an attempt was made to move them aside, so there was always the very real possibility of *Komet* being damaged beyond repair. The echo sounder worked overtime during this critical stage, confirming that Eyssen's earlier demand for a ship with a shallow draught was correct. There was no way that anything with more than seven metres of hull below the waterline would get through these incredible ice-covered shallows.

Progress was just getting better when things started turning sour elsewhere. First, *Kaganovich* announced that she would have to turn round to help a Russian survey ship that had got stuck and then, during a face-to-face discussion, it became apparent that there were others problems lurking among the far-off diplomatic channels. Exactly what these were has never been established and this happened a year or so before the German invasion of the Soviet Union, so the breakdown of goodwill between the two countries that launched Russia into the war was still far beyond the horizon. The Russians refused to take the German interpreter, Mr Kröpsch, back with them, leaving Eyssen with no alternative other than to keep him on board as a member of the crew. This was no real problem since he had become a highly respected member of the team. In the end, the commander of *Kaganovich* agreed to Eyssen remaining anchored in a sheltered position while he went back on his own to search for the survey ship. At this stage, considering himself to be a prisoner of the Russians, Eyssen made plans with his officers to give their escort the slip by absconding during a dark night and tackling the remaining 400 nautical miles to the Bering Strait on their own. The seas were more open with less ice than before, so the men thought they were in a good position to take this enormous risk. According to the Russians, this would have been suicidal because the narrows between Russia and Alaska were under constant surveillance of large surface ships; and submarines were also known to be patrolling those seas. To the Germans this massive amount of firepower in a lonely part of the ocean came over more as a scare story, and combined with the knowledge that the icebreaker had orders to bring *Komet* back to Murmansk, the officers agreed with Eyssen to go on alone without Russian help.

During these deliberations and the awkward negotiations with the Russians, Eyssen realised that he had got to where he was because luck had been very much on his side and there was no way that the tanker *Esso* would ever have got through the icy barriers. The deep feeling of satisfaction came when *Komet* passed through the Bering Strait into the ice-free Pacific and intercepted a signal from the icebreaker *Kaganovich* saying it had got stuck and was unable to move. Everybody aboard *Komet* breathed a deep sigh of relief and allowed themselves a good long sleep after all the exertions. It was 5 September 1940 that *Komet* arrived in the Bering Strait and found that neither propeller nor rudder had been damaged by the punishment received during their passage. Although the rudder survived the ordeal, the shaft connecting it to the powerful steering

When cutting a path through the ice it was necessary to find those areas where the ice was the thinnest and instead of going in a straight line there was a tendency to weave around like a drunkard.

motor did not. It was bent by ice and could not be repaired without heavy machinery from a dockyard. Unscrewing the motor and reseating it at an angle to balance-out the bend in the shaft eventually overcame this problem.

*Komet* passed through the Bering Strait during a clear night of 5–6 September 1940. Using the dark rocks of Siberia as cover the ship eventually anchored in the Anadyrski Bay to convert the disguise from the German *Donau* into the neutral Japanese *Manju-Maru*. Everybody on board was elated. It had taken 23 days to reach this spot. Nine of those were spent anchored, so the voyage took a total of fourteen days, covering a total of about 3,300 nautical miles (over 6,000 kilometres) of which more than 700 (1,300 km) were through thick ice. Eyssen recorded the event in his log by writing that he would never again volunteer to sail along this route.

Komet operated in the Pacific, Indian Ocean and Antarctic waters, eventually rounding Cape Horn on 10 October 1941 before heading home to return by sailing through the English Channel. She made fast in Hamburg on 30 November 1941 after having been at sea for 516 days and having reached both the most northerly and the most southerly points of all German warships. Komet was sunk in the English Channel by the British motor torpedo boat MTB236 on 14 October 1942, while trying to break out for a second voyage, this time under command of Kpt.z.S. Ulrich Brocksien. The number of ships sunk by auxiliary cruisers is insignificant because their main objective was to remain at sea for the longest possible time to tie up enemy forces.

# 3

# The First U-boats in Cold Waters

Germans of the Second World War era knew how to keep warm in cold weather and there was no need for anyone to join the navy or go to the Arctic to feel the bitterness of harsh winters. The continental climate assured that much of Germany was provided with plenty of snow, with temperatures well below freezing for weeks on end. Rivers, lakes and even the salty sea often froze solid so that wheeled traffic rather than ships could cross them. Those who did go to sea soon discovered that the typical cold winter dryness, where deep frosts of more than minus ten to twenty degrees Celsius removed all traces of wet water from their surroundings, did not necessarily apply to ships belonging to the navy. Despite pretty low heating, clamminess caused by condensation dripping down walls could also be felt, making people feel unpleasantly uncomfortable, even when the salty Baltic froze solid. Living in such conditions was horrendous. Standing on open bridges or in exposed lookout posts with winds whistling past your ears for four hours at a time and with little opportunity to move was nothing short of purgatory, worse than sheer hell on earth. To cope with such harsh conditions, the navy provided long johns, thermal undergarments and fur coats with protective waterproofs, but even with such superior equipment men still had to develop an indifference to the extreme harshness of winter. Being cold and feeling damp was part of everyday life. It was something that everybody accepted as part of the daily routine.

Going north into the cold Arctic did not fill the wartime generations with trepidation. Instead they looked upon such ventures with enthusiasm. The people of those times had grown up during the heroic age of polar exploration and the golden age of flying, where celebrities tried to walk and to fly to the poles. Stories of great achievements were told and retold in schools to ferment the imagination of children, and the men of the Second World War were well aware that even southern countries, such as Italy, had sent expeditions into the fascination of the Arctic to find the North Pole. It was a wild region, full of adventure and more difficult to reach than the deepest Africa or the high mountains of Asia. It was a place where dreams could still be materialised and where every explorer stood a chance of becoming king of this surroundings and a celebrated superstar when he returned home.

Yet, despite this Arctic coldness penetrating deep into Germany's cities, very little was done to adapt the naval hardware for such harsh conditions. It was more a case of battening down the hatches and waiting for the cold spell to subside, even when it did last for several months. Huge battleships doubled up as icebreakers when conditions demanded it, and the navy provided U-boats with special caps that were screwed onto the bows to protect the torpedo tubes. However there was no defence for the hydroplanes, none of which were retractable until the end of the war when the electro boats of Type XXI were commissioned. Propellers were protected from ice only by not using them. U-boats were towed far out to sea until they were clear of any obstructions floating on the surface. So, when the first U-boats ventured into northern waters, it was very much a case of collecting new experiences in conditions the majority had not faced before. Propellers striking hard ice suffered especially badly and to make matters worse, there were no dry dock facilities for U-boats north of Trondheim. Thus improvisation was going to be more than essential. The Germans quickly constructed a special repair facility near Narvik to prevent U-boats from having to go south to Trondheim or Bergen to have propellers replaced. This worked quite simply by reversing the boat into a steel cradle at high tide and then blowing the stern tanks and flooding the those in the bows so that a tug could come alongside at low tide to change the propeller. The supply and repair ships in northern Norway made an impressively significant contribution to the war and their engineers carried out a vast range of other complicated repairs with the most primitively improvised apparatus. Towards the end of the war these geniuses even got as far as rebuilding U-boats and fitting them with schnorkels.

Temperature was, of course, an obvious problem in cold waters and the first U-boats going north were provided with electric convector heaters. Unfortunately the machinery was already running at the limit of its performance and often could not generate the additional electricity to power them. This became especially critical once the diesel engines were shut off and the boat became fully dependent on its batteries. At that moment it was also necessary to turn off the electric heaters and suffer the extreme cold of the bitter Arctic. Apart from these heaters, there were hardly any other modifications for boats heading into Polar Regions. The top of the pressure hull, that part in which the crew lived, was usually at about the same level as the surface of the sea and therefore remained submerged even when the boat was fully surfaced. This meant it remained unenviably cold inside, even at the best of times.

An ocean-going type of U-boat moored in a home port during one of the cold winters in Germany.

Much of Germany is subject to a harsh continental climate where rivers, lakes and the salty Baltic Sea freeze solid during the winter. This shows U48 passing the high railway bridge over the frozen Kiel Canal in Rendsburg. It would appear that the men are waving to girls at the Colonial School, a tradition that had existed since early times. The girls would interrupt all activities including examinations to cheer and wave to passing ships from the German Navy. The bridge in the background is still standing and fully functional.

U48 having problems with the locks of the Kiel Canal. The ice is making locking rather cumbersome.

U657, a standard VIIC U-boat of the type that was employed in the Arctic, with the so-called bow protection cap in place. In an emergency the crew could unscrew the fittings on the upper (outside) deck so that the entire cap dropped into the depths. However, they were made from thick steel and were usually removed with the aid of a crane so that the cap could be re-used at another time. These caps were used only to help boats in and out of ice-bound ports and did not remain in position for operational voyages. The caps were usually removed in an ice-free port such as Heligoland, far out in the German Bight.

*Above:* U48 having the bow protection cap removed with the aid of a crane.

*Below:* An ocean-going U-boat of Type IXC with partly raised navigation periscope. These double-hulled boats had a series of tanks wrapped around the outside of the pressure hull, all of these were open to the sea at the bottom to equalise the pressure inside when the boat dived. The outside walls were relatively thin and could not have stood up to the harsh punishment from ice in Polar seas. This picture shows that the German home waters could be exceedingly cold in winter. Ice forming on all exposed metal structures could easily jam diving tank valves, making diving impossible until it had been removed. This was usually done by moving at fast speed through the slightly warmer sea while ballast pumps ejected the incoming water. The 105 mm quick firing deck gun has the barrel pointing towards the conning tower to produce the rather weird shape in the foreground.

*Above and below:* The bow protection cap only provided a cover for the delicate torpedo tube doors and U-boats moving through ice-infested waters could easily damage their hydroplanes, rudders and propellers. It was thought that rudders and hydroplanes were low enough not to be hurt by surface ice and the propeller was protected by not using it when ice abounded. Instead submarines were towed into ice-free waters as can be seen here.

U134 under Kptlt. Rudolf Schendel was one of the early boats to venture into the bitter north to join the first U-boat pack (Group Ulan) for a specific operation against Russian convoys. The other boats of this group were U454 (Kptlt. Burkhard Hackländer) and U584 (Kptlt. Jürgen Deecke). Running into Kirkeness on 12 December 1941 the men of U134 found themselves in a white world under a black sky, where the sun did not rise during the day. Around midday there was a faint glimmer of light on the southern horizon, making it possible to spot dark ships against a slightly lighter sky, but such conditions were rare and lasted only for a few hours at best. Fog was the dominant feature in much of the Arctic and helped to conceal each boat in its own small world.

Surrounded by low, barren, glacier smoothed hills and with Russia less than a dozen kilometres towards the south-east, Kirkeness experienced a vast number of air raids during the war. In all there were over a thousand alarms with the majority of aircraft flying on to some other target, but the tiny town did receive a powerful hammering on more than 300 occasions and was damaged to such an extent that only a dozen or so houses remained when Russian forces drove out the German army of occupation towards the end of October 1944.

The town did not have much to commend it when U134 called. It did not even have facilities for supplying torpedoes. So, it was a case of borrowing one G7a from U454 and moving the two torpedoes from the pressure resisting containers under the upper deck. This proved to be quite a problem. The one in the bows was moved easily enough, but the storage tube in the stern had leaked and with temperatures at around minus fifteen degrees Celsius meant that everything there had frozen into one solid lump, without any hope of doing anything other than resigning to the fact that warmer weather was required before this torpedo was going to budge.

Eventually, after having replenished some essential stores, U134 left the white shroud of Kirkeness at 15.30 hours of Christmas Day 1941 to head into the black waters towards the north. Trying to obey the instructions for joining the Ulan Pack proved to be impossible. To reach the patrol line U134 would have to cruise at a minimum of 12 knots, which proved to be impossible under the prevailing conditions. A bitterly cold wind was blowing from the north at Force 6 to 8 and with the sea whipped up accordingly meant that after less than one hour the lookouts were frozen solid, hardly able to move in the icy armour that had taken a hold on top of their raingear. The water froze instantly as it hit anything solid after having crashed over the top of the conning tower. On top of this, one of the engines failed and had to be shut down for repairs lasting four hours. It was hardly back in action when something similar happened and the boat had to continue for another five hours without the port engine. By this time the boat's colour had changed dramatically from the usual grey to looking more like some white monster. At this stage the periscopic rod aerial was raised to report the delay in arriving in the operations area. The lookouts on the bridge watched with profound surprise as it rapidly gathered a hard covering of ice. Raising it had already used considerably more power than usual, suggesting that the mechanism was also suffering from having been frozen solid, and lowering it proved to be impossible. The duty watch reported that the rod had increased in diameter by some thirty centimetres and shortly after that it was bent double by the power of the waves, without any hope at all of ever getting it back into its casing.

The men inside the boat did not fare much better than the exposed lookouts. The commander's attack position inside the conning tower, the central control room below it and the rear compartment with the electric motor controls as well as the bow compartment had a covering of ice up to one centimetre in thickness, despite additional heaters running at maximum power. The accommodation areas were just as cold, and only the cork and wood panelling prevented condensation from collecting on the walls. The U-boat had not reached its operations area yet when the men also discovered that their washing water had frozen solid and they were most surprised when they found that the internal tanks, such as the torpedo compensation tanks were frozen as well. These had been filled with washing water because it was thought that this would have been used up by the time torpedoes were going to be shot.

The next surprise was that some of the diving tanks had frozen as well, making it necessary to go through a complicated de-icing manoeuvre every half hour or so. This was done by slowly submerging the boat and continuing at fast speed through the slightly warmer water, to hopefully melt the ice that was jamming the vulnerable valves. With the sea temperature at not much lower than minus two degrees Celsius and the air at minus fifteen, this worked quite well as long as the ballast pumps could expel the water flooding into the interior of the boat.

Bear Island loomed into sight shortly before midday of 29 December 1941 at a distance of about 45 kilometres, confirming that U134 had reached its correct position in the Ulan Patrol Line. The rough seas of the previous days were calming steadily and the wind had slowed down to Force one to two, but was still blowing from the north-east with an unpleasantly cold bite. The brilliant visibility changed rapidly as well, with both rain and snow showers obliterating almost everything except the immediate area around the boat, and at times visibility was cut down to less than a hundred metres or so. Three full days were devoted to patrolling this desolate murk and it was not until six o'clock in the morning of 2 January 1942 that a ship suddenly appeared out of an intense snow

*Above left:* Tugs were often in short supply during war years because they were called in for all manner of support activities and any ship that happened to be passing was used to tow U-boats clear of ice. This could be a freighter or a special mine detonator that usually sailed in front of valuable ships to clear any explosives in the deep-water channel.

*Above right and below:* Standing watch for four hours in cold conditions was no easy job. The special waterproofs had similar seals to a diver's dry suit, so that theoretically water could not get inside. Yet, despite wearing two layers of fur coats and special thermal underwear underneath, condensation still accumulated and water usually found a way in, despite the special seals. In conditions like these the men became like robots, hardly able to move because of the many clothes and the outer layers being frozen stiff.

A lookout wearing a standard coat with the fur on the inside on a mild Arctic day when seas did not come crashing over the top of the conning tower.

The commander well wrapped up during a mild spell in the Arctic.

The officer on duty on top of the conning tower wearing warm cold weather headgear and a navy issue life jacket over his ordinary pea jacket.

Getting through narrow hatches while wearing full Arctic gear took some doing. Woollen bobble caps weren't a reminder from home but part of the ordinary naval issue.

This photo of action helmsman, Obergefreiter Otto Kloninger of U357 has been published elsewhere, but is of special interest because it shows just how cold it got inside the central control room of a U-boat. He is wearing normal Arctic gear and seems to have got so cold that someone has hung another coat over his shoulders. Either he is also serving as wardrobe stand for someone, but far more likely he is too cold to sit there in his ordinary gear. A motor that was controlled by the two buttons under Otto's hands moved the rudders. There are three speaking tubes in front him plus a gyrocompass towards the left and near his head is an indicator showing the position of the rudders.

Icy conditions somewhere in Europe, probably not much further than one of the Baltic ports.

shower, just like a well-performed conjuring trick. Since it was not much more than two kilometres away, it presented everybody with a severe shock. Schendel, the commander reacted by ordering action station and then he shot the rear torpedo. Nothing much happened, so the boat turned and another torpedo was shot from the bows. Again not much happened and it was the third shot that brought the target to a standstill.

Opening the outside torpedo doors had already been a problem, taking considerably longer than usual before the mechanics confirmed that everything was ready for action. The torpedo tanks were still frozen solid as well and everything seemed to be rather lethargic, probably due to oil having thickened. The great advantage was that it was dark. So U134 could go in for surface attack where torpedo tanks were not required. They allowed water to flood in when torpedoes were shot, to compensate for the sudden loss of weight, which would otherwise cause the submerged boat to rise. The men were under the impression that the extreme cold had reduced the efficiency of the batteries inside the torpedoes to such an extent that they were providing nowhere near their normal power.

Two far-off detonations were heard after a running time of about seven minutes, but the merchant ship did not react to this noise and continued running along its original path. It appeared to be relying on the eternal darkness to escape or everybody on board was either drunk or asleep. In the end, the British 5,135 GRT freighter *Waziristan* went down with all hands at 06.48 hours of 2 January 1942, shortly after that third torpedo had detonated. This success was a considerable improvement to U134's first sinking on 9 December, when Schendel sunk the German 2,185 GRT freighter *Steinbek* by mistake. Following this, the weather varied from cloudy with fog to brilliant moonshine and excellent visibility. The light was so bright that it was possible to read on the top of the conning tower without a lamp. More action followed and U134 did not return to Kirkeness until the early hours of 20 January 1942, proving that U-boat operations were possible in cold Arctic waters, even when there was a smattering of ice drifting over the surface of the water.

Not all of the mechanical problems were due to the weather or the extreme cold. Another U-boat nudged U134 hard enough in Kirkeness to damage the rear hydroplanes, making it impossible to move them much further than ten degrees and when they were moving they used considerably more electricity than before. The Junker Compressor for filling the air bottles did not work at all and, most annoying for the commander, was that the periscope had been raised while the water in the system had frozen solid, leading to several major failures. Nuts and bolts were torn off and the cable for raising and lowering it had slipped out of

An ocean-going U-boat of Type IX showing how U-boats looked in winter.

Clearing ships of ice was a difficult and backbreaking job because water that froze on exposed steel was often exceedingly hard and a great effort was required to remove it.

U98 in port. Ice did present a good number of problems for North Sea ports, but these were nowhere near as difficult as conditions in the eastern Baltic where entire dock basins froze solid for weeks on end.

The gun platform of a Type VIIC U-boat with the 20 mm anti-aircraft gun removed from its mount.

its fitting. It was thought that this could easily be remedied in future by using a de-icing fluid in the liquid, similar to that added to the cooling water in cars during the winter months. Periscopes had already presented some problems before this accident. The oil in the system had hardened sufficiently to slow the raising and lowering to a snail's pace. The men devised their own way of dealing with the extreme cold temperatures and made every effort to overcome the mechanical problems with their own improvisation. Interestingly enough the Naval Group Command North made the poignant remark at the end of the log book, saying it is urgently necessary to evaluate the effects of cold temperatures on U-boat machinery and what influence this could have on the weapons such as torpedoes. This knowledge together with possible convoy routes and the nature of the merchant ship traffic was still a major unknown during the beginning of 1942.

One did not need a university education to work out that the Allies were using the long, dark winter nights to best advantage for running their convoys into north Russia and that the chances of survival were pretty slender if one's ship was sunk. The chances of survival can perhaps be illustrated very well with the sinking of the *Scharnhorst* on Boxing Day of 1943 when the Royal Navy managed to pick up less than forty survivors from the 1,900 strong complement. In addition to this, just over forty U-boats were sunk in the Polar Seas and there were survivors from only seven of these. The chances of surviving in the water after abandoning ship were almost nil. Yet, despite this, U-boat men were given instructions in how to cope with such hopeless situations. They were told to discard only their shoes, to loosen any scarves and to keep their heavy clothing on. Surprisingly enough it was the men who jumped overboard without life jackets who managed to survive the longest. This was put down to the fact that they had to swim hard to prevent them from drowning, while those with a life jackets kept tended to dangle lifelessly in the water. Special survival clothing had not yet been invented and many men perished because rescuing U-boats could not spot them in the turbulence of the raging water, in any case, life expectations in such cold conditions were very short.

*Above and right:* U-boat decorated by the winter weather.

# 4

# Luftwaffe Weather Flights

Rudolf Schütze was a remarkable naturalist who became one of the first weather pilots some time before the Luftwaffe was founded. He grew up at a time when weather forecasting was changing from a mysterious art into a mathematical science and, at the same time, aircraft were starting to contribute even more numbers to the raw data consumed by forecasters. By the time the war started he had been a pilot for some five years with more than a thousand high altitude flights to his credit. As a civilian he had taken part in an eight-week-long course on how to operate anti-aircraft guns, but otherwise had no military training. What is more, he was not even a member of the Luftwaffe. The pilots and meteorologists of this Weather Flight (Wetterstaffel and later Wettererkundungsstaffel – Weather Reconnaissance Flight) were civil servants and only the technical staff and the ground crews belonged to the military, but all this changed in August 1939. Within a period of a few days the weather pilots and meteorologists found themselves coming under military jurisdiction to fly reconnaissance planes over Poland and France. This was a relatively simple affair of merely exploring what was going on ahead of the front line to give the ground troops some idea of what to expect.

The major weather forecasting problem was that the masses of raw data flooding in from worldwide sources petered out after the start of the war, and in order to forecast the weather in Europe it was necessary to know what was going on further afield. Schütze was soon promoted to the rank of warrant officer to become leader of a special detachment with the new name of Weather Chain North (Wetterkette Nord). This detachment was equipped originally with just three aircraft; each with a pilot, meteorologist, radio operator and flight engineer and every plane also had its own ground mechanic. Flying originally from Sylt, this group moved to Alborg in Denmark and then Stavanger in Norway, before settling into a remote airfield near Trondheim. From there planes flew for up to a thousand kilometres on a rough course of 270 degrees (due west) over the sea into incredibly hostile conditions. The first flight of this newly formed group in Trondheim took place on 21 May 1940, only a few months after the German occupation of Norway. The group was quickly enlarged so that later it was possible to have five or six aircraft ready for action each day.

On the one hand these weathermen lived in incredible opulence. There were no other military units near them, so they were accommodated in a hotel where they even had their boots polished and were given enough money to eat anywhere they fancied. Their task was to wait for their daily instructions before setting off. Usually just one aircraft would fly either west or northwest until it had reached the limit of its fuel. Then the only obvious thing to do was to fly back to base. Reporting the weather from an aircraft flying over featureless water was a good deal more difficult than trying the same trick over land and the men devised their own way of doing things. For example, they shot a few rounds into the sea ahead of

Two aircraft from the Luftwaffe's Special Weather Flights on Spitzbergen shortly after the British evacuation. The aircraft landed on flat ground by the side of the Icefjord to help establish a German radio station. *Photo: Franz Selinger*

them to determine both the force and the direction of the wind from the splashes. It was a case of taking a reading at sea level and then climbing up high to provide details from above the clouds.

At first the weather flight was supplied with Heinkel He111 aircraft and Dornier Do17 and later they also had some Junker Ju88. The first mentioned had a range of about 1,600 kilometres, the Do17 about 2,000 and the Ju88 about 2,700 kilometres. Their speeds and other vital performance data was hardly of interest since they were unlikely to encounter any opposition and their biggest enemy was going to be the extreme Arctic weather. The He111 was very much the preferred aircraft. Although slow, it sat so comfortably and steadily in the air that it was difficult to bring it into a spin. It also had the rather attractive feature of being capable of flying and maintaining height with just one engine. These aircraft flew from a dangerous 10 metres above sea level up to about 7,000 metres. The data they collected was coded with a Luftwaffe Enigma machine and then broadcast back to base, where the details were collated, re-coded with a more secure system and then passed on to Berlin. The technology of the day did not allow the aircraft to be heard by radio stations in the Reich capital, so the base radio station was a vital link in the chain. By this time the weather flight came under the jurisdiction of the Luftwaffe, but the immediate boss, Rudolf Schütze, was still only a warrant officer and most of the men did exactly what they liked. They did not get copies of the rule book, or if they did they disregarded the instructions on principle. These guys were very much dependent on each other and there was not anyone around who could match their flying ability. They flew whatever the weather and also took off totally blind in thick fog—something that was prohibited for the run of the mill pilots. Flying in such remote areas meant that their contact with base had to be so reliable that they could easily deviate to other airfields if the landing conditions at home were too bad.

The chances of being shot down were remote, but this lack of enemy contact did not make the weather flights an easy option. They flew through the most appalling conditions imaginable. They had to deal with serious icing of their wings, negotiate storms and cope with thick fogs. There were hardly any days when the daily flight did not get off the ground. The big problem was that flying over featureless sea, turning round and going home again did not provide any positive confirmation that their navigation was correct. To get over this, Schütze instigated flights to the Faeroe Islands so that the crew had a visual check of where they were. This was not particularly easy because the aircraft would be flying to the limit of their fuel capacity, but it worked well and it was not long before the engineering division found ways of adding more fuel tanks. This had

One of the first aircraft from the Luftwaffe's Special Weather Flight refuelling in Banak, northern Norway while en route to Spitzbergen during April 1941. *Photo: Franz Selinger*

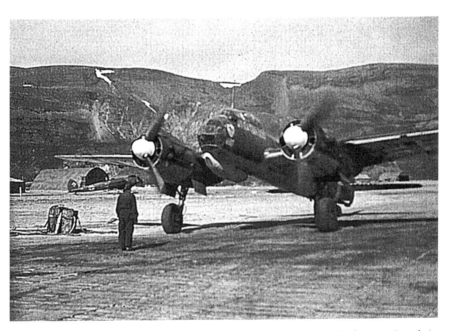

A Ju88 of the Luftwaffe's Special Weather Flight starting from the base at Banak in northern Norway. *Photo: Franz Selinger*

to be pumped manually into the main system and soon the weather flights reached Iceland as well. Besides being an incredible achievement for such comparatively small planes, the ventures also confirmed that the men's navigation was spot on.

Whilst the men were keen to penetrate far into the Arctic, there was always the question of what they would do if they had a mechanical failure. Shutting one engine down on purpose proved that none of their aircraft could muster sufficient power to climb with the remaining engine and they would be doomed, able to make headway but unlikely to get back to base. This drove the men into making their own evasion plans for possible mishaps. Radio connections to base were usually so good that those left behind knew exactly where their comrades were and another aircraft could fly out on a rescue mission. Yet, somehow the idea of sitting in an inflatable life raft up in the Arctic did not appeal. Conditions were usually rough enough for such a small target to be missed by a searching aircraft. In any case, the aircraft were designed for hard runways and none of them could land on water. In view of this it was decided that the weather flight should build its own emergency landing strips. Selecting suitable sites was not too difficult and testing the ground was easy as well. The men loaded a few large boulders into their bomb bay. If these bounced, then the ground was firm enough to hold an aircraft. The snag was that a ground preparation team had to be parachuted in to clear away obstructions to make a smooth runway before anything could land on those desolate islands.

Strange as it may seem, there were enough volunteers to take part in such harebrained schemes and it was not long before the first runway was ready. It was just long and wide enough for an aircraft. The plan was to mark the spot with cairns and all necessities for survival were placed in a well-marked position to make these quite attractive locations. Although this worked well, there were cases where aircraft landed with supplies and then got their wheels stuck in holes or soft ground that had been missed by the ground preparation team. So, the weather flights had to bring in timber and whatever else was needed to extract the wheels and then repair the damaged aircraft, to allow it to return to base. It was chaotic, very much against Luftwaffe rules, but the majority of the men could live exceedingly close to nature. Those that could not had to cultivate such qualities rather quickly or have a nervous breakdown. The achievements of these incredible weather flyers have hardly been documented but anyone delving into their history will be rewarded what must be one of the most exciting and unusual adventures of the whole war.

# 5

# Heinz Fritsch (U355) and the Red Fox (U255) versus Convoy PQ17

*Heinz Fritsch was a remarkable man who served as cook aboard U355, U548 and U1104. After the war he wrote a series of fascinating articles for Ernst Pfefferle's books* Kameraden zur See *and he left a considerable quantity of other manuscripts in the German U-boat Museum. Many of these are especially interesting because by the time he started this work he had access to original logbooks. Thus he was in a good position to present accurate facts and embellish these bare bones with the wealth of his own experiences. These are particularly valuable because other veterans visiting the Museum have confirmed that Heinz Fritsch did not colour his stories with his imagination, as has been done in so many other autobiographies. The Red Fox was the emblem used by U255 under Reinhart Reche. (Reinhart translates as Reynard, a name given to the fox.)*

U355 (Kptlt. Günter La Baume) left Kiel on the warm summer's day of 1 June 1942 for Skjomenfjord, an out of the way and secluded area to the south of Narvik in northern Norway. The technical division had been allocated one bunk for two men because they usually stood six hour long watches and the seamen's division had three men for every two bunks, but Heinz Fritsch had got so used to sleeping in hammocks that he strung one up between sausages and large joints of smoked ham. He preferred his own sleeping place rather than having to put up with the smell of other bodies in the bedding. This setup worked well until white-capped mountains and snow showers rapidly chilled the men's hearts. They had come through an exceptionally long, cold and bitter winter, had enjoyed the lush green during the increasing warmth of spring and were looking forward to a hot summer. Now, as they nosed into those calm waters guarded by incredibly high mountains, they found themselves sliding back into a most depressingly cold world.

The initial drop in morale was quickly improved when the men learned that they had been allocated special accommodation aboard the Norwegian royal yacht, the *Stella Polaris*, where they could enjoy hot baths and warm beds. A welcome change from what had rapidly become an uncomfortably chilly submarine. Yet the scenery was stunning, something the majority of men had never seen before and anyone looking closely along the bottoms of the deep valleys could see the dreariness of winter was being replaced by a distinct hue of green. Spring was also finding its way into those extreme northern latitudes.

The comforts of the royal yacht did not last and soon after U355 called on the Admiral Commanding the Northern Seas (Admiral Hubert Schmundt) in the town of Narvik for their orders. Following this, the boat headed into what turned into a powerful south-westerly of Force 7 and then slowly got worse. The lookouts were wearing their normal leathers with a 'large seal' (Grosser Seehund) over the top. This resembled a diver's dry suit by having boots incorporated into the trousers and the sleeves and neck had special watertight seals. Clambering to the top of the conning tower with such heavy gear demanded a special skill of first closing the hatch so that not too much water cascaded down into the central control room and then, quickly attaching the safety harness before the man was washed off by the next wave. This securing system was not uncomfortable and made it possible to stand upright and lean back slightly without having to hold on to anything, leaving both hands free to handle the binoculars. The men were provided with superb 7 x 50 night glasses while the duty officer had a slightly larger 8 x 50 or 8 x 60 set. Whilst the experience of

Heinz Fritsch, cook of U355, who compiled much of the information in this chapter.

Men from U355 in Narvik during August 1943, immediately after an Iron Cross presentation. The commander, Günther La Baume, is wearing a white cap. Next to him towards the right is the LI or engineer officer. The second from the right appears to be Heinz Fritsch whose notes were used to write a number of passages in this book.

A convoy at sea.

A modern ship battling its way through the waters around Spitzbergen in August, during the height of the Arctic summer. Even especially strengthened ships have to take great care not to damage themselves in such inhospitable ice. *Photo: Mike and Brenda Lyons*

being drenched in cold seawater was unpleasant, the men inside the boat did not fare much better. The vigorous movement tossed them against hard projections and the majority had to revise their own opinion of being hardened seamen. They had all considered themselves as such before this storm made it plainly obvious that the northern waters could throw far more at them than the seas nearer home. Heinz Fritsch and almost all the crew were severely seasick. One advantage with this was that it reduced the demand for food to such extent that the engineer officer suggested Heinz could retreat to his hammock until the torture subsided.

The men's appetite improved dramatically after the storm, with almost everybody calling at the galley, checking whether there were any goodies on offer. The big problem was not so much finding something to fill empty stomachs after several days of abstinence, but trying to find out where they were. They were far enough north for the sun not to set at night. So it did not get dark, but it did not get light during the day either. Sandwiched between a grey sea and low clouds, it was possible to see for over thirty kilometres over the water at times, but there was no sign of stars at night or sun during the day. For most of time they drifted through a grey murk over a calm sea, monotonous enough to make everybody most despondent. Once on the surface the men were allowed to move about as they pleased and the duty watch was delighted when new faces appeared up on the bridge to relieve the tedium of doing and spotting nothing. As visibility improved the men sighted U657 under Kptlt. Heinrich Göllnitz. Each boat had an ES board with the current identification signals hanging in the conning tower, making it instantly possible to work out whether any sudden appearance was a friend or foe and this meeting indicated that both of them were slightly off beam. (ES is short for Erkennungssignale or Recognition Signals.)

Shortly afterwards the men got a bearing on the extinct volcano on the Island of Jan Mayen, over a hundred kilometres further west, and also on the sun, making them confident that they could now take up their correct position in the newly formed Eisteufel (Ice Devil) Pack, awaiting a convoy from Iceland. Confirmation of its departure from Reykjavik had already arrived and the Luftwaffe had sighted a large oil slick along its expected route but that plane was shot at through the clouds and made off instead of exploring what was going on under the dense cover. Pack ice, already spotted a few days earlier, now started making life a little disturbing. Most of it was small enough not to damage the hull, but the noise it made as the chunks collided with the steel was annoying enough to make the engineering division concerned about their propellers, rudders and hydroplanes.

The noises filtering out of the central control room were even more unsettling. It started to look as if all the efforts of chugging through the severe storm were in vein and the convoy could well have slipped past the waiting pack by scraping along the edge of the permanent ice cap. The only real consolation was that many now felt the unsettling storm had finally cast off all feelings of seasickness and Heinz Fritsch was never troubled with this again. The men of U355 had won this battle against the natural elements and now they needed another enemy to flex their muscles on. Finding it, though, proved rather difficult.

The monotony of the daily boredom was usually only broken by practising this, that and the other, and the boat had been at sea for two weeks when the radio brought news of a cruiser having been sighted near Jan Mayen. Shortly after this sighting came details of Convoy PQ17 heading east towards Russia. The sloppiness with which the men had conducted themselves during the last few dreary days and the intensity of their card games came to a sudden halt. The new atmosphere was instantly sharper than any changes brought about by endless practices. Off duty men no longer lounged in moanful slumber but started looking for ways of checking and double-checking that everything was functioning properly. The convoy had to be somewhere close by, but no one knew exactly where that might be. All the boats of the pack were experiencing the most troublesome weather with constant fog sweeping over the waves, making it impossible to see very far and exceedingly difficult to work out accurate positions. Sailing by dead reckoning might work quite well over short distances, but this persistent fog was preventing the navigators from obtaining accurate fixes. Eventually, when U355 did manage to see the sun, the men discovered that they were almost fifty kilometres off course and drastic action was called for. This error in navigation explained why U355 had accidentally run into U408 under Kptlt. Reinhard von Hymmen. The two boats came close enough together to be told that two destroyers had attacked U408, but the men of U355 were not provided with any more news about the anticipated convoy.

Following this, U255 (Kptlt. Reinhart Reche) reported light enemy forces, meaning he had seen a couple of destroyers. It did not take too long before Reche made another report saying he had been attacked by two escorts and two destroyers and had consequently lost them. Kptlt. Heinrich Göllnitz of U657 also reported having been attacked by destroyers and then U456 under Kptlt. Max-Martin Teichert reported a depth charge attack. All this proved that the convoy with plenty of support was close by and the ether continued to erupt with a multitude of radio calls, but none of them helped in bringing the Eisteufel Pack any closer to the expected ships. In the end it was the Admiral for the Northern Seas (Admiral Hubert Schmundt) who ordered the pack onto a new course and to a high speed of 15 knots.

U355 was not exempt from attacks by small, fast warships appearing out of the foggy murk to force an emergency dive. The orders for the escorts were to push U-boats under and then, straight away, return to their protective position around the convoy. There were not enough escorts for prolonged pursuits. As a result the Germans experienced some depth charges and heard the sounds of fast warships passing overhead, but they were not often hunted to destruction. Yet this action also prevented them from getting close to their targets. Being driven under was often less nerve-wracking than having to surface again. Pushing up the periscope, all that the commander saw was more grey murk and not much else. The sound detector confirmed that there were no noisy engines in the vicinity, so U-boats usually surfaced in such a way that they could go straight back into another emergency dive if necessary. The lookouts stood ready dressed to go up to the top of the conning tower while the commander jumped up for a cursory look around to check that there was nothing lurking close by and following that he swept the seas in greater detail with his binoculars. Only when he had convinced himself that there was no one, with their engines shut off, did he call the others up. On this occasion, nothing much had changed. It was the late afternoon of 2 July 1942, everybody knew that Convoy PQ17 was only about thirty kilometres away, but finding it was still a problem and searching for it with the diesels hammering with an incredible din at fast speed did not bring any immediate results. The

Convoys at sea.

engine noise was so loud that talking in the galley was only just possible, but hearing anything anyone was saying on the other side of the sound-protecting wall was completely out of the question. The only consolation was that the seas were relatively cooperative by not punishing the men with too much water washing over the top of the conning tower, and the cooking pots sat quietly on the hobs without spilling their contents on the floor.

At this critical stage of coming close to the merchant ships, U88 under Kptlt. Heino Bohmann threw a spanner into the works by reporting a westbound convoy. Boats near him should instinctively have made a point of trying to find it, but the Admiral Commanding the Northern Seas nipped these standing orders in the bud by putting an immediate stop to such thoughts. Everybody was told to continue concentrating on the eastbound targets. The chance of being so close to valuable war materials heading for Russia was too good an opportunity to miss. The empty ships on their return journey could wait a little longer for an attack. Group Eisteufel obeyed, but none of the U-boats found any targets. No one, other than the two shadowing U-boats, even caught a glimpse of anything that might resemble a merchantman. All they saw and felt had something to do with the Royal Navy emerging out of patches of bad visibility before hitting hard, fast and furiously.

U355 had only just sent off a sighting report of the convoy on the horizon when a white painted destroyer was spotted heading directly towards it at fast speed. This had merged so well with its surroundings that it was already too close for running away on the surface and other drastic action was called for. The convoy appeared to be making for the murk that had concealed this nuisance and the situation left no alternative other than to dive and listen to some depth charges. These were luckily too far away to give too much concern and after that, when U355 surfaced again, everything was as peaceful as it had been before. There was nothing to see other than a grey murk drifting over a reasonably calm sea. The Luftwaffe in the Lofoten Islands broadcast details from their reconnaissance flights saying the convoy was made up of thirty-seven merchant ships, twelve destroyers, four corvettes and two submarines. Taking a deep breath the men in U355 guessed that these last two were the shadowing U-boats, something the aircraft would not have known about because they used a different radio code and therefore could not tune in to the general goings-on below them.

One U-boat was following an oil trace, but the others had no clue as to how they might find the merchant ships and it was not long before the two shadowers also lost contact. It was a case of fog getting thicker, speeds having to get slower, and everybody standing-by, ready for immediate action. At this critical stage of events, U255 (Kptlt. Reinhart Reche), spotted the convoy again and, knowing the awkwardness of the weather, immediately sent radio bearing signals for the other boats to home in on. This made the majority fully aware that they had been looking in the wrong areas. Obviously the convoy commodore had been making excellent use of the fog by twisting and turning into unexpected directions. Unknown to the U-boats, by this time the merchant ships would have been equipped with High Frequency Direction Finders (H/F D/F or Huff Duff) that told them the direction from which any U-boat radio signals were coming from. Therefore the constant use of radio by the wolf pack must have been exceedingly useful in determining the position of the escorts and the heading of the convoy.

The U-boats' main problem with many of the sighting reports was that even when three came more or less simultaneously there was still a difference of about thirty kilometres in their reckoning and it was anyone's guess which positions might be correct. The grey murk continued, reducing speeds and making all the U-boats use up the highly technical terms of their naval vocabulary in describing their surroundings and feelings. While the fog got thicker to reduce visibility down to less than 200 metres, the echo sounder was turned on to give some indication of the depth below the keel. The forty metres of water below U355 was not ideal for submarine activity, but no one counted on any enemy action in that thick fog and the most worrying point was accidentally bumping into Bear Island, which was known to be not too far away. When the echo sounder indicated a depth of only 20 metres, the fog suddenly lifted to show the southern tip of the lonely Arctic island, but there were still no clues as to where the convoy might be.

4 July 1942 merged into the previous day like every other. The men of U355 knew that the convoy was somewhere close by. At midday the Admiral Commanding the Northern Seas confirmed that there were no German surface ships in the area and any heavy units that the U-boat were likely to meet were therefore to be attacked without further ado. Some chases did occur, but for most of the time the majority of U-boats from the Eisteufel Pack did not make contact with anything more solid than the irritating fog that had accompanied them for the past few days.

It was shortly after midday when U457 (Korvkpt. Karl Brandenburg) reported contact with enemy forces and this was almost immediately confirmed by a Blohm und Voss reconnaissance plane. Consequently all the U-boats within striking distance ran up to a fast cruising speed of about 15 knots, making for where they thought the ships might be heading for. It was late in the afternoon when U355 spotted smoke on the horizon, but this single column disappeared quickly again and looked as if an escort had allowed a puff to escape up its funnel. It certainly could not have been more than a single ship and the men had no clues as to exactly where the others might be. The men of U355 were not too perturbed at not finding any targets because it was too bright for a surface attack and the water was now as smooth as a village duck pond on a calm day. The smooth sea with brilliant visibility would have made a submerged attack exceedingly difficult, because under such conditions it would have been too easy for enemy lookouts to spot the periscope. This high tension of knowing that the enemy was close by but not being able to find any targets was made worse at 1820 hours when six Heinkel 115 aircraft with torpedoes strung underneath were seen to be flying overhead. The men at the top of the conning tower watched as they circled and then lined up for an attack, coming down gradually to launch their weapons. At the same time it was possible to see bursts of black near them, making it obvious that the airmen were being given a hard time by anti-aircraft guns. This gave the men of U355 a definite indication where the convoy was, and the engines were once more run up to a high fuel guzzling speed to get in on the action. However, U355 did not make too much progress before the horizon was shrouded behind a violent snowstorm. This quickly turned to hail and later rain making it easy for the merchant ships to escape again.

U703 under Kptlt. Heinz Bielfeld then found the convoy, reported its position, speed and heading, indicating the ships had gone in an unexpected north-westerly direction. The men on U355 saw more aircraft, but somehow did not get any closer to any targets. This radio signal had hardly been digested when a submarine surfaced ahead of U355 and identified itself quickly as U88 under Kptlt. Heino Bohmann. Coming close enough for a quick message exchange the two commanders decided they would join forces to find the still elusive ships and the chase continued at fast speed. News of British warships that had been announced earlier over the radio now confused the issue. The operational command in Norway assumed that these were somewhere near the convoy and decided to split the U-boat pack by directing the nearby U-boats towards these ships. The exact positions were still being calculated when another radio call suggested that there was no point in directing the other U-boats towards the convoy because it could well have scattered. All that could be done was to continue hunting in likely places, but again U355 didn't get any positive help.

The second watch of 5 July 1942 had just come on duty at 0430 hours when things started to happen. The change over from one watch to another took the best part of half an hour. Only one man was exchanged at a time so that the new lookout could adjust himself and his eyes to the outside conditions. The last man had just come down when the sighting of mast tips on the horizon brought the commander to the top of the conning tower. Estimating their direction and speed was not easy over such long distances and the men still did not know what sort of ship this might be when Günter La Baume ordered a fast speed to get ahead and less than an hour later he dived for a submerged attack. The cook was not needed during action stations and Heinz Fritsch was the sort of chap who was tolerated everywhere in the boat, so he sat quietly in the open hatch by the radio room to watch the goings-on. This was the first time he had seen this for real, so this was indeed a most exciting moment. The euphoria did not last long, the target changed direction to run over the top of the submerged U-boat without noticing it. Once it was well out of range, the men were stood down from their actions again with the commander saying the ship had been a small fishing boat, almost certainly modified to act as escort but too small for a torpedo. Following this, the hunt for the illusive merchant ships continued in earnest.

On surfacing again U355 discovered that U456 (Kptlt. Max-Martin Teichert) had also lost contact with what was now called the cruiser squadron. Another signal from the Admiral Commanding the Northern Seas confirmed that these warships were also a priority target and every effort should be made to engage them. The big problem for the men in U355 was that nothing other than a Russian reconnaissance plane came into sight. It was infuriating, especially as the news had already come in that seven merchant ships had been sunk from the convoy. Everything indicated that rich pickings were to be had, if only U355 could find some targets.

Nothing happened amidst the chaos of not knowing exactly what was going on. U355 ran into U88 and U703 and all three commanders decided to form their own patrol line for chasing the illusive ships. The Admiral Commanding Northern Seas agreed with the plan and told the U-boats that eight Ju88 reconnaissance planes were also on their way to help. On hearing this Korvkpt. Karl Brandenburg in U457 found himself in an ideal position to lengthen the 'comb' in the west. Auxiliary *Komet* had by this time been back home long enough for the majority of commanders to know that the Matochkin Strait between the north and south island of Novaya Zemlya was so well marked that it was navigable without the need of a pilot. This made the men think that the merchant ships might be heading in that direction to avoid the onslaught from the torpedo bombers. The initial jubilation created by these new thoughts dissolved rather rapidly. The men in U355 had started to doubt their own luck, and despondency made a significant contribution to their reactions. Some of the men were already saying openly that at least those that are a long way from a shooting range have the opportunity of growing into old warriors. Novaya Zemlya came into sight by appearing to lift slowly out of the sea. Initially the men were delighted at being so close to the first part of Russia they had ever seen, but when they got nearer they were shocked by the incredible desolation of the coast, which was made up of nothing but rocks and mountains without the slightest indication of any human habitation. It is a weird feeling to experience this vast emptiness for the first time.

A convoy (UGF 1) under attack on 12 November 1942 with a detonation from a submerged attack by U130 under Kptlt. Ernst Kals. *Photo: Edward Rumpf*

A convoy seen from an escort.

U255 under Kptlt. Reinhard Reche. Although rather blurred, the boat's Red Fox emblem is at the front of the conning tower and the badge above the man bending to deal with the fender is the emblem of the 11th U-boat Flotilla.

The emblem of the 11th U-boat Flotilla as it appeared in a Christmas present in 1942 with the flotilla chief's (Korvkpt. Hans Cohausz) signature.

To the men inside the U-boat it was a day like any other. The first watch had come off duty and eaten, those on orderly duties were clearing up, Heinz Fritsch was smoking inside the conning tower because there were already too many men up on the top and then he climbed down to find an empty bunk to use as seat so that he could write the latest details into the galley's log book. Sitting immediately aft of the central control room, in the petty officers' accommodation and immediately forward of the galley and engine room, he was suddenly interrupted with the words, 'Smoke in sight. Pass that on to the engine room.' The message had hardly been conveyed when the telegraph demanded a faster speed and then the action stations signal sounded. 'A steamer with two masts, one funnel doing nine knots,' came through the loudspeaker system while the Obersteuermann (the warrant officer responsible for navigation) was making calculations on his tiny desk. Although the situation became tense, not much action followed and more than two hours passed before the lookouts came tumbling down from the top of the conning tower. The boat dived into an eerie silence where every man was left with his own thoughts. The hatches throughout the boat remained open, making it possible to see as far as the torpedo tube in the rear compartment and Heinz Fritsch watched the electro engineers react to different speeds called for from the commander's attack position inside the conning tower. The calm silence with its tense atmosphere and juggling of both speeds and periscope continued for some time until suddenly, without warning the order was given to discharge tubes one, two and three. Although almost unnecessary, the engineer officer ordered the compensating tanks to be flooded so that the change in weight would not make the boat rise to the surface. Voice tubes were all open and everybody knew the target was only 600 metres away, so every available stopwatch timed the progress. It was a weird feeling; far stranger than when this was first experienced on the Baltic shooting ranges. It felt as is time had stopped. Seconds had suddenly become awfully long, making it feel like an eternity before the first deafening detonation erupted throughout the by now stuffy atmosphere. Another bang followed almost immediately and then commander reported a hit by the forward mast and another in the engine room.

Neither seemed to have made much impact on the target. It stopped on an even keel and the torpedo in tube four was discharged as well. Slowly the U-boat turned. Things did not appear to be going too well and the commander finally fired the rear tube. Ten minutes later he reported the target to have sunk. At one minute before seven o'clock in the evening U355 surfaced amidst a sea of wreckage. The commander climbed up to the top, looked around without binoculars and then had another better look through his night glasses.

Kptlt. Reinhard Reche of U255 with a white cap on the right and on the left is Korvkpt. Hans Cohausz, Commanding Officer of the 11th U-boat Flotilla based in Bergen (Norway).

A lookout for convoys wearing standard U-boat leathers.

It was the First Watch Officer's duty to shoot torpedoes during surface attacks, but there were no hard and fast rules about this and often commanders or trainee commanders would aim torpedoes with the torpedo aimer at the top of the conning tower. This device automatically transmitted bearings down to the 'fruit machine' or torpedo calculator. The circular aerial of a radar detector can just be seen towards the left.

U405 under Kptlt. Rolf-Heinrich Hopman shortly after a tanker had been torpedoed.

Although the lookouts stood ready to follow him, the order was for navigator, first watch officer, engineer officer and Number One to come up. The situation started feeling most uncomfortable as if a cold drizzle was flooding through the boat. Men who were ordered to bring bread and rum up to the bridge were not allowed any further than the conning tower compartment either. They handed the goods up through the hatch. Even Heinz Fritsch, the provider of the food, was not allowed up top at first. Later, when he was given permission to witness the scene, he wished he had remained below. He could make out an overcrowded lifeboat with some injured men and none of the occupants dressed for the cold Arctic. 'This is not a place for the faint hearted,' said the engineer officer, 'but it's war.' The sinking of 5,082 GRT *Hartlepool* at 18.35 hours of 7 July 1942 was a depressing experience.

Later, once down in the depths again, the torpedo tubes were reloaded, giving the men in the bow compartment considerably more space. From then on they could eat their meals without having to hold their plates in one hand and a fork or a spoon in the other. Having completed this task, the next step was to empty the torpedo tanks by transferring an equal amount of water into the regulating tanks and then to trim the boat so that it sat comfortably level in the submerged position. While heading into a new operations area, U355 suddenly found itself running into heavy pack ice. This came as a surprise at first. The men had heard the noise of ice scraping past the hull before and were not too perturbed. The problem was that that these huge white sheets were constantly on the move and this time they came to surround the small submarine, making the men wonder how they were going to get out again. They need not have worried. The white accompaniment vanished as quickly as it had come. The more worrying point was the engineer's report that there were only twenty cubic metres of fuel left in the bunkers. The boat used three to four each day while cruising at an economical speed and considerably more when running at convoy chasing speeds, giving the commander no alternative other than to start heading for home (Narvik) where he made fast on 17 July 1942.

## The Fate of Convoy PQ17

The confusion as to what had happened with the battle for Convoy PQ17 was as thick as the Arctic fog that U355 had experienced and it was not until long after the war that it was possible for Heinz Fritsch to work out the end results. In all twenty-four of the thirty-six ships that left Iceland were sunk. Aircraft attacked exactly one third of this total and another third was attacked by U-boats, while the ships of the remaining third were sunk by U-boats after aircraft had disabled them. One reason for stopping or slowing down ships, rather than sinking them, was that aerial torpedoes were much smaller than those carried by U-boats. They had a diameter of 45 cm and were five metres long, whereas the naval version, the G7 had a diameter of 53.3 cm and a length of seven metres and could run some 10 – 14 knots faster than the aerial type.

The loss of Convoy PQ17 included valuable cargoes of more than 3,300 vehicles, over 400 tanks, 210 aircraft and almost 100,000 tons of other cargo. Perhaps one of the most amazing points about this battle is that all but one of the eleven-boat-strong Eisteufel Pack attacked and at least damaged one or more ships. The boat that failed in attacking, U657 under Kptlt. Heinrich Göllnitz, approached close enough to receive such a powerful hammering from depth charges that it had to withdraw with a leaking fuel tank. The question that still remains with this remarkable battle is: why did not the U-boats and aircraft not annihilate all of the convoy? This question can be answered to some extent by the logbook from U255 (Kptlt. Reinhart Reche) and by the convoy scattering into the Arctic wastes so that the wolf pack could not find the remaining ships.

Like U355, this was also U255's first operational patrol and afterwards the Admiral Commanding the Northern Seas remarked that the boat had a considerable amount of good luck, but he emphasised that the clear-headed thinking of the commander and him making the right decisions were also decisive factors. So, now step onto the bridge of U255 to join Kptlt. Reinhart Reche, the first to make contact with the convoy. Some sources would want us to believe that the boat left Kiel during the middle of June 1942 to operate against Convoy PQ17, but according to the log it put into Skjomenfjord, to the south of Narvik on 20 June and remained there next to *Stella Polaris* and the supply ship *Tanga* until the 23rd. Getting out of Norway and into the Polar Seas presented quite a challenge on this occasion. Lookouts spotted four drifting mines, which were destroyed by gunfire. Then, when U255 reached its operation area, things became only marginally better. Instead of mines the men found the sea to be laced with drifting ice. This might not explode on impact, but it provided even more opportunities for damaging propellers, rudders, hydroplanes and torpedo tube doors. Collisions had to be avoided.

The ice was thinning again when U255 ran into U251 (Kptlt. Heinrich Timm) and then U456 (Kptlt. Max-Martin Teichert). It was shortly after this meeting, on 1 July 1942 at 11.22 hours that a merchant ship was sighted. Immediately afterwards a couple of escorts and two destroyers came into sight, but failed in spotting the U-boat. This was plainly obvious when two of them passed over the top of the dived U-boat without attacking, leaving it in peace until it was safe to surface again. The Admiral Commanding the Northern Seas reacted instantly to the sighting report by ordering U334

A photo from the U255 collection showing German ships in a Norwegian fjord.

U225 leaving port.

(Kptlt. Hilmar Siemon) and U456 (Kptlt. Max-Martin Teichert) to the scene. U408 (Kptlt. Reinhard von Hymmen) had already reported a tanker and a corvette some two hours earlier, so the land-based operations room had ample time to evaluate the available data for immediate action by the boats closest to the convoy. The Operations Room for Northern Seas was also aware of information supplied by the B-Dienst (Radio Monitoring Service) under Kpt. z. S. Heinz Bonatz, which suggested that the convoy was underway and reports from air reconnaissance flights had confirmed that this group was definitely destined for North Russia, rather than making for the British Isles. As a result the Eisteufel (Ice Devil) Pack was formed to intercept it.

The first watch aboard U255 was changing at around 04.00 hours of the following day when the entry in the log stated, 'Convoy in sight. Keeping contact.' Following that Reche added that the escorts he had spotted the previous day kept coming too close for comfort while he and the duty officer were counting as many as twenty-seven heavily laden merchant ships. U255 was making every effort to get ahead of them by remaining at the limit of the constantly changing visibility. At first fog added considerable problems and things became even more irritating later on when large lumps of ice appeared as well to support those interfering escorts. Although U255 managed to make good progress, the escorts remained as insurmountable barrier and in the end Reche decided that there was no alternative other than having a go at the one nearest to him. It kept barring the approach far too often and a gap had to be created if he was going to get any closer. There were no other U-boats nearby at that time. Therefore it was not necessary to send continuous sighting reports or transmissions for radio direction finders. So, even if that escort had been equipped with a High Frequency Radio Direction Finder (H/F D/F or Huff Duff), this useful aid was not helping a great deal at this moment of time because U255 was not using its radio. Sadly for U255 though, the salvo of two torpedoes missed but they did not go unnoticed. The destroyer turned towards U255 and paid back with thirty-nine depth charges.

This highly annoying baptism of fire did not cause any serious damage, other than to keep U255 in the depths for more than three hours. After that it was not too difficult to make contact with the convoy again, but when the ships came into sight, it proved to be even more difficult to get close to them. U255 was pushed under immediately after having broadcast its sighting report. Reche did not know whether this came about as a result of an accidental meeting with the escort or whether the ship had homed in on his radio signal. Asdic foxers of Type Bold were discharged to help confuse the searching hunters. These consisted of tins that were ejected through a small tube in the stern of the boat. Forming a mass of bubbles in the water they helped to attract the chaser by reflecting Asdic impulses.

Once again U255 remained submerged long enough to have lost the convoy by the time it was safe to surface again. Yet, this time they were in luck. While still cursing naval oaths the men spotted a formation of twenty-three Heinkel 111 flying on a similar heading as the U-boat, suggesting that U255 was, at least, sailing in the right direction. This was confirmed a few hours later by an obviously damaged ship with a destroyer standing-by as lone sentry. Shortly after diving again it became apparent that there was no point in driving home this attack, the earlier aerial torpedo had obviously done its job well enough to deny U255 of a target. The damaged 4,841 GRT *Navarino*, belonging to the Glen Line of Glasgow, the same family as Alexander Glen, one of the Arctic explorers who is mentioned in the chapter on weather stations, dropped into the depths without U-boat assistance. It appeared that the escort, busy with taking on board the crew from the sinking ship, had not noticed the presence of the U-boat and Reche developed a strong urge to sink it. Unfortunately for him, the angle was not right for an immediate attack and by the time he moved into a more favourable position he found himself immersed in such thick Arctic mists that he could no longer see it.

Annoyingly the small ship was replaced by a much bigger one. Later in the day, when U255 surfaced again at around 22.30 hours, the men found themselves being shot at by a large cruiser. There was nothing for it, other than to go deep again and hope that the hunt would not become too aggressive. This incredibly large thorn did not show a great deal of interest in the U-boat and it certainly was not going to get close enough to provide U255 with an opportunity of shooting a salvo of four torpedoes. The sea was reasonably calm but by the time the boat resurfaced the men found that the earlier visibility of over twenty kilometres had been reduced most severely. Feeling their way through the thick murk, it was not long before U255 stumbled upon another merchantmen, confirming once more that they were on the right track. Navigating by dead reckoning worked well and the men were pleased when after several days of not getting an accurate fix they still found themselves in contact with the convoy.

Spotting the merchant ship through the periscope proved to be impossible, meaning there was nothing for it, other than going in much closer on the surface and hoping that there were not too many unpleasant surprises lurking in the sweeping fog. On this occasion the visual barrier was helping the opposition. Instead of providing adequate cover, it thinned into good visibility, exposing the U-boat to all and sundry. To make matters even worse, it was not an escort but a freighter that retaliated. The gun on its stern opened fire with amazing accuracy. One small hit would easily have put U255 out of action for good. Therefore Reche had no choice other than withdraw rather quickly, make another attempt to get ahead

U255 returning to Bergen where she spent the winter of 1943–44.

U255 at Novaya Zemlya.

U255 together with a supply aircraft.

of his opponent by running at fast speed on the other side of the horizon,
where he could not be seen, and then launch another submerged attack.
This worked well except that the freighter did not oblige by offering itself
as easy prey. Having driven the U-boat out of sight, it made such a drastic
change of course that the dead reckoning did not work on this occasion.

Finding nothing but empty seas, U255 dived to make use of its excellent
sound detector. This not only indicated that there was a ship on the other
side of the horizon, but also told the men approximately where it was.
Those merchant seamen were obviously no dummies. Every pair of eyes
would by now be focused on the surroundings seas, making Reche certain
that they were bound spot U255 if he approached too close. What was he
to do? Thinking that he was in an ideal position for a submerged attack,
Reche decided to remain in the cellar and go in as fast as possible. This
was going to be risky, leaving him in serious trouble with empty batteries
if he had to evade a long hunt afterwards. On the other hand, there had
not been any long determined hunts recently. The escorts usually only put
the U-boats down for a few hours so that they would lose contact with
their targets. The risk was worth taking.

The high speed brought U255 up to about six knots, meaning it would
reach the target over the horizon in a little over half an hour and perhaps
sight it before the battery condition became too critical. Yet all this
scheming did not work and it seemed likely that the ship made a drastic
change in direction. Instead of heading towards the North Russian ports,

it must have turned further away towards Novaya Zemlya. It was not difficult to guess that it was probably making for the Matochkin Strait to avoid both U-boats and the by now terrifying aircraft coming in with torpedoes and bombs. So, for U255 there was nothing for it, other than to surface for another spurt of fast speed to get ahead again. Not knowing exactly where the ship was making for, this became a matter of serious guesswork, but Reche was not going to give up easily. This was his first war cruise as commander, meaning he had to prove himself to his crew and he was not going to give them the impression that he was a soft nut. The chase lasted from 07.15 until almost 16.00 hours when he dived again. Half an hour after that Reche shot salvo of four torpedoes. He obviously was not going to allow this one to get away this time. Two hits were heard before U255 closed in to inspect three lifeboats from the 7,191 GRT *John Witherspoon*. It was a pitiful sight, despite the merchantmen having prepared their lifeboats as well as their incredible defence. They had adequate clothing and food on board, but conditions were by no means ideal for messing about in small boats.

It was almost exactly twelve hours later, at 04.33 hours that two more freighters heaved into sight. The first two torpedoes from a submerged attack missed, making it necessary for U255 to surface and race around out of sight of the target to get ahead again. It was much too light for a surface attack, so U255 dropped down into depths once more. This time a single torpedo brought one of the ships to a halt. Through the periscope Reche watched lifeboats being lowered and then he spotted another, much larger ship stopping nearby. A brilliant opportunity for U255, except that it was too easy for the merchantmen to work out that there must be a U-boat in the vicinity. The ship turned while making off at fast speed and with a too sharp an angle for another attack. Had the lookouts spotted U255's periscope? Two hours passed before Reche abandoned the chase to return to the stricken ship with a view of sinking it with gunfire. It was around midday of 7 July 1942 that the 5,116 GRT freighter *Alcoa Ranger* went down, leaving Reche with another chase on his hands to get in front of the other merchant ships. Seven-and-a-half hours later the lookouts spotted not ships but a lighthouse on Novaya Zemlya and another four hours passed before Reche prepared for the next attack. A single torpedo left tube one at 01.00 of 8 July 1942 to bring the 6,069 GRT freighter *Olopana* to a halt. Being so close to land did not feel comfortable at all, even if most of it was a barren wilderness of rocks and mountains. U255 surfaced immediately and the gun crew was ordered up on deck as soon as Reche had convinced himself that there was nothing offensive lurking nearby.

Meanwhile U457 (Fregkpt. Karl Brandenburg) had found the core of the merchant ships to send a sighting report. The problem was that U255 was now running short of torpedoes, meaning it was necessary to extract two G7a from their pressure tight containers under the upper deck, to load one into the bow and the other into the stern compartment. This must have been a hard task in excruciatingly cold conditions close to spray and water. Yet the men accomplished the feat in less than an hour and they were quickly down in the depths, searching for sounds with the hydrophones. Three freighters accompanied by five destroyers were sighted at 20.28 hours of 9 July 1942; almost immediately after this a German reconnaissance plane flew overhead and then the men on the top of the conning tower watched as several Ju88s attacked. The results were most dramatic; instead of just dropping out of sight, one ship started burning fiercely with a dense cloud of black smoke, producing the type of scene one usually sees only in films.

The action continued unabated without U255 coming within torpedo range of another target. Yet there was plenty going on. Perhaps most dramatic of all was an aircraft coming past that looked as if it was glowing rather than burning. There were hardly any flames and virtually no smoke. Expecting it to crash into the sea the men were surprised when it appeared to vaporize in mid-air and vanish from sight. U255 shot one more torpedo at another large freighter but missed. By that time it was 22.00 hours of 10 July and the action was rapidly subsiding, yet it was still not over. At 05.05 hours of 13 July the lookouts spotted what turned out to be an abandoned freighter stuck in ice, but with enough free water at one side for the U-boat to go alongside. It took a while before the men had convinced themselves that this was indeed an abandoned vessel. The IIWO (Second Watch Officer) and two petty officers were sent on board to salvage any interesting papers plus anything useful that they might find and having collected things from the obvious areas the 7,168 GRT Dutch freighter *Paulus Potter* was sunk with a torpedo from the stern tube. Later, after the war, the men learned that the ship had been abandoned eight days earlier on 5 July after a direct hit from an aerial torpedo. Following this U255 went home. It was the end of the battle for Convoy PQ17.

# 6

# Sailing without Convoy Protection

Following the disastrous losses from Convoy PQ17 in July 1942, when some 24 ships from a total of up to 36 were sunk a re-think was required. The convoy had been located by German forces on 1 July, after which it was shadowed continuously and attacked. In Britain, the First Sea Lord Admiral Dudley Pound, acting on information that German surface units, including the *Tirpitz*, were moving to intercept, ordered the covering force away from the convoy and told the merchant ships to scatter. However, due to vacillation by the German high command, the *Tirpitz* raid never materialized. As the close escort and the covering cruiser forces withdrew to intercept the presumed German raiders, the individual merchant ships were left without their escorting destroyers. In their ensuing attempts to reach the appointed Russian ports, these ships were repeatedly attacked by the Luftwaffe and U-boats. Of the initial 36 ships, only 11 reached their destination, delivering 64,000 tons of cargo. The disastrous outcome of the convoy demonstrated the difficulty of passing adequate supplies through the Arctic, especially during the summer period of perpetual daylight. As part of the rethink, the British Government went as far as encouraging shipping companies into paying officers a cash advance of one hundred Pounds and ratings fifty Pounds if they volunteered for service in the Arctic. Bearing in mind that this was more than their salary for several months, this was an attractive carrot. At the same time the Russians belittled the British and American war effort, with serious repercussions at highest levels. They did not believe that Britain had lost so many ships and suggested that the Royal Navy was not making the necessary effort to hunt both aircraft and U-boats. While this vocal war reached a high pitch, the Russians asked for two of their ships, the *Belomorkanal* and *Friedrich Engles*, anchored in Icelandic waters, to be sent home on their own. As a result they sailed on 11 and 12 August 1942. The first mentioned was a freighter of 2,900 GRT built in 1936 and the other a motor freighter of

3,972 GRT built in 1930. Russians manned both with the usual strong-willed characteristics of being prepared to put up with any amount of discomforts for the defence of their homeland. These stalwart men were well prepared for the hardships ahead of them, as U355 found out during its second war cruise. What happened was not only astonishing but also most unexpected and quite frightening for the U-boat crew.

Having taken part in the onslaught against Convoy PQ17, U355 (Kptlt. Günter La Baume) put into Narvik for replenishments and sailed again on 25 July 1942 to join the Nebelkönig (Fog King) Wolf Pack. Both Naval Intelligence and air reconnaissance had already announced that more convoys were being assembled in Iceland and Scotland and the U-boat men were looking forward to another set of great successes, where aircraft and U-boats could decimate the merchant ships. U405 (Korvkpt. Rolf-Heinrich Hopman), some ten days ahead, had reached the edge of the permanent ice cap when U355 was still in Norwegian waters and another six boats were stretched out between them, in the path of the anticipated convoy. The net was tight and the prospects looked good. Although Bletchley Park in England could not read the four-wheel Enigma code that these boats were using, the Submarine Tracking Room in London seemed to have been aware of the presence of the wolf pack. Whatever, U405 hardly caught a glimpse of the merchant ships and the height of excitement in U355 came when lookouts spotted a drifting mine. The commander ordered it to be sunk by gunfire from the 20 mm anti-aircraft gun.

U88 entering Kirkeness in northern Norway.

U88 near Kirkeness during April 1942.

U351 with the first watch officer, Karl Heinz Schmidt leaning against the 88 mm quick firing deck gun. He went on to command U17, U1103 and U3529.

While heading west across calm seas U355 encountered a mixture of rain and fog, with the latter always forming towards the end of the day to make the hours of darkness rather daunting. Nothing much happened. Progress towards the west was a monotonous routine of cruising on the surface, diving to listen for any noises and then surfacing again. Having reached its allocated operations area, U355 slowed down to the most economical cruising speed. So little effort was required for this tedious routine that one engine was switched off. This worked well except that the idle diesel was not to be allowed to stop for too long because it could take five minutes or more to start it from cold. So, it was a case of switching from one engine to other at frequent intervals so that both were ready for instant thrust as soon as the convoy was reported.

This dreariness of waiting was not terribly comfortable for the crew. With water temperatures at about five degrees, everybody was wearing two sets of underwear under their thick leathers, and even then they were still feeling rather chilled. The only relief from the daily monotony came from occasional exercises and the boredom continued for more than one week until U405 eventually reported the anticipated convoy near the edge of the ice. U355, and no doubt the other boats as well, turned towards the spot where they hoped to intercept the merchant ships, but this hive of activity, with everybody fully awake while expecting action, dissolved again a short time later when U405 sent another signal saying the ships had been lost in thick fog. By this time some nine U-boats were grouped around the possible convoy route, and constant changes of positions ordered by the U-boat Command in Norway interfered with the monotonous routine in each of them. During this chase U355 caught glimpses of Jan Mayen, Spitzbergen and then Hope Island—but all to no avail. The convoy remained as an illusive mirage that had just vanished into the vast Arctic emptiness.

It was around 19 August 1942, and U355 was close enough to land for the men to have a go at shooting a number of seabirds to add to their rather dreary menu. They tasted so awful that no one fancied more than a small sample and the cooked efforts were thrown overboard to feed the fish. At this stage the lookouts broke the daily tedium by reporting smoke on the horizon. Strangely, it was not the usual black cloud produced by ships, but bursts of small dark patches against the slightly lighter sky, looking almost like Red Indian smoke signals. This happened at 07.51 hours and immediately brought U355 to action stations, although the smoke was still at least some seven or more kilometres away. Dropping quietly into the depths, there was ample time to trim the boat for a perfect submerged attack and everything went well until the target was only two kilometres away, still heading straight towards the U-boat. Having kept its course for what appeared to be an eternity, the ship suddenly made a sharp turn to nip straight into a nearby fogbank that was approaching from the northeast.

La Baume was so dumfounded that he immediately ordered the best lookouts, irrespective of watch, to the top of the conning tower to see whether there was any chance of piercing the grey murk that had started to enclose them. Another full hour passed before a shadow was made out, but that vanished again so quickly that no one would even have sworn that they had seen anything solid. Then, while still wondering whether it had been the imagination, suddenly, without warning, at a distance of not more than 800 metres, a huge ship loomed up in front of them. The shock was still choking lookouts and the matter had only just been reported when a machine gun opened fire. To make matters even worse, the shells were immediately hitting the conning tower, making an impressive clang as they hit the steel. Luckily none of the shells were powerful enough to penetrate through the strong pressure hull, but no one needed any special orders for such a frightening shock. U355 instantly dropped into the cellar. It had hardly left the surface when something bigger, more powerful and much more noisy hit one of the diving tanks, causing the U-boat to glide out of control for a short period. La Baume's initial plan had been to remain at periscope depth for a submerged attack. The crew had now been at action stations for several hours. The forward torpedo tubes were flooded and a salvo could have been discharged within a matter of minutes or even seconds, but the unexpected blast made him abandon any thought of having a go at the monster. Instead he allowed his boat to drop deep, for the engineer officer to find the new trim and then to wait so that he could attack from a new, and hopefully unexpected direction. To do this, the boat was driven to a fast underwater speed in order to have the best control when coming up to periscope depth.

The process went well, the engineer officer caught the boat in the depths and was in the process of bringing it back to periscope depth when a single depth charge exploded behind U355. The painful noise from the deafening detonation was still ringing in the men's ears when a report flooded into the central control room that water was seeping in through the rear torpedo tube. There was enough of it to make the boat stern heavy, causing it to drop rapidly to the bottom where it bounced noisily off some rocks before scraping over them with an alarming screeching noise. Once again, the engineer officer had the situation under control and used compressed air and ballast pumps to lift the boat. After a while, when U355 eventually returned to the surface the men discovered the fog and the ship had vanished and a large area of brilliant visibility surrounded them.

The annoying point about this little cat and mouse game was that the freighter appeared to have had the upper hand, with incredible Asdic

*Above:* U302 running into Narvik.

*Right:* U584 in Kirkeness.

The wash thrown up by a U-boat's propellers.

equipment. The impulses from this were more powerful than the men had experienced before and seemed to have consisted of two sets working in tandem with one of them providing a general all round view and the other focusing far more accurately on the submerged U-boat. La Baume tried searching for differences in salinity or temperature but on this occasion did not seem to have been able to find anything that would hide the boat from the determined Asdic operator. The thought of meeting a merchant ship with Asdic and with radar was frightening. Radar must have played a role because the ship manoeuvred in front of the U-boat during the fog to get its gun crews to their action stations so that they could open fire the moment they sighted the U-boat. The steamer remained in the fog, where it vanished just as mysteriously as it had appeared. La Baume was convinced that this was no ordinary merchant ship, but one sent out especially to hunt U-boats, yet it would appear that it was the Russian freighter *Belomorkanal*, just an ordinary ship with a well-prepared crew that eventually made it safely home.

This determination shown by the Russians to retaliate against attackers played a far greater role on land, where the German army discovered that much of its progress was so precarious that every four men needed one in the rear to prevent surprise attacks by partisans. These were so frequent, thorough and well-aimed that special rear-guard units had to be formed to protect frontline troops. In the Arctic many U-boats found themselves being shot at by comparatively small guns hidden in such well camouflaged gun pits that the men in the U-boats could not spot where the shells were coming from. Despite the barren, cold and inhospitable environment, it would appear that individual Russians were more than determined to defend their homeland and make frightening sacrifices to do so.

Despite the considerable battering from the freighter, La Baume was not prepared to give up the hunt and determination drove him on to find this ship and to sink it. With thick fog making it impossible to see much more than a few hundred metres at best, the boat spent some time in the depths, listening for mechanical sounds and then surfacing to chase towards the source at fast speed. The Group Sound Detector, made up of a number of directional microphones (called hydrophones) was not accurate enough to give an exact bearing. So it was a case of heading into a general direction before diving again to hear more sounds. The device did not work terribly well while surfaced because water washing past the hull and waves masked the faint impulses coming from further away, but once submerged it was possible to hear ships that were too far away for lookouts to see from the top of the conning tower. On this occasion all the men in U355 saw was the southern tip of Hope Island. Being so close to it, they decided the steamer was going around the north of this rocky piece of land, but when heading off in that direction they realised that their assumption must have been wrong and the ship probably slipped past them by going the other way around the island.

Whatever, with the intermittent dense fog there did not seem to be any chance of catching it again and La Baume headed for home for more fuel. The earlier hunt for that illusive convoy, when the Northern U-boat Command in Norway kept directing the pack into different directions, meant cruising at fast speeds for long periods and therefore guzzling up vast quantities of the precious oil. All the torpedoes were still on board, making life in the bow compartment most uncomfortable. Two of them were lying above the floor between the bunks. This meant that tables could not be put up, and men had to eat their meals by holding a plate in one hand. To make matters worse, there were still considerable problems with the trim or balance of the boat and constant juggling was necessary to keep it on an even keel.

There was some relief on 21 August when a lifeboat was sighted. Not sure what to make of it, the men approached it with great caution until they discovered it was empty but of a highly superior quality with interesting modifications for the cold weather. The name on the side indicated it had come from the 7,177 GRT United States freighter *Daniel Morgan* that had been sunk by U88 (Kptlt. Heino Bohmann) on 5 July during the attack on Convoy PQ17. It even had an engine, which was possibly also used as a heating source. Trimming the submarine low in the water the men managed to haul it onto the upper deck for a thorough examination and found that the emergency provisions had not been consumed. A mass of American chocolate was distributed among the crew of U355. Chocolate was one of the first luxuries to vanish in Germany, so this was indeed a great treat. However, keeping the lifeboat on the upper deck for long was not possible. The waves washed it off again and it vanished into the wet desert without showing any signs of sinking.

Not all ships were as lucky as *Belomorkanal*. The independent sailing ships may have been heavily armed, but one must wonder what the defences were for. The 5,445 GRT SS *Chulmleigh* for example had a 4-inch gun on the stern, five anti-aircraft guns, two machine guns and a set of rockets when she sailed from Iceland. None of these helped her fight the natural elements or help with the difficult navigation in northern latitudes. The master, Captain D. M. Williams, knew his magnetic compass showed an error of about eight degrees, making it extremely difficult to find the right position through constant darkness where it was impossible to see the stars for much of the time. When a gap did appear in the clouds those taking bearings of the stars noticed there was also a Blohm und Voss flying boat in the sky. Anything like this, obviously out on reconnaissance, was bound to spot the freighter leaving a massive wake that was more blatant than any rude advertising hoarding. Aircraft did eventually appear, but not before the *Chulmleigh* had run aground off the southern tip of Spitzbergen. As it turned out the navigation error was only about twenty miles or so, hardly critical when crossing such vast seas under difficult conditions but fatal when there were rocks about. Running onto something like a knife's edge the ship remained locked in place, leaving the crew no alternative other than to abandon ship and their fate is mentioned in the chapter on Arctic Survival. The lifeboats had just got clear when five Ju88 tried to bomb the wreck into oblivion.

Messages from the reconnaissance plane and from the other aircraft were broadcast on the U-boat wavelengths, so U625 (Oblt.z.S. Hans Benker) could take an immediate interest. Turning towards the southern tip of Spitzbergen, the lookouts spotted the ship at lunchtime of 6 November 1942. There was no visible damage, other than that the stern appeared to have been a little lower in the water than the bows. There were also a few wisps of smoke drifting up, the lifeboats were missing and the two visible guns were unmanned. Closing in and then surfacing at 16.00 hours the men could see from close range that the ship had run into a semi-circle of rocks and had perhaps not noticed them because the entrance to this neat little trap was blocked with ice. To ensure that there was no danger of the ship being salvaged and perhaps being towed into port, Benker sacrificed

*Above:* U457 under Kptlt.Karl Brandenburg with the outside stern heads in use.

*Below:* U255 drying raingear.

two torpedoes, shooting both of them through gaps in the rocks. The first exploded on target. The other must have hit the rocks on the way in. Whatever, the torpedo disappeared without any noise. The bows of the ship rose slightly while the stern dropped, but the ship still looked in good condition. Therefore Benker ordered the gun crew on deck to hammer it with twenty 88 mm shells of incendiary ammunition. This was good practise for the men, but none of the many hits resulted in any significant fire and there was not even any impressive smoke. Yet the ship had taken on a definite list to starboard and by this time Benker guessed that it was firmly stuck to the rocks and was unlikely to be pulled off again. Turning round he headed back to his operation area a little further south. This was just as well. He had hardly got there when another lone target came sailing past that must have been carrying ammunition. The first torpedoes did not seem to do a great deal and it was the fifth torpedo that caused the dark night to light up as if it were day, with the ship, torn to shreds, flying high into the sky with a most impressive column of flames reaching several hundred metres up into the sky. Then, as the bits came falling down again, it looked as if the sea was boiling. That incredible experience was the end of the 7,455 GRT freighter *Empire Sky*, which went down at 22.24 hours of 6 November, the same day as the *Chulmleigh* had run onto the rocks.

The sad point about this whole set of episodes was that Convoy PQ19 had been cancelled because all escorts were required further south to help with Operation *Torch*, the North African Landings that took place on 8 November 1942. This was such a precarious operation that it could have had far-reaching consequences if it failed and therefore took priority over all other operations. Unfortunately for many who suffered or lost their lives, some naval authorities also demanded that the flow of goods to Russia had to continue at all cost. Therefore between 29 October and 2 November 1942 thirteen independent ships sailed from Iceland to North Russia. Three turned back, four were sunk by U-boats, running aground wrecked one and five others arrived. Going in other direction, between 29 October 1942 and end of January 1943 twenty-three ships sailed west from Russian ports. One of these (Russian *Donbass*, 7,363 GRT) was sunk by Z27 (Kptlt. Freiherr Wilhelm-Nikolaus von Lyncker) after it had been sighted by an aircraft launched from the catapult of the heavy cruiser *Admiral Hipper* and the rest arrived in Iceland. It was a heavy price to pay by 'ordinary' people with brave constitutions.

# 7

# Mining Cold Waters

The German thrust against convoys in the Polar seas did not start until almost the end of 1941, several months after the invasion of Russia. As a further guide, the famous massacre of Convoy PQ17 took place during June and July of 1942. This major attack, especially the support from the Luftwaffe, was so successful that the German command intensified its efforts to search for other convoys and the failure in finding them was put mainly down to uncooperative natural elements, such as fog and ice, rather than the ingenuity of the opposition. As a result the majority of U-boats sent north for these early onslaughts concentrated on searching for convoys and it was not until the summer of the following year that there was a drastic change in this approach, with 1943 seeing a heavier emphasis on mining activities. The acute absence of shipping in the Polar seas and the long time wasted by U-boat in hunting for ships sighted by air reconnaissance which then vanished was one of the major contributing factors for this change in attitude. The other contributing factor was Germany's withdrawal of Luftwaffe aircraft towards the end of 1942 to support operations in the Mediterranean.

It would appear that the first small-scale U-boat mining operations of Arctic waters took place in August 1942 when U589 (Kptlt. Hans-Joachim Horrer) mined the Matochkin Strait between the North and South Island of Novaya Zemlya and this was followed in October by U592 (Kptlt. Carl Borm) mining the Yugor Strait. The more intensive mining offensive of 1943 was launched in July with seven boats heading to different traffic knots and these were followed by another wave of five towards the end of August. Following this, in October and November another four sailed north with mines. During the following year (1944) there were at least six special mining operations to the Polar Seas. Finding target areas for mining was quite easy because there were many narrow and obvious focal points that could not be avoided by shipping. The approaches to Murmansk, the White Sea, the Matochkin Strait and the narrow channels between the mainland and Novaya Zemlya made obvious minefields where well-placed explosives could create havoc. Even if they did not sink shipping, they were still in a good position to shut those passages until the mines were cleared again.

All the U-boats mining the Polar seas were ordinary Type VIICs, meaning they were limited to use only special mines that could be ejected through torpedo tubes and could not carry shaft mines made for the large minelayer of Type XB or the special Type VIID with vertical mineshafts to the rear of the conning tower. There were three types of Torpedo Mines, versions A, B and C and these were known more often as TMA, TMB and TMC. The first two had a length of 2.31 m and a weight of 740 or 800 kg, meaning that three of them fitted into a torpedo tube. TMC was 3.39 m long and weighed about 1,115 kg so that only two fitted into each tube. The two main problems with using these was that the boats needed a special modification to the torpedo tubes and the commander had to have extra training, but they could be dropped by a surfaced or submerged submarine in comparatively shallow water. Placing them was not an easy task.

Although these torpedo mines were comparatively small, they were quite something and might have inflicted considerably more damage had the Luftwaffe not presented Britain with a magnificent opportunity of neutralising this magnificent weapon. The great advantage with these mines was that they were not cleared away by existing methods, and minesweepers could pass over the top without influencing the magnetic detonator. Unfortunately for Germany, in November 1939 the Luftwaffe dropped an aerial mine of similar type into the river Thames near Southend-on-Sea in Essex and Lieutenant Commander J. G. D. Ouvery walked out to it during the following low tide to make rubbings of its screw heads and fastenings. Germany could not have chosen a better location for presenting this valuable gift to the Royal Navy. There were military workshops nearby, and by the next low tide Ouvery went out once more with a set of freshly made tools to dismantle the mine. By doing this Britain learned that the trigger system was different to how British magnetic mines were detonated and the Royal Navy could take immediate measures in neutralising what was at that time a highly successful weapon.

One major difficulty with mining activities was highlighted frequently enough by the commanders of supply U-boats in the Atlantic, who discovered that there were a good number of U-boats that could not steer a steady straight course alongside the tanker and this resulted in some refuelling operations having to be abandoned. This got so bad at times that some tankers sent their charges home because it was too difficult

*Right:* Map showing Arctic Mining Targets.

*Below:* Oberbootsmaat Gerhard Jungclaus of U377 showing a sighting device fitted to a magnetic compass on the top of the conning tower. Compasses turned out to be most unreliable in the Arctic, but they were mounted in gimbals and therefore remained fairly steady and were ideal for taking bearing of landmarks to help calculate accurate positions. Finding the right positions was essential for many mining operations, where it was easy to place the deadly loads in shallow water rather than in the main shipping channels.

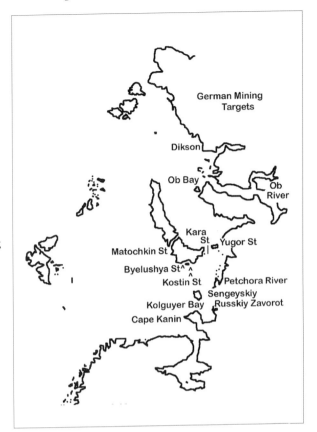

German Mining Targets

Dikson
Ob Bay
Ob River
Kara St
Yugor St
Matochkin St
Byelushya St
Kostin St
Petchora River
Sengeyskiy
Kolguyer Bay
Russkiy Zavorot
Cape Kanin

*Above:* A torpedo mine for U-boats being lowered by crane onto what appears to be a standard Type VIIC. The 'V' on the side of the conning tower is the emblem of the 24th U-boat Flotilla based in Trondheim (Norway).

*Below:* A torpedo mine being lowered onto U373.

to supply them. This may sound absurd, but one has to remember that German U-boats were designed to be operated by crews with the minimum of training and some of the men could not cope with the accuracy needed for dropping mines in exactly the right spot. When attacking convoys there was always the opportunity of going in closer to fire torpedoes and one could see the target, but there was nothing to guide you when laying mines. So precision was a major element and only proven boats could be sent on such difficult operations.

What was probably Germany's first mining operation of Polar Seas went ahead towards the end of August 1942 without too much of a hitch, except that the Mining Depot in Tromsö was not equipped to deal with the special torpedo mines and did not have the appropriate gear for loading them. As a result it took rather a long time to load sixteen TMC mines into U589 (Kptlt. Hans-Joachim Horrer). The next step, up in the Polar Seas, was even more unsettling for the crew. The boat had to be prepared for special shallow water operation, which involved attaching scuttling charges, laying secret materials in places where they could be quickly destroyed and assuring that every member of the crew had his submarine escape apparatus to hand. The coding machine was often dismantled and each bit distributed among the men, who were told to throw their bits away if they had to abandon ship. Although air temperature sometimes reached into double figures when fresh southerly winds were blowing, the water always remained incredibly bitter even during the height of the summer and the knowledge of perhaps having to swim in those cold temperatures made the men more than just apprehensive. Even in summer men in the bow torpedo compartment wore two layers of underwear in addition to their Arctic thermals. It never really got warm so far away from the main heat source—the diesel engines.

Even the officers and lookouts, who were in a position to see what was going on outside, were nervous as they nosed nearer to Novaya Zemlya. Nothing—Nothing at all was known about possible hazards ahead, of the possible defences, or of what sort of sentries might have been posted. No one had been there before. No one had approached so close to known Russian hotspots, making this a frightening step into the unknown. As it happened the approach to the shipping channel through the Matochkin Strait was calmer than anyone had imagined and most of the land was hidden behind that magical veil of fog, making it possible to see the mountains but not identify any features on them. What was also unsettling at first was that the old Russian charts the boat was using—some of them dating back to 1901— did not seem to be very accurate and several structures marked on them were missing. This added a worrying element until the men confirmed that their navigation was correct, and they came to the conclusion that the

Part of Spitzbergen's inhospitable coast showing the type of conditions faced by U-boats that approached close to the coast to lay mines in shallow water. *Photo: Mike and Brenda Lyons*

way markers had probably been demolished to slow down any German intrusion. In the end U589 got close enough to make out what looked like a pilots' station with meteorological office but without any signs of military installations and no visible defences. This last point did not mean much at the time and there was no way that the men were going to take any chances. They had heard enough rumours of hidden gun installations suddenly opening fire from such cleverly concealed positions that even the smoke from the guns did not make it possible for observers to spot the source of the irritation.

To be on the safe side, when arriving at the mining destination, U589 dived some ten kilometres off the coast for a close-up submerged survey through the periscope. This was not the easiest of tasks because there was not much space between the bottom of the sea and the surface of the water and it was much too easy for top of the U-boat to protrude into the air without anyone inside noticing this until someone peered through the periscope. The fog bound shore and a noticeable heavy swell made it rather difficult to keep the boat at the correct periscope depth and in the end the boat accidentally broke through the surface of the water on at least two occasions. These most dramatic incidents were put down to strong variations in salinity of the water. Kptlt. Horrer was under the impression that this happened when they moved from a fresh water rich layer to one containing more seawater, thus allowing the boat to rise on its own. On both occasions a dramatically concerted effort had to be made to keep the superstructure below the surface and at one stage all spare hands were ordered into the bow compartment to balance the boat. It was a tricky time for the engineer officer.

The boat also touched the sandy bottom on several occasions, making a weird, almost high-pitched screeching noise as it slid over the bed. Other than frightening the crew, it did not seem to damage the boat. Steering through those inshore waters was indeed so difficult that the course had to be corrected after the dropping of each mine and at times it was next to impossible to keep the bows in the desired direction. Instead it felt as if some huge hand was continuously twisting the boat into the wrong direction. What was strange was that when U589 had completed its task and started running out to sea again there was none of this natural interference at all and the boat distanced itself from the coast without any hiccups.

What was probably the second attempt to mine North Russian waters took place under highly contrasting circumstances in October 1942 when the long Arctic night had taken a hold and when the surface of the sea already acquired a new coat of rather thin ice. The winter had not yet got such an extreme hold to prevent shipping from running along the Siberian Sea Passage. This time the Yugor Strait, between mainland Russia and Vaigach Island to the south of Novaya Zemlya was singled out for attention. U592 under Kptlt. Carl Borm had on board twenty-four TMB mines, three G7e and two G7a torpedoes plus a generous allowance of artillery ammunition for this far-flung outpost of the Russian Empire.

The first major task was to determine the general conditions between Novaya Zemlya and the mainland Russia. As with U589, the boat was prepared for instant scuttling before approaching the shallows of the Strait. The depth of water of only twenty-five metres made this rather unsettling and then, at the critical moment, an aircraft was spotted, making it necessary to remain on the seabed for some time. This was not as easy because there was a strong northerly current and the clearness of the water combined with a mirror smooth surface made the men apprehensive in case their shadow was spotted from the air. Visibility was so brilliant that navigation errors could be ironed out by taking positive sightings on a number of well-defined landmarks while they were illuminated by a brilliant display of Northern Lights. Following that, everything ran like well-oiled clockwork with the mines going in exactly the right places.

Having dealt with the tricky bit of the operation Borm was no longer worried about advertising his presence and took on the second part of his challenge to destroy a land-based radio station at 70° 24′ N 58° 48′ E during the following day.

Despite everybody on board feeling somewhat relieved at having come through the special operation in shallow waters unscathed, the natural elements did not continue with their obliging assistance. The sea remained calm the following day, but incredibly thick snow showers swept over them, making it virtually impossible to make out anything on land and it was not long before the men realised that they must have overshot their target. Once again the men caught enough glimpses of landmarks to confirm that they had gone too far along the coast and then the snow showers were also interlaced with thick fog patches, making it somewhat dangerous to go in close to the radio station. No one on board had any idea whether there would be any retaliation and in the end Borm decided the whole idea was just too risky. The fact that the starboard diesel engine was giving some trouble and the port engine had already been repaired several times encouraged him to break off the attempt to return to Kirkeness to stock up with more torpedoes and fresh provisions.

It would appear that if the records are right that U601 (Kptlt. Peter-Ottmar Grau) was the first to launch the 1943 mining offensive in the Polar seas and this time the loading process ran considerably smoother than a year earlier when it was necessary to collect the mines from more than one port. The target was the south-west corner of Novaya Zemlya with the immediate seas there serving as operations area after the mining attempt. Not much happened, other than meeting a number of drifting mines in areas where they were of hindrance to the opposition rather than interfering with German traffic. Meeting mines in Norway was far more thrilling because they added some excitement by being blown up by gun fire, but high up in the Arctic it was a case of avoiding them and keeping a sharp lookout for the next one. There were three of them; one after the other during the morning of 19 July 1943, and shortly after lunch there was an even bigger surprise when lookouts spotted what turned out to be a signal tower at Cape Kostin. This called for an immediate navigation check. Everything was correct. Although this isolated tower was still more than fifty kilometres away, it stood out as well defined obstacle above a mirror calm sea. It was an incredible sight with no wind and with an air temperature of 14 degrees Celsius, even warmer than the 10 degrees when they had left Tromsö. It was not possible to enjoy the view for too long because a column of smoke also came into sight and after the boat had dived this was identified as a Russian sentry. U601 did not have enough power in the batteries to tackle it nor sufficient torpedoes in the tubes.

Therefore the only option was to turn away, to continue with the main objective of laying the mines.

Nothing terribly exciting happened other than the two mines from tube three did not drop out as expected and the second time this happened it was not noticed right away so that the chain did not have all its links evenly spaced. The sentry spotted the day before was lying at a pier and construction machinery nearby suggested the small harbour was being modified. There was enough activity to make Grau cautious. In addition to this, air cover proved to be more than a little troublesome. There were enough aircraft to prevent him from having a go at the small ship. It was too tiny to risk any lengthy retribution in this shallow water where he could not dive deep enough. The opposition was obviously making every effort to prevent any intrusions, even in this barren and remote spot. In the end it was thick fog that prevented further action and Grau returned to Hammerfest.

It is astonishing how the experiences of different boats varied, even when they were not too far apart. U212 under Kptlt. Helmut Vogler, for example, found conditions fairly straightforward and was only harassed by four drifting mines, two of them probably left over from the First World War. A couple of planes passed at a distance of about twenty kilometres without apparently noticing the U-boat, but nothing much else upset the plans. Yet at the same time and in around the same area U586 under Dietrich von der Esch was confronted with considerably more problems than mere drifting mines. On 23 July 1943, while passing through the Barents Sea under low clouds with a few lighter patches further away the boat suddenly found itself under attack from two Russian PB100 aircraft that dropped from the clouds to rake the boat with gun fire. U586 had already been fitted with a radar-warning device and had the anti-aircraft gun manned to immediately return fire but there had been no warning on the electronic device. Even more disturbing was that these relatively small planes with a crew of only three had a powerful sting, shooting with something in the region of a 40 mm gun. The rate of fire was slow but incredibly annoying and the German were lucky that none of the shells hit. To make matters worse, the Russians did not let up after this attack and U586 encountered strong and most annoying air interference during the next few days. They were obviously making a concerted effort to hunt the U-boat.

Later, when conditions were ideal with a brilliant blue sky, the boat was left in peace. The radar detector produced some weird irritation inasmuch that the magic eye used to tune it suggested someone was on the prowl in the vicinity. Yet the warning noises associated with the set did not follow and all it did was to produce a mysterious crackle. As U586 approached closer to its destination the lookouts spotted a buoy that had not been marked on the German chart, making the men wonder what it was supposed to signify. They thought it might be a temporary marker for the summer period to guide ships into port or, perhaps, it indicated new shallows that were constantly being washed into the sea by the comparatively huge rivers. The featureless land in the distance did not help by providing easily identifiable landmarks for navigation, so progress was not easy.

It was during the middle of the afternoon of 27 July 1943 when the starboard stern lookout reported a haze in the distance. Approaching at a fairly fast speed, it was immediately identified as heat from a ship's funnel and the rate at which it was closing in suggested there was a small fast warship underneath; putting U586 in a dire predicament. There were just nine metres of water below the keel and the only good way out of this awkward situation was to go north, exactly where the intruder was coming from. It was only a matter of ten minutes or so before it became obvious that the U586 was not only in an embarrassing but also in a most dangerous situation. It definitely was a warship. There were a good number of large buoys and beacons around, so for a while the Germans hoped that the U-boat might be mistaken for one of these. Yet remaining on the surface was not to be recommended and at around 3 o'clock in the afternoon with still brilliant sunshine and a warm temperature of 12 degrees Celsius, von der Esch was lucky to have found enough water to dive gently into it.

The boat immediately jerked onto the seabed, sliding over what appeared to be soft mud. The strange thing was that the sound detector did not hear the ship and it was not possible to see it through the periscope either. Eventually, when von der Esch did spot it through the sky or navigation periscope, the one with the large head lens, he identified it as a small escort with three guns. The snag was that the torpedo tubes were full of mines. Luckily the ship did not come any closer and remained well out of attack range. There was nothing for it, being so close to the mining destination, U586 continued and eventually, at around 05.40 hours of the following day, surfaced to start dropping the mines in 17–18 metres of water close to 69° 00´ ´N 55° 00´ E, leaving a gap of about 300–350 metres between each one. Once the last mine dropped out, there was nothing for it other than running away at fast speed and making another visual check with landmarks to confirm that the mines were in exactly the right positions.

The first operation of the first mining wave of 1943 had taken place towards the end of July and such undertakings continued until the end of September as given in the table below. Each one of the second wave had a name prefixed with the word 'See' (sea) and suffixed with the

Roman numeral I, suggesting that more operations had been initially been planned. The next wave for autumn 1943, named Eistorte and starting with U636, went ahead but the rest were cancelled because it was thought that the boats could be employed more profitably in other areas. The main U-boat Command (located in Berlin since March 1943) was very much against these operations in Arctic waters because the number of targets sighted per U-boat at sea was abysmally low when compared with other areas further south; where convoys were avoiding wolf packs because each patrol line was thought not to contain enough boats. Arctic mining operations resumed again in September 1944.

D-Day, the invasion of Normandy, starting on 6 June 1944, had a profound influence of the war at sea with such heavy losses that only schnorkel boats stood a reasonable chance of survival. As a result six boats of Group Dachs (Badger) were sent into the Polar seas for another bout of special mining operations.

U992 under Oblt.z.S. Hans Falke went north on a mining operation for the boat's 7th operational cruise. It had been in action since the beginning of April 1944, had operated with the Trutz Group, helped with setting up an automatic weather station on Jan Mayen and been depth charged by a Sunderland flying boat, so the men had ample experience when they ventured deep into the Arctic seas with mines. There had been considerable changes to the war at sea and it was no longer a case of just avoiding a few ships that sometimes appeared on the horizon or the occasional aircraft that happened to be passing but failed in spotting the U-boat below. By this time the lookouts had almost taken on a secondary role with two radar warning devices of Type Naxos and Wanze giving the first warning of approaching danger and this very often came in the form of a large fast-flying aircraft rather than an antiquated rusty ship squelching forth a great deal of black smoke. Large land-based aircraft were not the only problem. Small single and twin engine aircraft were also a feature, confirming that an aircraft carrier had be somewhere close to the Norwegian coast. Despite having had their anti-aircraft armament strengthened, the autumn of 1943 had already demonstrated quite clearly that this new firepower was insufficient for tackling the new fast-flying, land-based aircraft. The problem with these was that the puny 20 mm shells from a Type VII U-boat could not do a great deal of damage to the comparatively small sheets armour in front of the vital aircraft components, and once these were side-on to the guns, they flashed so fast past the gun sights that hitting them was near to impossible. So, for most of the time, all U-boats could do was to dive before the aircraft came too close. Taking them on in combat was risky and rather dangerous with the aircraft usually gaining the upper hand.

U992 left Hammerfest during the afternoon of 29 August 1944 and had not got very far when two single engine aircraft were spotted flying over the low rocky islands that guarded that part of the coast. They did not come any closer, but when they had gone Falke used the opportunity for testing the men's reactions by ordering an emergency dive. After supper the boat had hardly surfaced again when the Wanze detector indicated radar activity in the vicinity and the men vanished below the waves again, hoping they had left the surface before the aircraft's radar was close enough to receive an echo from the U-boat. Unfortunately they had no way of knowing the distance between them and the aircraft, but radar impulses were picked up some time before the opposition got so close that the echo from their target would bounce back.

The two radar-warning devices paid for themselves following day, on 30 August 1944. U992 surfaced at 00.57 hours to find a night-time temperature of 14–16 degrees Celsius, very little wind and visibility of over twenty kilometres. Dawn broke just over an hour later at those northerly latitudes and at 04.52 hours came the first radar-warning signal on the Naxos. Consequently U992 dived without being molested. Remaining submerged until after midday U992 dived again less than two hours later and this up and down process continued as the boat headed east through the Barents Sea. Mines were laid on 2 September without surfacing and therefore without interruptions. Surfacing again to ventilate the interior and to recharge the batteries also went well without interference, but aircraft once again became an irritating part of the return journey to Hammerfest.

Arctic Mining Operations
(Compiled by Reinhart Reche with help from Prof. Dr. Jürgen Rohwer)

| Name | Boat | Commander | Date | Place |
|------|------|-----------|------|-------|
| **Year 1942** | | | | |
| | U589 | KL Hans-Joachim Horrer | 28 August | Matochkin Strait |
| | U592 | KL Carl Borm | 13 October | Yugor Strait |
| **Year 1943** | | | | |
| Alster II | U601 | KL Peter-Ottmar Grau | 20 July | Byelushya Bay |
| Nelke I | U625 | KL Hans Benker | 20 July | Yugor Strait |
| Gladiole I | U629 | OL Hans-Helmuth Bugs | 27 July | Petchora Bay |
| Tulpe IV | U586 | KL Dietrich von der Esch | 28 July | Petchora Bay |
| Veilchen I | U212 | KL Helmut Vogler | 31 July | near Kolguyev |
| Narzisse I | U639 | OL Walter Wichmann | 1 August | Petchora Bay |

| | | | | |
|---|---|---|---|---|
| Rose I | U636 | KL Hans Hildebrandt | 3 August | near Sengeyskiy |
| Lilie I | U629 | OL Hans-Helmuth Bugs | 10 August | Russkiy Zavorot |
| Seebär I | U625 | KL Hans Benker | 13 August | Yugor Strait |
| Seehund I | U639 | OL Walter Wichmann | 21 August | Ob Bay, Kara Sea |
| Seekuh I | U636 | KL Hans Hildebrandt | 23 August | Yenisey – Dikson |
| Seevogel I | U960 | OL Günther Heinrich | 28 August | Matochkin Strait |
| Seeadler I | U629 | OL Hans-Helmuth Bugs | 5 September | near Amderma |
| Seeschlange I | U960 | OL Günther Heinrich | 23 September | near Dikson |
| Seemöwe I | U601 | KL Peter-Ottmar Grau | 23 September | near Dikson |
| Eistorte I | U636 | KL Hans Hildebrandt | 14 November | Yugor Strait |

**Year 1944**

| | | | | |
|---|---|---|---|---|
| Dorsch I | U425 | OL Heinz Bentzien | 1 September | Pechora Bay |
| Sprotte I | U992 | OL Hans Falke | 2 September | near Kolguyev |
| Butt I | U956 | OL Hans-Dieter Mohs | 3 September | Byelushya Bay |
| Lachs I | U968 | OL Otto Westphalen | 4 September | Cape Kanin Noss |
| Hering I | U995 | KL Walter Köhntopp | 4 September | Yugor Strait |
| Forelle I | U636 | OL Eberhard Schendel | 5 September | Pechora Bay |

# U31

Loch Ewe, the British assembly point for many Russian Arctic convoys, was mined on two occasions by U31 (Kptlt. Johannes Habekost), an ordinary Type VIIA and a remarkable holder of several records. U31 was the first U-boat of the Second World War to be sunk by an aircraft without any form of outside help, it was the only U-boat to be sunk twice by enemy action, the first U-boat of that war to attack a convoy (OB4) and possibly the only U-boat to be a target for three Royal Navy submarines during one operational voyage.

The first sinking of U31 took place on 11 March 1940, more than a year before the first Arctic convoys sailed. Having undergone a thorough refit the boat moved out of the naval dockyard in Wilhelmshaven for some simple diving trials in the approaches to the harbour. On this occasion there were eleven dockyard workers and two flotilla engineering assistants on board. Once far enough out with sufficient water under the keel, a red warning flag was attached to the extended periscope before dropping into the depths. At that critical moment, when everybody inside the submarine was concentrating on the dive in their own home waters, Blenheim 'O' from RAF Squadron 82, skilfully piloted by Squadron Leader M. V. Delap burst out of the clouds and immediately straddled the unfortunate boat with four bombs; two of which were seen to hit before it disappeared

The memorial stone by the sea entrance of Loch Ewe in Scotland with the inscription, "In memory of our shipmates who sailed from Loch Ewe during the Second World War. They lost their lives in bitter Arctic sea battles to North Russia and never returned to this tranquil anchorage. We will always remember them." Standing by the side of the piper is one of the veterans who attended the Russian Arctic Convoys Reunion in 2013.

from view. Circling, the observers in the aircraft spotted a large oil slick where the boat had gone down. A while later a passing ship gave the red flag a wide berth so as not to interfere with the diving tests, which were a common feature in the approaches to this busy naval base with full-blown shipyard. Judging by the wash around the extended periscope, the submarine appeared to be making good headway against the tide. Yet, in reality everybody in the submarine was probably already dead, either drowned or killed by poisonous gasses that form when seawater is mixed with battery acid. The boat was already stuck on the bed with the wash around the still extended periscope being created by the tide alone.

As it happened a passenger aboard a ferry running to Wangerooge Island saw the aircraft dive and circle in the far distance, but the crew were used to all kinds of military activities and did not take any notice or report the matter. Being somewhat disturbed, once on land one of the passengers telephoned the dockyard in Wilhelmshaven, where he worked, to report what he considered to have been suspicious aircraft activity, suggesting that the aircraft might have laid mines in the deep water channel. Eventually, when an investigating boat with divers reached the spot they found the conning tower crammed full of people who obviously had tried to escape from the flooding down below. A ventilation pipe had been left open for poisonous gases to seep up from the battery compartments. Everybody on board was dead. The boat was raised, re-fitted and commissioned a second time by Kptlt. Wilfried Prellberg to be sunk once more on 2 November 1940 when HMS *Antelope* rammed it. This time forty-four survivors were picked up and only two men died to the north-west of Ireland.

The incidents with the three submarine attacks during a single voyage are rather unusual inasmuch that a complete is day is missing from the logbook. It is, of course always possible that the typed sheets got lost somehow, but on the few previous occasions where this has been noticed there was something 'interesting' known to be going on and it looked as if the details were removed on purpose to prevent prying eyes from finding information. The first meeting with a British submarine took place a long way west of Northern Ireland on 28 September 1940 while Prellberg was hunting convoys. Unfortunately for him those convoys that had been reported were too far away and U31 was chugging through calm seas with very little wind when, at 14.48 hours, a lookout spotted the shadow of what appeared to be a submarine. The duty watch was already clambering down for a quick dive when it became apparent to Prellberg that the submarine had spotted him as well. Still diving, he turned to silent drive to head towards the intruder, hoping he might have been mistaken and he might just meet it again as decent target. Yet this was not to be. Instead, the high-pitched whine of a torpedo was heard to pass behind the U-boat. Surfacing again at 20.00 hours all Prellberg could do was report the incident to headquarters. Other U-boats were known to be in the area and it would have been rather unfortunate if one of them fell foul to this marauding attacker.

A couple of days later at 03.16 hours of 30 September 1940, U31 was running at comparatively slow speed through a calm sea with little swell because strong luminescence was creating rather obvious giveaway flashes of light. Suddenly, without warning the Second Watch Officer ordered full speed ahead and a sharp turn to starboard. Prellberg had just spotted the cause of his alarm, when another torpedo was seen to be running towards U31 as well. It was time for taking a deep breath, but not enough to say goodbye to the other men on bridge. The luminescence made both torpedoes plainly obvious. One of them passed within a metre of the U-boat. Definitely a close shave.

The third incident, this time on 8 October 1940, was even more impressive than the first two encounters. Running from Wilhelmshaven to Lorient in France, U31 was by this time within sight of the French coast when Lieutenant Commander G. M. Sladden in HM Submarine *Trident* fired a salvo of four torpedoes from a range of 1,500 yards (1,370 metres). All of them missed. Then opening fire with its deck gun the submarine reported a hit on the base of U31's conning tower. This was not recorded in U31's log, so it is likely that he missed. While this was going on two more salvos of two torpedoes each were shot, but again they missed.

To look at the same incident of meeting HMS *Trident* from the German angle: U31 was having some troubled times at that moment. First, one of the diesel engines was out of action due to having some bearings replaced and, secondly, there were a good number of small fishing boats about, adding to the problem of running towards the rendezvous with the escort that was due to take U31 into Lorient. It was 06.15 hours of 8 October when the duty watch at the top of the conning tower reported a light that was at first taken to be another one of these irritating fishermen. A quarter of an hour later came a report that a shadow had been sighted that did not look like a fishing boat. Scrutinising it carefully, it was eventually identified as a submarine and at that point the lookout for the sector informed Prellberg that he had seen it ages ago, but assumed it had been a rock. It quickly became obvious while giving the lookout a sharp lesson in reporting sightings that the submarine had seen U31 as well. Two torpedo tubes were flooded with seawater by opening the outside doors, something that brought a few repercussions a little while later. At the same time U31 went to top speed with the remaining working diesel engine. The other submarine was now immediately behind U31, at a rather sharp angle for an attack, so the men in U31 felt relatively safe, thinking it was unlikely that the opposition would fire torpedoes from such an acute angle. They were mistaken. Soon afterwards they had to avoid a salvo of two. Turning to run exactly parallel to the torpedoes, one passed some fifteen metres on the starboard side while the other on the port side was only an uncomfortable three metres away. Just to infuriate matters further, the anti-aircraft gun jammed before it fired a single shot. While digesting all this quick action, the commander had to turn his attention to two more torpedoes speeding towards him. Again U31 succeeded in outmanoeuvring them, although they passed closer than the other two. Just to cap it all, the other submarine started shooting with a large deck gun of about 3-inch (7 cm) calibre. Prellberg had enough and dived. Through having flooded the torpedo tubes from the outside U31 had taken on some additional water, making the bows a little heavier than the last time the engineer officer trimmed the boat. As a result U31 hit the bed rather hard while the opposition made life more uncomfortable by dropping what were thought to have been either bundles of hand grenades or small depth charges. Later there came some grinding noises that were taken to been mines. Whatever they were, U31 did not sustain any damage and eventually surfaced again to report the presence of what was obviously a hostile submarine. After meeting the escort, the U31 made fast in Lorient later that same day.

# Mining Loch Ewe

The first operation to mine Loch Ewe in Scotland started shortly after midday of 21 October 1939 when U31 under Kptlt. Johannes Habekost cast off from the Bant Submarine Base in Wilhelmshaven. This was a momentous period of time. Four days earlier U47 under Kptlt. Günther Prien had returned to a noisy reception from the famous raid into Scapa Flow where the battleship HMS *Royal Oak* had been sunk. Something that was irrigated rather strongly in the local bars. Despite the euphoria, U31 did not get off to a good start. The boat had hardly cleared the sea locks when both diesel engines came a juddering halt. This was more embarrassing than dangerous because with the batteries topped up to capacity it was possible to continue with electric drive. It turned out that some seawater from the storage bunker had got into the main tank below the ceiling of the engine room that held a day's fuel and was quickly removed again. It took only half an hour before U31 was back on diesel power. A few hours later the men got an enormous boost in confidence when, during the darkness of the night, U31 passed the Second Minesweeping Flotilla, without anyone noticing the submarine's presence. Everything was going well. Even the dreaded narrow stretch, the so-called 'Hole' between the Orkney and Shetland Islands was negotiated without any serious interference. Two ships on the same course as U31 prevented the first dash through during early evening, meaning it was necessary to wait a while until the coast was clear. The second attempt just before midnight of 24 October 1939 went without a hitch and without any meddling from guards. There was only a ship coming the other way that was spotted while still a long way off, enabling U31 to merely drop into the depths to run under it.

The men were a little peeved with the weather though. It seemed as if the seas to the west of the Orkneys were on a different planet. Suddenly, without any warning the barometer dropped rather rapidly while the waves and the wind increased exceedingly quickly to Force six. To make sure that everybody was fully aware they were running towards the wrath of Cape Wrath, the weather controller sent along a mixture of rain and hail showers as well. Despite rather poor visibility the men later confirmed their navigation first from the lighthouse on Rhy Stoer and then by sighting the northern tip of Shiant Island, to the east of Lewis. The idea of lurking comfortably on the seabed, as U47 had done before entering Scapa Flow,

*Above and below:* The Fisheries Protection Vessel *Minna* at the Russian Arctic Convoys Reunion of 2013 in the sea entrance of Loch Ewe.

for the purpose of some impromptu reconnaissance did not work out at all. The hard seabed created a nerve tingling scraping noise as a strong current dragged the boat over it. So, U31 moved further east to get a good view of the entrance of Loch Ewe. There was not much going on. Naval Intelligence had informed Habekost that the loch was likely to be used by the British fleet in preference to Scapa Flow, but on this particular occasion it was all quiet and calm and just to emphasise this point the storm settled down as well. There was no way that anyone in Germany, especially in the navy, could have missed hearing about U47's penetration of Scapa Flow and many minds concluded that this bold action would drive the Royal Navy out of its famous anchorage in the Orkneys. What the Germans did not know was that having predicted this attack; the local authorities had an old wreck of a ship ready, waiting for the right conditions to sink it in the only possible hole in the defences, through which U47 had slipped. So there was no need to evacuate Scapa Flow, despite the Admiralty having designated Loch Ewe as an alternative to their northern anchorage.

There was an occasional steamer going through The Minch between the Isle of Lewis and the mainland of Scotland and a multitude of small fishing boats kept the men of U31 on their toes. Many of these ships were small enough to have been carried by rail from the east coast, meaning they were too small to make a great deal of noise for the hydrophones to detect. U31 remained in position, assessing the situation around the mouth of Loch Ewe, until shortly after 07.00 hours of the following day, the 27 October, when the mines were made ready. The strange point about this operation was that Habekost had planned to go in submerged during daylight, rather than wait for darkness to cover his presence. The plan was to penetrate into the loch for a couple of miles to the Island Sgeir an Fharaig to the north-west of the large inhabited Isle of Ewe. Habekost wrote that the discharging of the mines should have been completed by 1830 hours so that he could use the last vestiges of daylight for a submerged retreat out of the loch. A full moon was due to illuminate the region and he did not fancy tackling the navigation in the dark, when observers on land could easily spot the U-boat if it had to surface.

Having observed the entrance of the loch for one and a half days without spotting any large naval units or small ships that might prevent a withdrawal, made him confident that he would get away again without interference from warships. Deep down there was always the hope that a large cruiser or battleship might be lurking further inland, hidden behind the islands near the entrance. Habekost knew that nothing had prevented Prien from reloading his torpedo tubes while lurking in Scapa Flow, so there was always hope of great excitement in Loch Ewe. While contemplating these thoughts he found himself in a rather exposed position

The military remains from the Second World War around Loch Ewe are most impressive and incredibly abundant.

The road running along the side of Loch Ewe.

with what looked like a cross channel ferry from the Harwich–Flushing route approaching from behind to enter the loch. 'What's he doing here?' he wrote in his log. At least that proved that there were some large ships around.

The approach was nowhere as easy as had been thought. Closing in on the coast, it quickly became apparent that a strong current was driving the boat to the west. This was rather unexpected, as it had not been mentioned in the sailing handbook or in the atlas showing water currents. The other big problem was that the coast was as wild as one could imagine, without any obvious landmarks for a foreigner. Locals who could identify individual headlands negotiated these waters without difficulty but for an outsider each bit of the coast looked exactly the same as any other, without obvious man-made additions for easy identification. The navigation chart was not much of help either. It was a British one, dated 1906 with different water depths marked on it to the ones the boat registered with its echo sounder. On this occasion the current was so strong that U31 could not maintain its pre-planned schedule and then, eventually when the boat was in the right position to start ejecting mines, a fishing boat appeared close to the shore.

At that critical moment, with a boat nearby Habekost spotted a row of exceedingly shallow buoys in the water ahead of him. He had for some time been running at a fast-submerged speed that produced a white wash around the expended periscope and now the buoys forced him into a quick halt. Full speed in reverse and rudder hard to starboard did not help. The men in the bow torpedo compartment reported an ominous scraping sound shortly before it became obvious that the boat had run on top of the net. By going hard in reverse U31 could easily rise to the surface and wriggling too hard was going attract attention as well. It was a delicate if somewhat unenvious position, and just to crown it all another small fishing boat came close past the submerged submarine without noticing it. It was now shortly after 18.00 hours, with almost total darkness over the water, making it tricky to find a gap in the protective netting. Eventually, having pulled himself free, Habekost surfaced to find the waters further out from the coast full of lively nautical traffic. The snag was that no one could determine for certain whether these were fishing or on patrol. There was nothing for it, Habekost did not have a great deal of choice, instead of penetrating into Loch Ewe, U31 blocked the main channel with eighteen TMB mines before blowing a hurried retreat. While mining, the boat moved at 1.5 knots so that the gaps between each mine would be 150 metres.

U31's mining operation to Loch Ewe was by no means a one-off affair. The beginning of the war had taken the German Navy with such surprise that there were not enough torpedoes and therefore even the U-boat

The splendid isolation of Loch Ewe.

Command was happy to fall back on its generous stock of torpedo mines. In all, more than fifty mining operations were carried out by U-boats close to the British coast between September 1939 and the Norwegian offensive of March 1940.

Having returned to Wilhelmshaven on 30 October 1939, U31 was sent out once more to the Orkney area; this time with torpedoes. Coming back from that voyage Johannes Habekost was hit with some significant shock when he was asked to go to Loch Ewe for a second time. The U-boat Chief, Karl Dönitz, had a habit of not giving his commanders direct orders, instead he tended to ask them whether they considered the proposed task to be possible. Leaving Wilhelmshaven on 15 January 1940 was no easy matter. Ice in the Jade estuary could easily have demolished the U-boat's propellers, so there was no way the U31 could risk going out alone. The old battleship *Schlesien* went on ahead as icebreaker and then U31 followed in tow of the tug *Geeste* until the little squadron reached the open waters of the North Sea. The torpedo doors in the bows were protected with a special ice guard that prevented damage to that delicate area. This huge steel covering could have been jettisoned in an emergency, but on most occasions U-boats were clear of ice by the time they were away from coastal waters. U31 went on alone as far as Heligoland to a spot where Habekost had hoped to meet an escort and pilot to help him into the naval base for the removal of the ice cap. On this occasion, something had gone wrong with the communications system. There was no support waiting and U31 got into the comparative safety of the small harbour on its own. The boat had not been long in port when the weather turned into a foul north-north-easterly gale with snow, hail and rapidly dropping temperatures with enough ferocity to delay departure.

The following pages of the logbook are blank with only details of position, weather and the remark 'nothing observed'. We do know that the torpedo tubes of U31 had been especially modified to take the new type of mine known as TMC that has been mentioned earlier. On this occasion the navigation lights along the edges of the Minch were burning to help guide U31 to its destination and the mine laying process started at three o'clock of the afternoon of 21 January 1940. Conditions were good, with hardly interference from obverse weather or from fishing boats and the whole process was over in a couple of hours. U31 made fast in Heligoland again during the afternoon of 3 February before going on to Wilhelmshaven.

It was not an easy operation and neither the commander nor his men were terribly happy about the turn of events. Oblt.z.S. Wegener, the watch officer responsible for leading the laying of the mines would have loved to have rehearsed the loading process with training mines of the new type, but such items were not available and to embitter the men even more they were not given much time to try out anything with the new mines before leaving. This was the first time that U31 had used the torpedo mines of Type C, that were slightly longer than the older Types A and B. To make matters worse, the discharging mechanism in U31 only worked when boat was submerged and the old British chart from 1906 was not anywhere near accurate enough for such delicate navigation and manoeuvring. During the earlier operation Habekost had already discovered that the depths marked on the chart did not correlate with those obtained from his echo sounder.

This time the plan had been changed from the previous occasion to make matters a little more difficult for minesweepers. The idea was to deposit one line close to the entrance of the loch and another a little further out. This presented some quite challenging navigation of a submerged U-boat along what was a rocky coast with strong currents and little margin for error and, once again, there were no easy landmarks to help establish accurate positions. To test the men to their limit, the gauge indicating the position of the bow hydroplanes failed after the 7th mine had been dropped, meaning some delicate juggling was necessary and, in the end, Habekost had no idea exactly where the last mines actually ended up. Yet, despite the problems the men found everything went better than expected.

Even the fast loading system for the mines worked better than it had done with the smaller earlier mines. Habekost also made the comment that there were enough opportunities and space along the mouth of Loch Ewe for a double set of mines.

The first mining operation resulted in the sinking of two minesweepers that had been converted from fishing boats, HMS *Glenalbyn* and HMS *Promotive* on 23 December 1939 and the battleship HMS *Nelson* was damaged on 4 December. It would appear that the second set of mines was cleared without having caused any damage, or, what is even more likely is that they are still lying where U31 dropped them all those years ago.

The name Loch Ewe rolls easily off the tongue and is quickly lost in the highland wilderness of its own surroundings, yet this place has got to be one 'the' most fascinating areas in the United Kingdom with remains of many military installations from a stirring past. What is more, much of this history still lurks in the barren undergrowth, waiting to be discovered. The area was divided into an incredibly large number of small crofts during the 1840s to resettle people evicted from their homes as a result of the Highland Clearances and it remained as an isolated backwater until naval activity after the First World War resulted in the area being connected to the rest of Scotland by an all weather road, rather than the existing unsurfaced cart track. This single-track road with passing places has since been replaced by a fantastic new highway that allows even lorries to pass each other along much of its length. Yet even today, with tourism high on the list of priorities, it is still easy to miss the area all together. The only main road forms a huge twisting loop through what must be among the most isolated parts of the United Kingdom without any highly significant traffic knot at each end, so one is unlikely to accidentally go past Loch Ewe as a result of getting lost elsewhere.

The majority of travellers heading west from Dingwall or Inverness are far more likely to end up on an 'A' road that loops back upon itself to come out just a couple of miles away from it started or the other follows the railway to Kyle of Lochalsh. This tiny port on the mainland side of the sound separating it from the Isle of Skye served as harbour for ferries running out to the Hebridean islands and still carries all manner of local cargo in addition to an ever increasing number of tourists. The rails of the passing places along this single-track system are so wide apart that trains carrying fishing boats could pass each other. Many of these were nothing more than converted out-of-date lifeboats from large ocean-going ships. The military installations around Loch Ewe, the natural splendour and the enthusiastic welcome from locals cannot be described in a few words and require a book for themselves. The area is more than fantastic.

# 8

# Land-Based Targets

## U355 in Icefjord on Spitzbergen

There were two distinctly different types of Arctic exploratory operations. One was to find information about the lie of the land, ice conditions and the depth of water in unexplored areas; the other was to see what was happening in an already reasonably well charted location. The latter was usually centred on a known settlement, and involved some type of demolition work because enemy activity had been suspected in the area. Pitching U-boats against land-based objectives was not unique to the Arctic, but the incredibly small size of the targets made some of the operations there quite exceptional. U-boats attacked ships in far-flung harbours along the African coast, they shelled oil installations in the Caribbean and perhaps most remarkable of all, the first underwater rockets were launched against oil tanks along the shores of the Black Sea. Some of these targets might have been difficult to locate, but they were all of considerable size, while in the Arctic, U-boats were pitched against something that may not have been much bigger than an oversized garden shed that had not yet been marked on the navigation charts the boats were using to find it. Landing parties, demolition crews and infantry units were usually made up from ordinary members of the boats' crews, which was not difficult because many of the men had excellent marksmanship qualifications. Yet, being cooped up inside the cramped confines of a submarine did not provide them with opportunities of exercising, and many found the physically hard work of climbing over difficult terrain quite taxing. Often they also lacked hobnail boots for dealing with mountaineering objectives.

U355 under Kptlt. Günter La Baume set out from Trondheim in Norway on 6 July 1943 for one such special mission to destroy what was thought to have been a deserted radio station. On the way the boat was due to test a new radar detector with an aircraft flying nearby. These experiments went ahead without too many problems, but the boat had not got far when the engineer officer discovered a problem with the fuel in the external bunkers. This oil must have been stored at one stage in a newly painted tank. Whatever the actual history of the fuel, he found sizeable flakes of paint floating in it, similar to those cheap ornaments that when shaken looked like a snow scene, and this was useless for injecting into engines. There was no other option than to return for fresh fuel.

This took a few days and it was shortly after lunch on 13 July that U355 left for the second time to head towards Spitzbergen. The weather was brilliant; hardly any waves and with crystal clear visibility. The boat was still more than twelve kilometres from its objective, Barentsburg, when the bridge was cleared for a controlled dive to periscope depth. This turned out to be less than easy. The x 6 magnification was not working and the commander was not keen on using the large sky or navigation periscope until he was sure that there was no lurking reception committee. The sky periscope could only be viewed from the central control room, meaning the huge conspicuous head lens could not be raised as high as the other

U355 in St John's Fjord of Spitzbergen during the July 1943.

This photograph is an example of 'strange things' one can find in dusty corners of museums. It must have dropped out of a file in the German U-boat Museum before it was discovered at the back of a bookshelf. There is obviously a Type VIIC U-boat offshore and the type of hut found in the Arctic in the foreground. The fact that there is a child's bed in the middle would suggest this was occupied a family, rather than a bunch of soldiers and the high mast towards the right indicates that the hut was also used as radio station. The large number of canisters by the boat towards the left look suspiciously like those used by land-based automatic weather stations, but a close-up shows that they are wooden casks.

U668 with what looks like a landing party having gone ashore.

periscope, so he had no choice other than to use the standard, almost zero, magnification of the attack periscope. From a distance of about two to three kilometres, the shore and the settlements all looked deserted. Gliding silently along the coast and penetrating into Icefjord, La Baume gave a continuous commentary of what he saw. Things were so promising that after a while he came down from the commander's control room inside the conning tower to use the other periscope with the larger head lens. Later, at 05.15 hours, he felt confident enough to surface.

What happened next was a weird experience for the lookouts. Following the coast slowly they moved from one centre to another, all the time keeping a sharp eye on a multitude of small isolated huts dotted all along these almost 'over inhabited' shores. All was curiously silent, without movement, without any form of interference and no signs of anything having recently been occupied. Feeling confident that they were alone in this barren wilderness, a rubber dinghy was made ready on the deck while a landing party was kitted out. Eternal daylight, with the sun still shining at midnight, had settled in some time ago, so there was little difference between day and night and no darkness to limit or aid activities. Then, without warning, the serenity was broken by a frightening sound. A combination of a large shell whistling overhead and a loud, echoing bang from some impressive calibre. Even the lookouts that faced in the opposite direction ducked and momentarily turned to gape at the source of the interference. All they saw was a smoke cloud rising up from somewhere on land. The shell hit the water with a dramatic splash not much more than a hundred metres away. As a result the dinghy was hurriedly stowed away again before U355 dropped down out of sight. This spine-chilling interference made it more than obvious that this was not a good spot for promenading. Had the crew of what appeared to have been a three or four-inch gun kept its cool and allowed U355 to approach closer they could have hit it without difficulty. As it turned out they had given U355 an easy opportunity of running away.

Risking the submarine to deal with a well-camouflaged single gun was not on the agenda and since the spot was easily avoided, all La Baume needed to do was to register the matter before going on to his next objective of destroying a small radio station on Calypso Bay. At this stage there followed a spectacular change in the weather. A strong and strikingly cold wind started blowing down the fjords towards the open sea, driving the waters before it so that turbulent currents, often faster than a cyclist, gurgled away from the land-enclosed salt-water arms. At the same time the earlier crystal clear visibility that had been so helpful while reconnoitring the coast now had a distinct veil of heavy mist drawn through it. The advantage of carrying out this type of work in a submarine was that it could dive and then come to rest in a safe location for the crew to enjoy a meal and to sleep. Putting off the task in hand was an easy decision as both the severe currents and the intensely cold wind made a landing impossible. It was definitely advisable to hang around until better conditions prevailed.

The men of U355 did not have to wait for too long. It was 06.00 hours of 21 July 1943, the third day after the gun incident, when the rubber dinghy was ready once more and the first watch officer and three men set off to demolish a radio mast. There were no signs of the accompanying buildings having been used recently, but there was always the possibility of the opposition later coming along with a portable radio transmitter and that would not be much good to them if they did not have the high up aerial. The demolition team was only just back on board when two drifting British mines were sighted and destroyed with the anti-aircraft gun. Creating such loud detonations was always a good opportunity for some relief from the daily boredom, although only a few people on the top of the conning tower could enjoy the spectacle. During the next few days a considerable number of mines made it clear to the men of U355 that they were at the end of the Gulf Stream where the floating garbage from two continents ended up.

Once more there was a change in the natural conditions. The waters had been relatively clear until the boat entered Hornsund, which has a number of glaciers at the far end. Large enough chunks of ice had broken off to make a detailed examination of the waters inadvisable. There followed even more excitement on 30 July when U355 approached a wreck near Cape Borthern. A metallic grinding noise associated with shipyards rather than Arctic desolation told the men that not all was well. Even if there had been a deaf person on board, he would have been aware of the severe rocking as the boat obviously hit something hard. This happened just after midnight and U355 continued without too much trouble, other than it was not responding in the usual way. Some twelve hours later, when the sun was higher in the sky, La Baume looked for a quiet spot to send down a diver. Volunteering for such an arduous task was not difficult. Usually the man would be supplied not only with hot coffee but also some alcoholic central heating and U-boats carried so little brandy that they did not have to make do with the cheap varieties. The waters were crystal clear, making the dive easy. It did not take long to report that both propellers looked to be in good condition but the starboard rudder was definitely missing. This was annoying but not highly critical. The boat could get home without it.

Icebergs.

*Above and below:* U737 under Kptlt. Paul Brasack waiting for the next high tide after having run aground on Spitzbergen. The partly extended attack periscope jutting up at a most peculiar angle should normally be vertical, indicating that the boat was lying at a most precarious angle on 1 July 1944.

# The Radio Station on Bear Island

Friedrich Stege (Watch Officer of U212) has illuminated the boat's log in one of Ernst Pfefferle's books *Kameraden zur See* for when he was detailed to lead a landing party on Bear Island in June 1943. The commander, Kptlt. Helmut Vogler, was not renowned for making detailed entries to his log, yet many of his pages contain some general details of what was going on. This changed in June when his log contains many blank spaces despite the boat having been at sea. Each time it returned to the depot ship *Black Watch* in northern Norway, Vogler made the pertinent comment that U212 was in a state of readiness to go to sea at four hours' notice. After one such return, U212 put out again shortly before midday of 3 June 1943 and later joined U622 under Kptlt. Horst-Thilo Queck and then U586 Kptlt. Dietrich von der Esch, who were also economical with the entries to their logs. The few comments that there are suggest that U212 had a new type of radar detector on board, possibly for receiving signals sent out by convoy escorts, so it is possible that they were part of a new and highly secret patrol line trying to intercept a group of merchant ships on their way to North Russia. U212 was patrolling an area to the south-west of Bear Island, ideally placed for intercepting such convoys. Of course, the serious U-boat losses of Black May were still happening, so it could

*Above and opposite:* Setting up the Kreuzritter Weather Station on Spitzbergen's north coast.

well be that the commanders were being especially cagey about possibly giving their position away. Whatever, some ten days passed without serious entries in log and then, suddenly the calm was smashed during late afternoon of 13 June when the radio reported a destroyer moving at high speed towards the west. It was 03.06 hours of 16 June when U212 also sighted such a ship. Instantly the men went to their action stations while Vogler tried following it through a rain squall and shortly afterwards reported his sighting to headquarters in a code that every other U-boat at sea could read as well. The chase was on, But not for long though. The target turned out to be an iceberg with an uncanny resemblance to a small warship.

The next significant action took place shortly after five o'clock in the afternoon of 18 June and took the form of an unusually long radio message. Although not mentioned by Stege or in the log, it would seem this was an 'officer only' signal that had to be decoded twice so that a casual eavesdropper on other U-boats would not have understood the message.

*To Vogler.*

1. *A radio station on the north coast of Bear Island, probably not occupied by the enemy, has been bombed by the Luftwaffe. People were not spotted.*
2. *As soon as possible when weather condition permit and with sufficient care, land an armed landing party to investigate. It might be possible to land by the pier near Tunheim.*
3. *Absence from your patrol area is to be as short as possible.*
4. *Vacating your operations area and completion of mission are to be reported by short signal.*

U212 was submerged at the time when this signal arrived and a quick look through the periscope confirmed that the thick fog that driven the boat below was still going to make progress rather difficult. So, all the men could do was to get ready. Second Watch Officer Stege was detailed to lead the landing party together with a warrant officer, two petty officers and four men who were equipped as follows:

Each man was to wear a life jacket.
Each officer – 1 machine pistol with four full magazines, pistol with fifty rounds, 1 double barrelled signal pistol with five green, five red and five white star cartridges, four hand grenades and a pair of binoculars.
Each petty officer – 1 machine pistol with ammunition, one pistol with fifty rounds, 4 demolition charges with time fuses, four hand grenades and a set of special tools in the life belt pocket.

One man – one pistol with fifty rounds, four hand grenades and 200 rounds of ammunition for the automatic machine pistols carried by the officers.

Signalman – a set of semaphore flags and a pair of binoculars.

Two seamen – one pistol with fifty rounds, 4 hand grenades, three hauling lines (ropes for throwing) and one thicker rope for making the rubber dinghy fast.

The second watch officer aboard submarines was usually responsible for any outside activities especially those that involved leaving the boat. The third watch officer was also the Obersteuermann or navigator, a warrant officer rather than a commissioned officer and he would have served for some ten years among the lower ranks before starting his special officer training and this was a much too valuable experience to risk losing. So the difficult job was given to the officer who usually had the least experience and whose jobs other men could perform. Training for commissioned officers usually lasted about three years.

The plan as to what to do, and what role every person was going to play, was discussed more than once and a system of signals and emergency actions established if things did not work out as scheduled. All this went well until the men had assembled on deck to pull the rubber dinghy out

This photograph showing the gun that fired on U307 under Kptlt. Friedrich-Georg Herrle. Men from the U-boat landed to set the gun crew's hut on fire. There were a good number of such simple gun emplacements along the Arctic shores, some of them so well camouflaged that U-boats could not make out their exact positions, despite each shot producing a good cloud of smoke.

*Above and below:* Men from U307 have set a hut on fire to prevent the opposition from using it.

of its special watertight container. This was located between the wooden deck planking and the pressure hull. These containers were not big and putting anything into them, especially while the boat was at sea, was not easy. On this occasion the men discovered that the stowed bundle was slightly smaller than the container and thus had ample opportunity to slide around so much during the past few weeks that some parts had worn rather thin. At least, one did not need a highly technical education to work out that inflating the heap of rubber would result in some rather big bulges and possibly in a loud bang as well. Since none of the men fancied being aboard when this happened, they either had to give up their objective or improvise. The last mentioned appeared as the most practical and a raft was built on the upper deck from shoring-up timber and life jackets. Although looking like a rather precarious contraption and nowhere large enough to support the entire team, it was decided that Stege should go it alone with only one man. The commander was going to support the two unfortunate paddlers by bringing up two large machine guns for mounting on the top of the conning tower and manning both the 88 mm deck gun in front of the conning tower and the 20 mm anti-aircraft gun on the wintergarden. The objective of the exercise, clearly visible from the conning tower, did not seem to be inhabited, so this came over as a reasonable compromise.

The two men completed their mission, although bringing down the radio mast proved too much for the few explosives they could carry, but the mast did take on a new angle and no longer looked in its prime condition. The close inspection on land came up with rather indecisive results, making it difficult to decide whether the place was occupied or not. Stege thought that there might be some men nearby that had taken to keeping their heads down because they must have seen the fairly powerful array of U-boat artillery pointing in their direction. There was no sign of anyone living near the few buildings, but it was possible that there was a camouflaged camp nearby whose occupants occasionally walked around the deserted radio station. The two U-boat men remained on land for some ten hours, making it quite some energy-robbing activity and then after all that they still had to paddle back on their improvised contraption.

## U586 and the 'Radar' Mast

Although it has not been possible to find the original author of the following interesting account, the basic facts correlate well with the logbook, so one can assume that the anonymous story is correct. U586 under Kptlt. Dietrich von der Esch was already one of the longest serving

Arctic U-boats when the men spent two weeks doing nothing other than trailing back and forth somewhere near Bear Island. On this occasion they knew exactly where they were. Weather had been perfect and they even checked their navigational details with a sighting of the lonely island. Having done this, a homecoming U-boat reported having sighted a radar mast on the top of a cliff. This was towards the end June 1943, a time when 'radar' had become a tantalisingly rude word and the German backroom boffins were struggling to come to terms with a number of new electronic inventions. Germany had been leading in the field before the war, but had now dropped so far behind with its research that anything new was investigated with great vigour. On this occasion, U586 was given the precise position of the new radar installation and told to investigate and to destroy it.

Since the boat had been at sea for some time any change in the boring routine of doing nothing was welcomed. The only problem was that this sort of thing had not been planned; meaning improvisation was going to be essential. Virtually everybody aboard volunteered to join the landing party; it sounded too exciting to miss. While the men were looking forward to anything different, the commander was a little more apprehensive and counted with the possibility of not all of them coming back. After all, the opposition was unlikely to leave such an important new installation at the mercy of a few ill-equipped seamen and would have fitted it out with impressive weapons. Therefore his first order was that only men that were 'double' should be considered. He could not risk leaving a blatant gap in the firm's functional ability. Having chosen the team, it was kitted out with the necessary items for the task, weapons, emergency provisions, first aid kit and some explosives. Everything was ready and the six 'killers,' as the rest of the crew had dubbed them, were ready and waiting as U586 used the lighting of the early dawn to close in on the target. Imagine the nerve tingling situation—six fully armed men with a large rubber dinghy at the ready—absolute silence. Hearts pounding with anticipation and fear and then among all this tenseness the commander suddenly burst out laughing. Others on the top of the conning tower started laughing as well. What they saw was not a radar aerial, but a huge wooden cross that had been put up years ago to mark the grave of a seal hunter who had probably succumbed to nothing more than an overdose of vodka. The commander turned the boat around, headed back to Narvik where he reported to the Flag Officer for U-boats that nothing significant had happened except that the men had eaten all the food on board.

# Port Dikson and the Sterlegova Radio Station

On 2 August 1944 at 10 o'clock in the morning four U-boats slipped their moorings in Hammerfest (North Norway) without much ado to glide into the comparatively warm Arctic summer. They were well clear of the coast and had vanished into a grey veil hanging over the water by the time they turned onto a general heading of 60 degrees. Later they were joined by two more U-boats to complete the newly formed Greif Pack, heading east on a special mission far into the Siberian Seaway. This group was made up of U278 (Kptlt. Joachim Franze), U362 (Oblt.z.S. Ludwig Franz), U365 (Kptlt. Heimar Wedemeyer), U711 (Kptlt. Hans-Günther Lange), U739 (Oblt.z.S. Ernst Mangold) and U957 (Oblt.z.S. Gerd Schaar). All of them had been to the Arctic before and were therefore well-acquainted with the severe conditions ahead of them. They were also all ordinary VIIC boats without any significant modifications to cope with ice. As a result, by the beginning of September the group was whittled down to three, mainly due to ice damage. Only one boat was lost due enemy action, the rest eventually returned home. U362 became the boat that was sunk the furthest east in the Arctic when it was attacked near Krakowa Island at 75° 51′ N 89° 27′ E by the Soviet minesweeper T116 (Kptlt. K. L. Babanov) on 6 September. Comparing this position with a better known region, this longitude runs through the Bay of Bengal between India and Burma and passes not too far west of Dacca, indicating that these boats did indeed penetrate a considerable distance along their torturous icy route. It was not an easy undertaking and many days of nothing much happening passed before any of the pack saw any serious action.

U957, having been the last to leave Hammerfest on 7 September, had the advantage of considerable experience in front of it and thus it managed avoid a good number of pitfalls and dead ends leading into permanent ice. Not much happened to the boat at first. A drifting Russian mine was dispatched with a few shots from one of the bridge mounted machine guns, otherwise nothing was sighted while covering between 168 and 237 nautical miles per day, most of it on the surface. Navigation was not easy and the men took several opportunities of checking their calculated position with identifiable landmarks. Conditions started to change when U957 came close to land on the eastern side of the Kara Sea, a long way beyond Novaya Zemlya. In addition to pack ice and more dominant icebergs, the lookouts were surprised when they spotted a solitary Catalina aircraft ahead. It may have been too far away to take any notice of the intruder, but it did unsettle the men inside the U-boat. They had not expected a modern American aircraft in such a far-off region.

U739 (Oblt.z.S. Ernst
Mangold) loading a
torpedo from the depot ship
*Kamerun* in Norway.

One wonders how good German naval intelligence had been at the time
and whether the U-boat crews knew that the Kara Sea Naval Base had
been founded in Port Dikson earlier in 1944. What was more, despite being
in one of the most remote regions of the world; the Naval Base was not
supplied with obsolete junk from the active front. The Catalinas and ships
stationed there had arrived only a few weeks earlier as a special delivery
from the United States. Port Dikson, with Dikson Island in front of it,
was originally not much more than an elaborate fishing village that also
provided a few facilities as a stopover for anyone attempting the hazardous
Siberian seaway. The pocket battleship-cum-heavy cruiser *Admiral Scheer*
had bombarded it two years earlier during August 1942, and now it seemed
very much as if the boot was on the other foot, with enough Russians
determined that such humiliating event would not occur a second time. As
a stopgap measure, the Northern Task Force of the White Sea Fleet was
stationed in Dikson shortly after *Admiral Scheer*'s attack until the Kara
Sea obtained its own naval unit in 1944. There may not have been any
heavy ships or impressive guns along the coast, but getting close to the port
proved more than just difficult. Air cover intensified as U957 approached
closer and so did the floating sentries. These were a considerable nuisance

inasmuch that many were so small that some would have been sunk by the sheer weight of a torpedo inside them and disposing of one with heavy artillery could easily have caused others to pay back with depth charges. The approach was indeed tricky with every effort having to be made to remain unseen until worthwhile targets appeared.

This Russian move of defending its Arctic sea routes was not confined to the coast. Towns far enough inland for seagoing ships not to be able to reach them were fortified to resist possible attacks by German special troops making their way along wide but shallow rivers. From the Russian point of view this did not look as absurd as it might to people living in Western Europe. Many of Russia's important factories had been overrun by the German invasion, meaning it was necessary to move the vital armaments industries further east. It was far easier to set up machinery to out-of-the-way locations than to unsettle established workforces by moving people in the opposite direction and then having to provide accommodation for them.

By the time U957 spotted those irritating Catalina aircraft in the distance, the other boats of the Greif Pack were already a considerable distance further east, leaving the Port Dikson area free for U957. Yet, being there did not feel comfortable at all. The men of U957 wondered whether earlier action by other boats had annoyed the opposition so much that everything Dikson could muster was now out guarding the coast, perhaps waiting for their return. The snag was that all of these potential targets were not much bigger than two hundred tons and many were considerably smaller. There was not anything obvious to hit at and 'no special observations' became a standard phrase in the logbook. U-boat Command with the Admiral for Polar Seas in northern Norway, must have guessed that there was not much happening and sent new orders to conserve the little hitting power that had survived the ravages of the ice. On 14 September Hans-Günther Lange of U711 was ordered to take command of that part of the group that was remaining further east than Dikson, while others were told to operate off Dikson or head further west.

Russian sentries, all consisting of those small boats mentioned earlier, continued to spoil the relative peace of the area and those irritating Catalinas also helped to make patrolling the Dikson approaches most tedious. Then to crown it all, when frustration had reached a peak, the radar-warning device in U957 suddenly went to more than the usual full alert. Instead of its normal nerve-wracking squeaking it screamed at a high pitch for several minutes without the operator being able to calm it. In the end he brought it to its senses by switching it off and then a little further investigation showed that the device had suffered from a short circuit, rather than input from enemy radar in the vicinity.

U673 with one of the double barrelled 20 mm anti-aircraft guns in the foreground.

The Russian sentries were not terribly methodical either. They would go along in a straight line for a while, then suddenly drive the German nerves to fever pitch by zigzagging for no apparent reason or sending wild Morse signals that no one in the U-boat could understand. U957's previous mission had involved taking specialists from the B-Dienst (the naval radio observation service) along the North Russian coast to explore the radio traffic there and these men were still on board. Yet for much of the time these experts, who spoke fluent Russian and could also understand the codes, could not make much sense of the goings-on. Then, when someone did crack the Russian radio system, they found that the news was not good. One of the guard ships had issued a general warning on a high priority setting to all units in the area. Still not sure what was said, it was thought that something had been spotted to warn shipping of German activity in the area. It took a while for the Germans to realise that U362, among the spearhead of this thrust, had been sunk early in September, driving the Russian defences onto a high alert. The absence of good targets and tiny patrol boats being used for guard duties finally drove U957 east of Port Dikson, into an even more remote area. Even that did not help a great deal. The Catalinas seemed to be following, although none of them took any interest in the U-boat and it seemed highly likely that they did not even spot it—but they were still there, flying overhead.

During the early morning of 16 September 1944, U957 sighted Bjelucha Island and at around the same time took up an underwater telephone connection with U711 under their new commander, Hans-Günther Lange, who had just a few weeks earlier been promoted to Kapitänleutnant. Thus, unfortunately for Oblt.z.S. Gerd Schaar, it befell to the men of U957 to bring their commander over to the senior boat for a face-to-face conference to discuss what to do next. (It was usual for junior officers to call on seniors.) This cold and wet escapade ended with both commanders assuming that already assembled Russian convoys were possibly waiting for the right ice conditions and, perhaps, also for confirmation that U-boats had vacated the area before sailing. So the decisive factors for the immediate future were patience and remaining unseen while other boats were already heading for home. In the end it was decided that since U957 had most fuel, it should go on further east alone to search for any waiting convoys and then call up others when and if conditions demanded it.

The weather had so far been reasonable; no great storms and none of the dead calm conditions that made it difficult for U-boats on the surface. The sea was rough enough to make the average day-tripper decisively seasick, but such boisterous conditions were just part of the ordinary day's work for sailors in small boats. That by now famous Arctic mist hung over the water to reduce visibility from about five to ten miles; not ideal and somewhat unsettling, yet it was something deemed to be normal for the area at that time of year. Heading east under such conditions U957 found the seas very much the same as before, other than there was a greater abundance of ice, especially large icebergs rather than flat sheets of ice. Sailing along with a number of icebergs within sight U957 did meet a convoy but could not get into a favourable position to shoot at it. Schaar decided it would be best to remain unseen rather than make a mess of the attack and arouse the opposition's vigilance. Following the ships for almost a whole day U957 was frustrated every time, usually by ice preventing it from getting into the right attacking position.

Eventually it was shortly before eight o'clock in the morning of 18 September that the attack appeared to succeed. The big problem was that this was not the first time that a U-boat tried this trick of attacking from a submerged position and Schaar knew full well from previous occasions that he could not make use of his periscopes due to the ice floating above him being thick enough to bend them. Eventually, when he did give the order to fire, it seemed likely that all he hit was some of the hard ice and that detonation was loud enough for the opposition to pay back with a few depth charges. Unable to surface or to see what was going on, all Schaar could do was to rely on his sound detector that had been working very well by providing him with the basic data for adjusting his firing settings. Now all he could do was to run away, nurse his wounds and hope that his ego was not too blemished. He did eventually, a few days later come to shoot at a set of ships, sinking the Soviet 550 ton corvette *Brilliant* (renamed No. 29) on 23 September 1944 at 76° 10′ N 87° 45′ E.

To make things difficult, the ice was constantly in motion at such a speed that one could actually see it move, presenting the U-boat with a series of rather difficult problems and making it look as if U957 was surrounded by a fleet of icebergs that locked it in place, unable to move in any direction. Luckily eternal daylight was no longer a feature, so it was possible to wait for darkness to survey the situation and then come to some decision about the best possible action. This paid dividends. U957 managed to extract itself from this rather precarious predicament, although despite the earlier caution the periscope was bashed hard enough against some ice to bend it. The periscope was strong enough to easily hoist a man into the air, yet a single knock from the pack ice bent it like as if it was nothing more than a matchstick. The bow torpedo tubes had suffered as well and only the stern tube remained operable with the bows doors buckled and jammed by the ice. The annoying point was that not long after this several ships came past, advertising their presence with dense black smoke, and there was little that U957 could do about it other than to satisfy itself by hitting at the small escort instead of some rather sizable merchant ships.

On 20 September U957 supplied U739, which had been at sea for fifty days, and U711 with fuel and provisions and then hung around to act as ice reconnaissance vessel for the other two, which were still fully operational. There had been good opportunities for the commanders to meet for face-to-face discussions about what they should do next and to discuss one other objective among their list of orders, and that was to destroy a radio and weather station on Sterlegova Island. Trying to locate this on the average western atlas is virtually impossible and the nearest marked natural feature is the Taimir or Tajmyr River to the west of Cape Chelyuskin at about 100 degrees east. This longitude runs close to Bangkok in the Gulf of Siam and then on through Malaya to pass some distance west of Singapore and on to Sumatra. It is a long way east.

Attacking the radio station on Cape Sterlegova might sound easy until one realises that the Germans had no details of the coast and had no idea what to expect under the surface of the water, so, it was very much a stab in the dark. Eventually it was decided to send over eleven men in two rubber dinghies from U957 and U711. This went reasonably well except that the Arctic seemed to be playing the game as well. The men had hardly stepped ashore when the wind increased, the temperature dropped and fearsome waves started lapping against the hulls of the still surfaced U-boats. To make matter even worse, this mini gale brought along a heavy snowstorm of the type not normally experienced in Britain or Germany. It was now around midnight. Not too dark; there was snow on the land reflecting an eerie glow and the sea was choppy and dark to cover the approach of the attack. Once again patience was required. Those men on the top of the conning towers could see that according to the signals the landing corps had the situation under control. Yet there were many lights flashing around, dogs were barking, a sledge was seen to be on the move, smoke was pouring from some chimneys, making it all looked rather chaotic; the sort of confusing situation where it is good not to be in command. The landing party had set out at 22.25 hours of 24 September and was not back on board until 17.45 of 26 September and, to complicate matters the men brought with them what they thought was almost the entire population of the radio station plus three dogs. Now, having evacuated the staff, it was possible for the landing crew to identify the important buildings and direct the U-boats to destroy them with gunfire from their 88 mm deck guns. Even far more valuable than that, the two boats also brought home a considerable haul of Russian codebooks. It definitely had been a successful undertaking.

The German U-boat Museum has a typewritten Russian manuscript by V. Jaroslavcev about Lev Eduardovitsch Venckovskij, who was a radio operator at the Sterlegova radio station when the Germans raided it. It would appear that the staff there was made up of a number of highly contrasting units. There were trained meteorologists, radio operators, soldiers and others whose devotion to duty varied considerably. Especially the men in the military team gave up their duties long before their observation tasks were due to be shut down for the dark winter. The weather and radio teams were kept busy all the time with the sending of at least four reports every twenty-four hours and at times the details had to be sent hourly. The commanding officer's report about the apathy among the military section did not receive a reply and the place degenerated into further chaos as the winter progressed. There was certainly no shortage of work and the rest of the staff did not have the time to take on the military observation duties as well. It was necessary to keep the pier on the Lenivaja River fully operational in case a ship needed to make fast there before the sea froze solid and it was also necessary to keep the runway in such a condition that an unannounced incoming aircraft could land on it. Bearing in mind that many of the men there were not highly technical, they already had their hands full with keeping the wind powered electricity generator fully functional.

Although the place was rather isolated, there was always plenty to do until things slowed down due to the winter freezing the ice solid that it was no longer necessary to keep the coastguard lookout in position. Ironically some of the staff at Cape Sterlegova was replaced during August 1944 when the 200-ton survey ship *Nord* appeared without notice, bringing in fresh supplies and new staff. The men whom the commanding officer had complained about were still on board when the *Nord* came into the sights of U957 on 26 August 1944 to be sunk at 75° 35′ N 89° 50′ E. (This happened during an earlier voyage, before the operation where it attacked the Sterlegova radio station.) Following the sinking of the *Nord*, U957 returned to Hammerfest on 3 September and left again on the 7th to join the Greif Pack and later to attack the Sterlegova radio station during the night of 24 September 1944.

A few days before the arrival of the German landing party, the radio station was ordered to search the coast for stranded mines and also for any remains from the missing survey ship. It would seem that the new military division was just as apathetic as the men they had replaced and it was Grigorij Buchtijarov, the man in charge of the watering area for seaplanes and one other man who set out with a dog sledge to carry out this latest order. The watering area was now so full of ice that it was no longer operational. On the day of the German attack, it was already well past midnight when the duty meteorologist Dmitrij Markov handed in the latest report for transmission to Port Dikson. This had just been completed when the door was thrown open, emitting a cold wind and several men wearing fur coats. It would seem that these were just as frightened as the residents. Using a little excessive force they quickly subdued the radio station's staff. Several men were in their underwear, already asleep in bed with their weapons still dismantled after a thorough cleaning. The Germans brought an interpreter who spoke good Russian, therefore there were no problems with communications and the situation quickly settled into an amiable but tense meeting with the Germans controlling the situation with their pistols.

The weather had now deteriorated so badly that no one could get back to the two U-boats lying offshore and not wanting to attract attention to their presence the Germans ordered the usual radio transmissions to continue. Since the Russian speaker did not seem to understand Morse, it was not too difficult to inform Port Dikson about what had happened by squeezing the details into the middle of the usual report. Unfortunately for the Russians, the other end did not respond to this warning part of the message and later, when there was another opportunity to send a second warning the words were taken to be a joke. No one reacted or offered any help. The Russians had some hope of Buchtijarov and his colleague Nogaev, who were still out searching for mines and remains of the survey ship, possibly saving the situation. However, this did not work out as expected. The dogs pulling the sledge had the ability to run at a fast speed and at the same time make the most fearful barking noise to frighten an entire housing block in a built up area. So, with ample warning, the Germans took up hiding positions,

One of the Baltic bases during a hard winter.

aimed their guns and merely waited for the sledge to drive into their trap. As it happened the arrival of the sledge was just what the Germans needed and they used it for transporting masses of captured material to the beach for transfer by rubber dinghy to their U-boats. As expected, none of the Germans had the faintest idea about how to drive a dog sledge. They must have known that it was rather difficult to spur the dogs into motion and if they did this too enthusiastically the animals would run out of control, spilling whatever was on the sledge. Therefore they employed the two men to deal with this tricky part and that gave them the opportunity to escape and to hide among the barren emptiness near the beach. They were later found by a Russian reconnaissance plane and taken back to Dikson by a minesweeper that had been sent to assess the general situation.

Following the evacuation, the Germans found sufficient fuel for setting many of the buildings alight and later used their large deck guns to destroy the more solid and important parts of the radio station. The Russians were taken on board U711 and eventually on to Oslo in Norway and from there to a prisoner of war camp in Poland where they were later repatriated when it was overrun by the Red Army at the end of the war. These men learned about the sinking of U957 and they met a number of men from the radio station that had survived the sinking of the survey ship *Nord* as well. The whole experience can hardly be described as pleasant, but they did survive the war and Lev Eduardovitsch Venckovskij, who had lost his left arm towards the beginning of the war, became a renowned Doctor of Philosophy at the Institute of Scientific Information in Moscow. In point of fact, U957 did not sink. It was decommissioned on 21 October 1944 following serious damage during a collision with heavy ice and all of the crew survived. Oblt.z.S. Gerd Schaar, the commander, was awarded the Knight's Cross on 1 October 1944 and promoted to Kapitänleutnant on New Year's Day of 1945. He survived the war and was released from prison of war camp in September 1945.

# 9

# Large Warships and Aircraft in Norway

## The Threat

| Type of Ship | Name | The Threat's Power |
|---|---|---|
| Battleships | *Tirpitz* | Size: 52,600 tons<br>380 mm: 8<br>150 mm: 12<br>105 mm: 16<br>37 mm: 16<br>20 mm: 12–58<br>Torps: 8<br>Speed: 31 kts<br>Range: 8,870 sm @ 19 kt |
| | *Scharnhorst** | Size: 38,900 tons<br>280 mm: 9<br>150 mm: 12<br>105 mm: 14<br>37 mm: 16<br>20 mm: 10–38<br>Torps: 6<br>Speed: 31 kts<br>Range: 7,100 sm @ 19 kt |
| Pocket Battleships** | *Admiral Scheer /*<br>*Lützow**** | Size: 15,900 / 16,200 t<br><br>280 mm: 6<br>150 mm: 8<br>105 mm: 6<br>37 mm: 8<br>20 mm: 10–28 |

| | | |
|---|---|---|
| Heavy Cruisers | *Admiral Hipper /*<br>*Prinz Eugen* | Torps: 8<br>Speed: 28 kts<br>Range: 10,000 sm @20kt<br>Size: 18,200 t / 18,750 t<br><br>203 mm: 8<br>105 mm: 12<br>37 mm: 12<br>20 mm: 28<br>Torps: 12<br>Speed: 32 kts<br>Range: 6,800 sm @ 20 kt |
| Light Cruisers | *Köln / Nürnberg* | Size: 7,700 tons / 8,350 t<br>150 mm: 9<br>88 mm: 6 double barrel<br>37 mm: 8 double barrel<br>20 mm: 8–18<br>Torps: 12<br>Speed 32 kts<br>Range: 5,700 sm @ 19 kt |

Size = When fully laden, calibre of guns, Torps = number of torpedo tubes, speed = maximum, range = maximum at fast cruising speed.

\* Scharnhorst was classed as battle cruiser in Britain.
\*\* Pocket battleships were re-classed as heavy cruisers after the start of the war.
\*\*\* **The name** *Deutschland* was changed to *Lützow* after the start of the war.

Battleship *Tirpitz*—the lonely Queen of the North. The ship spent most of its time behind anti-submarine and anti-torpedo netting in Norwegian fjords and only once fired its large guns in anger against the opposition. Yet, this ship presented such an enormous threat to Allied shipping that Britain mounted many attacks to sink it.

*Right:* The destroyer *Anton Schmidt* in southern Norway.

*Below:* The light cruiser *Köln* long before Hitler came to power flying the old Reichsmarine flag, showing how difficult it was for large ships to negotiate angry seas. Now imagine a small fishing boat having to cope with similar conditions.

The heavy cruiser *Prinz Eugen* fighting its way through horrendous waves that must have been pure hell for small escorts.

# The Presence of the Treat

*Tirpitz*

| | |
|---|---|
| January 1942 | *Tirpitz* moved from Wilhelmshaven to Trondheim in Norway. |
| March 1942 | *Tirpitz* became the flagship for Vizeadmiral Otto Ciliax for the ship's first cruise into the Arctic and engaged against Convoy PQ12 and QP8. The accompanying destroyer Z14 destroyed an empty Russian freighter. Otherwise no success. Following this there were several training cruises in the Trondheim area, but all operational voyages against convoys were cancelled at around the designated sailing time. Towards the end of the year the ship spent some time in dock for repairs. |
| March 1943 | Tirpitz was moved to near Narvik and shortly after that to Altafjord in northern Norway. This put it beyond the reach of British bomber aircraft. |
| | Once in Altafjord *Tirpitz*, *Scharnhorst*, *Lützow* and six destroyers formed a new battle group. This prompted the Admiralty in London to postpone convoy sailings to Russia until after the summer of 1943. |
| 6 September 1943 | *Tirpitz* and *Scharnhorst* and several destroyers sailed to Spitzbergen under Admiral Oskar Kummetz to evacuate people and to destroy Allied bases there. |
| 22 September 43 | The British attack by several midget submarines (X-Craft) put *Tirpitz* out of action for the rest of the war. Following this there were further British aircraft attacks and *Tirpitz* moved to Trondheim for repairs. Following this, on 5 April 1944, Tirpitz was attacked again by a large number of planes flown off aircraft carriers and there was another air raid on 17 April when one bomb hitting the bows put the ship out of action for the rest of the war. |

*Scharnhorst*

| | |
|---|---|
| 11 February 1942 | *Scharnhorst, Gneisenau* and *Prinz Eugen* left the French port of Brest for the by now famous Channel Dash. *Scharnhorst* was damaged and remained in dock for repairs. |
| March 1943 | Moved to Altafjord to join the task force led by battleship *Tirpitz*. |
| 6 September 1943 | Sailed with *Tirpitz* to Spitzbergen and after that remained in North Norway without any further engagements until the end of the year. |
| 26 September 43 | *Scharnhorst* was sunk during the Battle of North Cape. |

*Admiral Scheer*

| | |
|---|---|
| February 1942 | *Admiral Scheer* was moved from Germany to Trondheim in Norway and two months later to near Narvik. |
| July 1942 | *Admiral Scheer* and *Lützow* formed a new battlegroup with six destroyers to attack Convoy PQ17, but were re-called when the convoy was scattered. |
| 16-31 August 1943 | Operation *Wunderland*. *Admiral Scheer* sailed into the Kara Sea, which culminated with the bombardment of Port Dikson on 27 August. Following this *Admiral Scheer* returned to Germany. |

*Lützow*

| | |
|---|---|
| May 1942 | Moved to Trondheim and later to Narvik. |
| July 1942 | Damaged as a result of grounding. Returned to Kiel for repairs. |
| December 1942 | Moved to near Narvik and then Altafjord. |
| 30 December 1942 | Joined *Admiral Hipper* and six destroyers to attack a convoy near Bear Island. The action was broken off when the ships met a British cruiser squadron with destroyer escort. |
| September 1943 | Moved back to Germany after several months of inactivity in northern Norway. |

*Admiral Hipper*

| | |
|---|---|
| 19 March 1942 | Moved from Germany to Trondheim to anchor close to battleship *Tirpitz* and shortly afterwards sailed to Narvik and from there to Altafjord. |
| 7 July 1942 | Joined *Tirpitz* and *Admiral Scheer* for a convoy attack in the Arctic seas, but did not find the convoy. However, this action caused the escorts to leave the merchant ships and made it easier for U-boats and aircraft to attack. |
| 30 December 1942 | Sailed to attack Convoy JW51B. This was abandoned when the Germans realised there was a British cruiser squadron nearby. *Admiral Hipper* was damaged and moved back to Germany in March 1943. |

*Prinz Eugen*

| | |
|---|---|
| 23 February 1942 | Torpedoed by HM Submarine *Trident* shortly after having arrived in the Trondheim area. Returned to Germany with serious damage. |

*Köln*

| | |
|---|---|
| July 1942 | Moved to Norway |
| 6 August 1942 | Arrived in Narvik to relieve the heavy cruiser *Lützow*. |
| 10 September 42 | Moved to Altafjord with *Admiral Scheer* and *Admiral Hipper* to prepare for an attack on Convoy PQ18, but these orders were cancelled by Hitler. |
| February 1943 | Moved back to Germany. |

*Nürnberg*

| | |
|---|---|
| November 1942 | Moved to Narvik to replace the heavy cruiser *Admiral Scheer*. |
| May 1943 | Recalled to Germany. |

# Destroyers in North Norway

*Friedrich Eckholdt* *
*Friedrich Ihn*
*Hans Lody*
*Hermann Schoemann* *
*Karl Galster*

*Paul Jacobi*
*Richard Beitzen*
*Theodor Riedel*
Z24
Z25
Z26*
Z27
Z28
Z29
Z30
Z31

The number of destroyers varied. There were usually never more than a dozen at any one time.
* Sunk by enemy action in the Polar Seas.


# Air Power in Northern Norway

(Based on the British Naval Staff History: Arctic Convoys 1941–1945 and approved by the Lords Commissioners of the Admiralty in December 1954.)

From March 1942

| 60 | Ju 88 | Long-range bombers |
|---|---|---|
| 30 | Ju 87 | Dive-bombers |
| 30 | — | Fighters |
| 15 | BV 138 | Torpedo carrying floatplanes* |

From June 1942

| 100 | Ju 88 | Long-range bombers |
|---|---|---|
| 30 | Ju 87 | Dive-bombers |
| 40 | He 111 | Torpedo bombers—increased by 35 in autumn |
| 8 | FW 200 | Very-long-range reconnaissance bombers |
| 22 | Ju 88 | Long-range reconnaissance bombers |
| 44 | BV 138 | Very-long-range floatplanes* |
| 15 | He 115 | Torpedo carrying floatplanes* |

Aircraft came under Luftwaffe command except those marked with a star (*); they belonged to the Naval Air Arm and came under naval administration. Meteorological flights are not included in the above figures.

Before the war the Commander-in-Chief of the Luftwaffe, Reichsmarschall Hermann Göring, took the view that everything that flies belonged to him and he did not see it fit to create a torpedo-carrying arm. It was not until December 1941 that this type of aircraft was developed in significant numbers and crews trained.

In March 1942 the Fliegerführer Nord (West), Oberstleutnant Hermann Busch of the Naval Air Arm had five flights with the following aircraft:

| | |
|---|---|
| Do18 / BV 138 | 2 aircraft with 1 operational |
| He115 | 8 aircraft with 2 operational |
| BV138 | 10 aircraft with 2 operational |
| He115 | 6 aircraft with 6 operational |
| He115 / Ar196 | 12 aircraft with 5 operational |

Following the first major success against Convoy PQ13 towards the end of March 1942 these numbers were increased so that the total number of Naval Air Arm planes reached 55 aircraft with 42 of them being operational at any one time.

Aircraft were first sent to Norway to help protect German coastal convoys and to carry out reconnaissance of the waters as far west as Scotland and Iceland and later to assist mountain troops fighting on the land. This last mentioned role became more critical after Russia joined in the war, when land forces tried fighting their way as far as Murmansk, Archangel and the railway line connecting these ports with the hinterland. During that period bombers were used to attack a vast number of targets in Russia. To get there, it was first necessary to build a number of new airfields in isolated positions. The majority of these were close to saltwater arms so that they could be supplied by ships. Whilst Luftwaffe bombers were withdrawn towards the end of 1942 because they were required in other areas, the Naval Air Arm remained at around this strength for much of the war and at one stage acquired a total of about eighty aircraft of which over sixty were usually operational.

German bases in northern Norway were in the hub of a huge wheel with Allied convoys having to sail along the rim. This made it possible to approach convoys sideways on rather than having to meet them end on and the distances the Germans had to travel were considerably shorter than in the more southern regions of the Atlantic. The shortest distance from Glasgow or Loch Ewe to Hammerfest in northern Norway is about 1,100 nautical miles, to Barentsburg on Spitzbergen 1,400 nautical miles and to Murmansk 1,600 nautical miles. Of course many convoys sailed on long detours to avoid contact with German forces and even if they took the shortest route, the convoys still had to spend an exceptionally long time within a relatively short range of German bases. Most of those convoy routes could be reached by large warships in a period of about ten hours sailing time. The damage these battleships could have inflicted on a convoy is not difficult to imagine. One only needs to look at the few occasions where big ships had met groups of merchant ships in the North Atlantic, such as the legendary last stand of the auxiliary cruiser HMS *Jervis Bay*. Their presence posed an enormous threat to British defences. This importance can also be illustrated with the fact that it is possible to describe battleship *Tirpitz*'s actions against shipping on not much more than one page of paper, yet the British actions against this huge giant fills several books. It was of paramount importance to British shipping that these heavy German ships were neutralised. The term 'British' rather than 'Allied' is significant here because the Russians were not particularly perturbed about U-boats close to their shores. At first they even went as far as prohibiting the British Navy from setting up its own hospital in the Russian ports. It was not until March 1942 that the British cruiser *Nigeria* sailed to Murmansk under Rear Admiral Harold M. Burrough, with the aim of persuading the Russians to do more to help with the defences of the Arctic seas.

Alta Fjord in northern Norway, where the German battleship *Tirpitz* was moored for some time. The buoys holding up the anti-submarine and anti-torpedo netting can be seen stretching across the water. Attacking shipping in fjords like this was exceedingly difficult because the mountains made it difficult for planes to spot and to attack shipping. Both the shores and the ships anchored in the fjords were often provided with artificial fog making apparatus, making it virtually impossible for bomb aimers to find a definite mark for dropping their bombs.

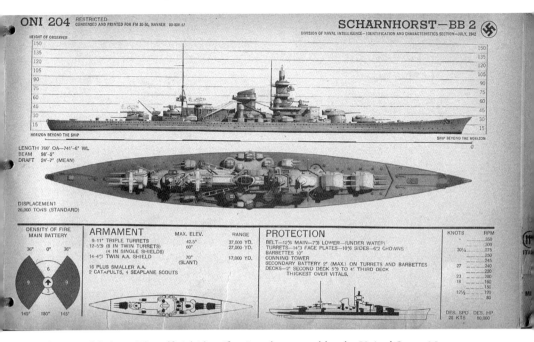

*Above and below:* The official identification sheets used by the United States Navy to identify German warships.

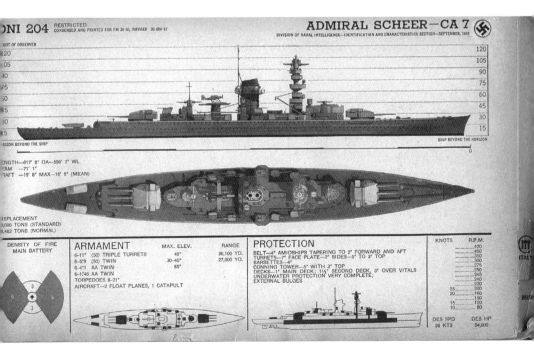

It has already been said elsewhere in this book that Germany's heavy warships were sent to Norway as a result of Hitler's hunch that Britain was going to invade the country. The U-boat Command was not interested in the Arctic as an operations area and asked for the accompanying U-boats to be returned for duties in the North Atlantic convoy routes rather than have them stationed in Norway, where they were doing very little. ('Very Little' was defined by the U-boat Command as tonnage sunk per U-boat at sea. The boats in the Arctic were fully operational and enduring extreme hardships but often finding only a few targets.) Having dispatched battleship *Tirpitz* to the Trondheim area, it cannot have taken long for Hitler to realise that there was no way that his navy could actually employ the ship for any meaningful duties. Yet he was adamant, saying any ship not in Norway is in the wrong place. The four destroyers that had accompanied *Tirpitz* to Norway were immediately recalled to return south to help with what was to become the Channel Dash, where *Gneisenau*, *Scharnhorst* and *Prinz Eugen* made their way back from Brest in France to Germany and it had been planned that they should continue on to Norway.

The big problem was that there was a dire shortage of both tankers and the type of oil required by *Tirpitz*. So rather than sending this big ship to sea, the Germans hid her in a fjord some fifteen miles east of Trondheim by covering the obvious stark outline with camouflage netting. Tirpitz was later moved further north to Altafjord and apart from shooting down British aircraft, the only time when this huge giant battleship fired its main armament in anger was during the sortie to Spitzbergen in early September of 1943. It is most significant that almost all the actions of the German heavy units have been mentioned elsewhere in this book because they supported other naval 'sideshows' in the Arctic. The single significant action that has only briefly been mentioned is the famous Battle of North Cape and even that huge scuffle would have merged into the insignificance had it not been for the sinking of the battleship *Scharnhorst*.

The Battle of North Cape centred on the 19 ships of Convoy JW55B that left Loch Ewe in Scotland on 20 December 1943 and 22 ships of Convoy RA55A that left Russia three days later. Both had an impressive escort of ten destroyers and four other escorts. The eastbound convoy was discovered by German air reconnaissance not long after leaving and the nature of intercepted messages suggested that the conditions were right to encourage battleship *Scharnhorst* to leave her Norwegian refuge to launch an attack. Decrypting this information in Britain made it obvious that the three cruisers (HMS *Belfast*, HMS *Sheffield* and HMS *Norfolk* under Vice Admiral R. L. Burnett) sent north to cover that area where the two convoys would pass each other were not sufficient and Admiral

*Above, below and overleaf:* The German destroyer *Hans Lody*, still afloat long after the war in Norway. This incredible model was built by Ivar Berntsen in Skjeberg (Norway). *Photos: Ivar Berntsen*

Fraser was dispatched from Iceland with the battleship *Duke of York*, the cruiser *Jamaica* and four destroyers to support any developments at North Cape. In the meantime the fact that German aircraft were shadowing Convoy JW55B prompted the British high command to send another four destroyers to its aid. The British Admiralty was also holding its breath as far as the other the westbound convoy was concerned. So far it appeared that it had not been discovered.

Admiral Erich Bey aboard the *Scharnhorst* received orders on Christmas Day of 1943 to engage the convoy, but his orders also told him to retreat if heavy ships were encountered. The Supreme Naval Command had been bombed out of its offices in Berlin during the previous November and it was only a few weeks before Kpt.z.S. Heinz Bonatz, the chief of the Radio Monitoring Service, was moved away from his rather important post. This suggests that Germany was not doing well as far as reading British signals was concerned. Whatever was going on with signals intelligence, the German Naval Command had not yet realised that a number of impressive heavy warships were also converging on the Bear Island area.

Convoy JW55B, sighted by U601 under Oblt.z.S. Otto Hansen during the morning of Christmas Day was then instrumental in ordering a U-boat pack to assemble while U601 continued to shadow the merchant ships. This was rather a vital constituent because the weather had now turned into such a raging gale that all German aircraft were grounded. Even if the weather had been better, there were now so few aircraft left in northern Norway that they could no longer inflict the serious punishment on convoys that they had done earlier in 1942. On this occasion, however, the Germans did get an air strike of Ju88s into the air before the bad weather put an end to flying, but not a single plane managed to break through the convoy's defensive screen. So, it seems highly likely that the British defences had got so strong that even the bomber intensity of a year earlier would not made much difference to the outcome of the battle. The weather continued to degenerate to such an extent that the destroyers supporting the *Scharnhorst* could no longer keep up and Bey asked his High Command what he should do next. Should he abandon his hunt or proceed without them? Neither the new Grand Admiral, Karl Dönitz, nor the Naval High Command came up with any positive help, other than approving him to go on alone, if he thought such action was appropriate.

The usual seven hours of Arctic twilight each day that might have produced a faint glow on the southern horizon did not help anyone while the action of the battle was unfolding. The storm, intense enough to scatter the westbound convoy, assured that the dull blackness of the Arctic night was going to rule whatever was going to happen and that can be summed up with only a few words. Some brief action did occur before Bey realised that he was surrounded by a number of heavy units during quite appalling visibility that allowed even small destroyers to get close enough to launch torpedoes. The British officers summed up the situation by saying that the punishment *Scharnhorst* endured without blowing up before sinking was remarkable. Despite an intensive search in the darkness, they picked up only thirty-six survivors, who were brought back to Britain. The following day, when U-boats were ordered to search for survivors they found the seas empty. There were not even any floating corpses supported by their lifejackets.

By the time *Scharnhorst* went down at 18.40 hours of 26 December 1943, *Tirpitz* had been put out of action by midget submarines called X-Craft. *Admiral Scheer* was being used as a training ship in the Baltic, *Lützow* (ex-*Deutschland*) was also in the Baltic, having sustained heavy damage, *Prinz Eugen* had been damaged in Norway and the light cruisers did not fare much better. Despite what Britain recognised as a gallant effort, the heavy ships of the German Navy did not do much more in Norway than consume massive Allied resources in case they came out of their protective lairs to decimate a convoy. Even the convoy that gave rise to *Scharnhorst* putting to sea, JW55B reached its destination without loss and the counterbalance convoy, sailing from Russia to Loch Ewe also reached its destination. This meant that even the U-boat pack that had been established to intercept JW55B did not make any impression other than provide historians with some highly exciting incidents to weave into their accounts.

# 10

# Voyages of Exploration

Germany's biggest problem with the expansion into Arctic waters was that very little was known about anything in that area and much of what was known was rather variable, based on calculated deduction rather than solid facts. It was already common knowledge that the North Polar Ice Cap was not sitting on a solid mountain, but floating; constantly moving from east to west so that timber from Siberia ended up on the islands to the north of Norway. The German Navy had some reasonable charts showing positions of islands, but there was hardly any accurate information about the depth of water, the currents or the irritating different layers of salinity and temperature within the water. These influenced the sensitive sound detectors to such an extent that at times it was possible for a noisy ship with brass band on deck to pass over the top of a submerged submarine without being heard and, of course, Allied Asdic operators were driven mad by the unusual acoustic interference. In addition to this, no one in Germany knew what happened to the ice in summer, where the boundaries were or where it might be possible to sail convoys. It was therefore necessary to devote considerable resources to nothing more than acquiring some basic information about the lie of the land, the sea, the ice and the traffic.

Whilst individual U-boats were bringing back valuable reconnaissance information, more was required, so several exploratory expeditions were sent north, to penetrate deeper into the Arctic seas. One of the biggest of these was Operation *Wunderland*, which set sail during the summer of 1942. The amazing point about this was that U-boats were accompanied by long-range reconnaissance aircraft and by the pocket battleship *Admiral Scheer* under Kpt.z.S. Wilhelm Meendsen-Bohlken. One reason for choosing a pocket battleship instead of a heavy cruiser or other large ship was agility. Each propeller shaft was driven by four large diesel engines and in a tight place it was possible to set two of these running forwards, while the other two were started to run in reverse. Then it was a case of merely clutching from one set of engines to the other to make the ship perform the most amazing manoeuvres to get itself out of a tight spot without help from tugs. Marine diesel engines could be made to rotate clockwise or anti-clockwise, but the many ships did not have a gear for switching from forward to backward without reversing the engines. Instead it was necessary to stop the engine and re-start it in the other direction. The term pocket battleship is important in this context because although these had been re-classed as heavy cruisers shortly after the start of the war, the two types had totally different propulsion systems. It should also be remembered that the heavy units had been sent to Norway because of Hitler's hunches. He was still expecting an Allied invasion in the north and he was not too keen on them being away from this defensive role for any length of time.

Arctic Exploration and Destruction—Operation *Wunderland*

| | | | |
|---|---|---|---|
| 1. | 19 August 1942 | ÄF 8932 | U601 met *Admiral Scheer* |
| 2. | 20 August 1942 | ÄF 0739 | U251 met *Admiral Scheer* |
| 3. | 12 August 1942 | ÄG 8186 | U255 supplied a BV138 with fuel |
| 4. | 2 September 1942 | AT 3215 | U255 shelled Radio Station Shelanija |
| 4. | 27 July 1943 | AT 3513 | U255 sank *Akademik Sokalski* |
| 4. | -- August 1943 | AT 3277 | Cape Sporyy Navolok |
| | | | U255 supplied BV 138 aircraft, met |
| | | | U601 and other U-boats. |
| 5. | 6 September 1942 | ÄF 9943 | U255 sighted Lonely Island |
| 6. | 12 September 1943 | AF 7563 | U307 rescued crew from BV138 |
| 7. | | | Belyy Island |
| 8. | | | Port of Dikson |

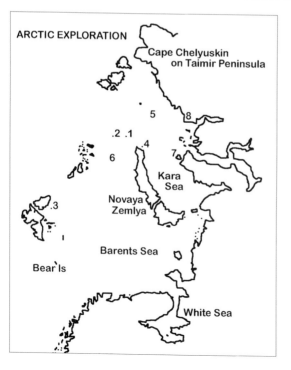

ARCTIC EXPLORATION

Cape Chelyuskin
on Taimir Peninsula

5   8

.2 .1
4
6       7

Kara
Sea

Novaya
Zemlya

.3

Barents Sea

Bear's Is

White Sea

This show a massive chart that U377 used when setting up weather stations on Cape Mitra near New Alesund. Although it will be impossible to make out the details in this picture, it does show how little was known about Hopen Island and East Spitzbergen compared with Bear Island and Spitzbergen's west coast. The tiny dots in the sea indicate the water's depth and one can see quite clearly that there are a vast number of such soundings in some areas and others are almost completely devoid of any water depth information.

One of the big conundrums of the time was the Kara Sea. So far German military activity did not reach far beyond the boundaries of the Barents Sea, where warmish waters from what started out as the Gulf Stream penetrated even during the winter months, making part of the North Russian coast ice free all the year round. Novaya Zemlya, that massive strip of land of a thousand or so kilometres in length, prevents this warmish water from flowing further east and during the Second World War it was already well known that the Kara Sea was considerably whiter for much of the year. It was also well known that Russia had been developing the shipping routes through it for a long time, but nothing at all was known about the traffic that might be there and in 1942 it was thought that this might make a considerable contribution to Russia's war effort. The term 'warmish water' in this paragraph must be taken with a large pinch of salt because with its temperature hovering around freezing point means that it is still pretty cold but not cold enough for the salt water to freeze solid.

Operation *Wunderland* started at three o'clock in the afternoon of 16 August 1942 when *Admiral Scheer* weighed anchor near Narvik and proceeded out to sea. To make sure that Meendsen-Bohlken understood his orders correctly, he was given written instructions that he was not to put his ship at risk and he was to break off any action if there was the slightest danger of running into trouble. His written orders also emphasised the importance of surprise. None of the vessels going into the Polar seas were to use their radio and every effort had to be made to remain unseen. This, of course made it impossible to provide the pocket battleship with any up-to-date reconnaissance information from U-boats which were already at sea, and three days later *Admiral Scheer* met with U601, whose commander, Kptlt. Peter-Ottmar Grau, was not the happiest of mortals at that time. Just to confuse the issue, there were two people with the same name on board. Peter Grau, who later went down with U1191 to the south of Torquay (Devon) joined U601 as 2WO (2nd Watch Officer) in October 1942 and was later promoted to 1WO. Peter-Ottmar Grau, the commander, survived the war. The last mentioned had called at the Naval Command Centre in Kirkeness for his final orders, but the telex system was not working well and there was no way in which he could get answers to the many questions he wanted to ask. He did get the general bearing of what he was supposed to do, to potter around as far north as he could go and to find the summer limit of the pack ice around Novaya Zemlya. The code words 'Operation *Wunderland*' did not mean anything to him at this time and he headed off without any real objective or knowing what lay ahead. What made things even more obscure was that Grau was told not to report any of his findings until asked to do so over the radio. So, it very much sounded like 'an urgent operation but don't disturb us if you find anything exciting.' Grau was emphatically calm and never showed any outward signs of being confused or ruffled, so his crew could not guess that they were going to do anything other than hunt convoys. U601 had arrived in northern waters during the middle of July, some three weeks earlier and had already hunted the remains of Convoy PQ17, attacked one ship and shelled a Russian radio station at Karmakuly, so everybody on board was fully aware of the difficult hunting in their area.

Sighting the north-west coast of Novaya Zemlya was hardly unpleasant. There was a moderate north-easterly wind of Force four to five with visibility up to a white haze at about 15 kilometres from the boat and no sign of any opposition. The sea was more or less devoid of ice. There were only a few pieces in some of the more sheltered bays and later exploration indicated that the pack ice did not start until more than a 100 kilometres to the north; so all was well. Grau received orders to send his findings as a short signal and after following the edge of the ice for two days, he received another message to meet with *Admiral Scheer* to the north of Novaya Zemlya and until then he was free to do what he liked but he was to attack only valuable targets.

Sighting *Admiral Scheer* came as surprise to the crew of U601 and what was even more unusual was that they went alongside for Grau to meet with Meendsen-Bohlken, to discover that they were part of Operation *Wunderland*. After giving a detailed account of his experiences, Grau was told to go further east to explore the ice conditions off the eastern side of the Kara Sea. If possible he should ascertain the condition around Port Dikson, some 80 degrees east. (As far east as Ceylon or Sri Lanka.) Going as far as White Island on the tip of the Yamal Peninsula presented no great problems. There was no ice, but no sight of any of the expected traffic either. Earlier radio reconnaissance from Berlin had suggested considerable volumes of shipping were moving through those seas throughout the summer.

Crossing the Kara Sea to Dikson Island produced a most unexpected surprise on 22 August when a zigzagging freighter came in to sight. Its helmsman was either drunk or, far more likely, expecting an attack in this incredibly remote region. At 17.35 hours with a steady north-easterly of Force four to five and with visibility up to some twenty kilometres, it looked like an easy target for a submerged submarine. Unfortunately for U601, somehow, when the boat dived, the ship just vanished as if it had been part of a convincing conjuring trick. At first the men assumed that stark differences in salinity or temperature were preventing them from hearing it, but a few hours later when U601 surfaced again the ship had disappeared without giving any indication as to where it might be going. It seemed weird that the ship was fully prepared for an attack and took

The pocket battleship *Admiral Scheer* sometime before the beginning of the war. By the time it sailed into the Kara Sea as part of Operation *Wunderland*, it had been refitted with a different command tower.

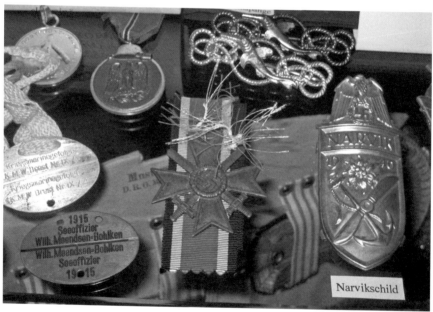

The identification disc or dog tag that once belonged to Admiral Wilhelm Meendsen-Bohlken, commander of Operation *Wunderland*. Officers had their name on these discs while other ranks had their service number engraved on it.

This rather poor quality picture was taken during the war from Novaya Zemlya and appears to show three U-boats. The one in the foreground is partly submerged with only the conning tower protruding above the surface and the long boat is in fact two with their conning towers almost overlapping.

Part of Kingsfjord near New Alesund taken from U377 showing the sort of conditions encountered near land.

every opportunity of avoiding it, despite being so far away from any large habitation centre. The men thought that it might be heading for a small, unknown port along the coast and decided it was better to give up the hunt in order to continue with the main objective of reconnoitring Dikson Island, which was sighted towards the late afternoon of the following day.

Having reached Dikson Island at about eighty degrees east, both *Admiral Scheer* and U601 went into action and although the U-boat managed to get close enough to sink one target (the 2,332 GRT freighter *Kujbyshev*) so quickly that it did not have an opportunity of sending a distress call, the pocket battleship was not so lucky. Her presence was well advertised and even the bombardment of Port Dikson and the suspected total destruction of the radio station there, all resulted in comparatively meagre pickings for such a huge ship. It was thought that the attack would help make the region unstable, force the Russians to escort ships and make them devote more resources to the defence of that desolate coast. This was wishful thinking by the German higher command. Russia did not divert too many resources into the Arctic seas. Instead the Russians used the vastness of their land to best advantage. It very much looked as if shipping at sea was merely shut down and kept in port or in isolated sheltered bays and it was anybody's guess which ships might be in which port. Germany was not even sure where all the Russian ports were. This vastness can easily be illustrated by merely heading north along the motorway from Moscow where signposts

Large icebergs were a definite nuisance in the Kara Sea.

Ice as seen from an aircraft.
The amount of ice was measured by 'Ball', where 10 meant complete ice cover and 1 equalled one tenth of the sea covered by ice.

show the directions to towns more than a thousand kilometres away. This empty vastness combined with extreme weather was indeed a major hurdle for any European venturing into that desolation.

On 25 August 1942, *Admiral Scheer*'s only Arado seaplane crashed so seriously that it was of no further use and strangely enough there was no replacement on board. The aircraft had paid for its worth by having provided a constant picture of the ice conditions, which turned out to be far more serious than Peter-Ottmar Grau's first report. The situation around Novaya Zemlya had been easy and progress through the Kara Sea was not too difficult either, but after a while heavy ice started play such a destructive role by coming in from behind that progress was becoming incredibly difficult and air support was more than essential. The natural conditions gave *Admiral Scheer* no alternative other than to break off the military action so that the ship could concentrate on finding a way back to more open waters. Searching for the right conditions was difficult, even from the top of the high command tower where the massive three-dimensional optical range finder was being used as extra set of eyes. Much of the horizon tended to be hidden behind what looked like a whitish net curtain.

Two pests of German Arctic exploration, heavy ice and Russian aircraft. The aircraft often took no notice of U-boats, yet they did not appear to be coming from anywhere specific nor going to any known destination, so it seemed that they were out searching for something and at times drove U-boat men to abandon objectives long before reaching them.

The famous typical Arctic mists hanging over the sea to make it difficult to spot anything and impossible to take bearings on sun or stars. Navigating for days on end under such conditions made it difficult to pin point positions and dead easy to bump into rocks and ice.

Several of the U-boat landings took place in large areas of shallow water where boats and rubber dinghies grounded a long way from dry land, making it necessary to carry packages through ankle to knee deep freezing cold water, where the waves were often deep enough to wash over the tops of boots.

Realising that both U601 and *Admiral Scheer* had proceeded a long way east, the Admiral for Northern Seas sent another U-boat, U251 under Kptlt. Heinrich Timm, to reconnoitre the shifting seas through which the pocket battleship would have to pass on her way back. *Admiral Scheer*, with the call sign SC, had now been given the name *Zeus* to help confuse possible enemy forces listening in to radio messages. *Scheer* supplied U251 with fuel on 20 August 1942 but the general situation was not good. Shortly after this meeting Timm ran into what looked like a submarine chaser and, in addition to this, he was forced to dive to avoid reconnaissance planes on several occasions. The Germans were well aware that it was not unusual to spot Russian planes. For most of the time, they appeared to pass overhead while on some other mission, other than chasing U-boats. Those that were now being spotted did not appear to have come from any known base and did not seem to be heading for anything specific either, so they were obviously just searching the seas. Their presence suggested that there were going to be difficult times ahead.

The other, rather serious problem with Operation *Wunderland* was that the weather during the outward-bound part had not been objectionable for the Arctic and made progress relatively easy. However, once on the way back, *Scheer* ran into long periods of poor visibility, often with quite bright conditions, making the men fear that the shadow of the huge pocket battleship could easily be spotted from the air without lookouts on ship being able to see the very much smaller aircraft and the consequences of that scenario were not encouraging for life assurance salesmen, especially as ice was becoming a worrying nuisance.

The initial worry with the aircraft catapulted off the pocket battleship was that it had only one engine and a breakdown in those hostile waters could well result in total disaster if ice prevented the ship from reaching the wreck. Being aware of this anxiety, the navy went as far as sending a Blohm und Voss flying boat to help out. The BV138 had been designed for long-range reconnaissance by the famous ship builder. With three engines providing a cruising speed of about 155 mph, it had a range of about 2,500–3,000 miles. And, most important, it could continue flying if one of the engines failed, so the chances of survival in the Arctic wilderness were considerably better than the single engine Arado carried by the pocket battleship. The difficulty was that the Siberian Sea Passage was so vast that aircraft's range seemed puny over such long distances, and initial proposals put many of the essential flying areas beyond its reach. As a result plans went ahead for a BV138 to operate in far-off regions in conjunction with a U-boat for accommodating the aircrew and supplying the necessary fuel. The aircraft was powered by Junker Jumo diesel engines, meaning it was not necessary for the tanker U-boat to carry highly volatile aviation spirit.

*Above and below:* Moderate seas with a strong wind may have been no problem for large ocean-going ships but they were a real pain to U-boats that had to approach close to land and then unload masses of goods or equipment on isolated coasts.

Incessant polar fog hanging over and ice field not far from Spitzbergen. Making progress under such conditions was exceedingly difficult and at times most dangerous. Yet, the monotony of the weather was sometimes broken by weird atmospheric occurrences such as solar halos hugging the bright sun. *Photo: Michael and Brenda Lyons*

This may sound good, but the system had a major flaw inasmuch as high-octane aviation petrol was necessary to start the engines when they were cold, and the fuel could only be switched over once they were hot. This, of course, became rather critical in those Arctic latitudes and provided a major stumbling block until special arrangements were made to carry more than the usual quantities of petrol.

The first trials with such a joint aircraft and submarine undertaking were carried out around the time of Operation *Wunderland*. On 12 August 1942, U255 under Kptlt. Reinhart Reche supplied a BV138 under Oblt. z.S. Karl Dierschke with a cubic metre of fuel near Spitzbergen. It was essential to try this out in a comparative safe location so that the aircrew would not perish if the refuelling did not run according to plan. This first refuelling worked well, the aircrew was accommodated in the U-boat for a while and Dierschke then decided to fly to a German base on Spitzbergen before heading back to Tromsö. However, he watered (landed) again much earlier than expected. The BV138 took off, circled over the U-boat and then, without much warning dropped out of the sky like a stone for the pilot to make a breathtaking emergency watering. He obviously knew how to fly.

Seas breaking over a German minesweeper. U-boats could avoid such difficult conditions by diving, which also provided some rest for the crew, but convoy escorts had to endure such harsh conditions without finding any nook to get away from the vigorous movement. What was more, many escorts had the crew accommodation forward and the galley aft without an internal corridor connecting the two.

The reason was that two engines stopped without warning and this made things rather difficult because none of the airmen were well-versed in engine maintenance. Even the flight engineer usually left such intricacies to the ground maintenance teams. Now it was a case of getting his hands dirty, but he had ample support from the U-boat's diesel crew and it was not long before the men discovered the fuel tanks contained some seawater in addition to the oil. This had never presented a problem in submarines because any water coming through the U-boat's pumping system was merely allowed to drain out of the bottom of the tank. The U-boat storage bunkers filled with seawater, not air, when the fuel was pumped out. Furthermore, the diesel outlet pipes were at the top, not the bottom of the tanks. The fuel for daily use was usually pumped into a tank below the ceiling of the engine room and this had a glass tube along one side so that it was possible to see what and how much was inside it. The aircraft did not need such facilities because it was rare for them to be supplied from bunkers that were open to the sea at the bottom. Getting the water out of the aircraft's tank was not easy as there was no obvious drainage tap. Therefore the men had no alternative other than to tow the BV138 to a calmer location where they could tackle the necessary remedial work. The first two attempts failed due to the hawser breaking. If this was not bad enough, the BV138 floated on its ship-like hull with a stabilising float under each wing. One these then snagged on the towing rope, causing the aircraft to turn over and sit on the water like a protesting duck with an injured wing. Seeing it was going to be impossible to repair the damage, there was no alternative other than to take the crew on board the U-boat and to sink the aircraft by gunfire. No one was very pleased.

A year later, during the summer of 1943, Germany made a more determined effort to reconnoitre those Arctic wastes and got as far as setting up a temporary U-boat base on Novaya Zemlya. This was quite a complicated operation inasmuch as two U-boats were required in different locations because there was no guarantee that the weather would allow the aircraft back to where it had started. U255 was now under command of Oblt.z.S. Erich Harms. The boat's first commander, Reinhart Reche, had moved on to become an Admiralty Staff Officer with the Flag Officer for U-boats in Norway. Harms had originally joined U255 as Second Watch Officer in November 1941 and progressed to 1WO before becoming a fully pledged commander. He had been on board during the earlier escapades and was probably in a better position to deal with these delicate Arctic operations than many of the other, older commanders.

This new venture, codenamed Wunderland II, started on somewhat better prepared foundations than the earlier attempt and Harms was in a brilliant position of assuring that the earlier teething problems would

*Above, below and next page:* The Arctic Seas around Spitzbergen could be worse than hell on earth, yet they also had an incredibly pleasant side with a deep magic that enthralled those who had the privilege to experience this cold world of rich wonder.

not occur a second time. Not only did the navy provide more essential equipment, but the admirals also provided one aircraft with two crews and each with their own meteorologist who could interpret the complicated data that they were going to collect. U255 was backed up by U601 under Peter-Ottmar Grau, who was initially going to look after the alternative landing area. The idea was to place one boat on the eastern and the other on the western side of Novaya Zemlya. Bearing in mind that both boats were some eight hours flying time from Norway, the rendezvous was indeed in a most isolated location and there was no way the aircraft could get back to German occupied territory of it failed in finding the one of the two U-boats. The fact that the BV138 was too fragile for landing on the rough conditions usually prevailing over the open sea, meant it was more than essential that there were no hiccups with navigation or with any other part of the operation.

U255 was a standard Type VIIC with a bunk for four officers, four warrant officers and eight bunks for thirteen or more petty officers so these additional bodies were indeed an enormous burden on the already overcrowded U-boat that had already been filled beyond capacity with provisions and additional stores. Surviving in those exceedingly cramped conditions for weeks on end called for a high spirit of cooperation to make the venture tolerable and the only consolation was that the airmen were used to working in tight surroundings without much space to move. In addition to this, they were used to being tossed about by the outside elements and therefore put up with the hectic conditions without complaining.

Finding that a safe landing area was not as easy as the men had imagined. Harms must have had considerable trepidations, because a year earlier U255 discovered that strong currents pushed the boat onto rocks and this time the men found similar conditions during an ebbing tide. The situation turned out to be manageable and the boat was pulled free on the next rising tide without damage, but there was no way the men could get as close to a beach as they had hoped and there was no chance of docking anywhere as near to the land as the men had wished. Finding that illusive spot became a major headache.

The search for a more suitable re-fuelling area was brought to an abrupt halt when the lookouts spotted a tiny Russian ship of about 300 tons (*Akademik Sokalski*), apparently surveying the same area. There was nothing for it, other than to take on the Russian in an artillery combat. It was too small and the water too shallow for an expensive torpedo. The gun crew was obviously in top form for they did not have to expend too many shells before their target turned turtle and sank. What surprised

*Above and next page:* U377 in Norway with lookouts spellbound by the natural wonder of their surroundings.

the men was that a large proportion of the more than thirty people who took to the lifeboats were women. Some post war researchers were even more surprised to discover that the Germans could tell the difference over such a considerable distance. A number of veterans at an Arctic convoys meeting near Loch Ewe said they found it difficult to work out the difference between male and female in Murmansk because they looked almost identical, wearing the same type of baggy clothing without any feminine features.

The sinking of the survey ship was an emotionally horrifying experience where Harms made a point of sending everybody who was not needed below decks. It was war and orders were orders. It was essential to continue the search for a more suitable landing and refuelling place without regard to any humanitarian issues that might get in the way. The next suitable location was not much good either. It may have looked good a year ago when the area was briefly surveyed from the air, but it was rather exposed without any opportunity of hiding the aircraft when it was 'in port.' To make matters worse, the men also found the remains of a boat together with a floating corpse—not the ideal invitation to set up a base.

Following this, lookouts spotted people on a beach. It was possible that these had come from the ship that U255 had sunk the previous day. The critical factor was that these characters were reasonably active and the

*Above and following page:* U255 under Kptlt. Reinhard Reche refuelling a Blohm und Voss flying boat in the Arctic seas.

Germans could see that they were making every effort to escape into the barren rocky wilderness rather than surrender to the U-boat. The survivors had a fire near the beach, making it look as if they were well prepared for their ordeal. The trouble was that they also seemed to have had the determination to get back to civilisation and possibly create problems for the U-boat by sending out a hunting party to sink it. Leaving the survivors to their own devices could spell disaster for the entire reconnaissance mission, so it was necessary to somehow fix them to the land, to prevent them from raising the alarm. Harms did not have much choice. He was certain that these people were survivors from the ship that he had sunk and therefore they were making excellent progress, taking every opportunity to make good use of the meagre resources available to them. It seemed likely that they would find their way back to civilisation too quickly for his liking. It was obvious that they needed to be slowed down and the inflatable was made ready to capture their large sturdy lifeboat. It had occurred to more than one person aboard U255 that this was just the sort of aid that they could do with for servicing with any incoming aircraft. So the order was to appropriate it. U255 dived under it, allowed it to float above the partly submerged deck and then surfaced again with the prize high and dry.

Two days later, on 31 July 1943, with the captured lifeboat on deck, U255 stopped almost half a kilometre from a high cliff, hoping to find a suitable refuelling area, but the bay on the north-east coast of Novaya Zemlya was still full of rather solid ice and this, together with the shallow water, made it impossible to get in close to the land. Although not ideal, the protruding headlands made it difficult to spot the submarine from the sea and therefore this was going to be the first Arctic aircraft refuelling location. A lookout post with a good pile of provisions was established on the top of the cliff, the lifeboat was sent out to determine the depth of water in the bay and the U-boat was camouflaged with matting brought especially for the purpose. This did not just drape over the top of the superstructure like a flimsy net but provided enough space underneath to man the 88 mm quick-firing gun on the foredeck and the 20 mm anti-aircraft gun. There were a number of rocks breaking through the surface of the water and by the time men finished the U-boat looked similar. Later the airmen congratulated the crew for their brilliant camouflage. The first of these arrived during the afternoon of 4 August and left again the following morning at 0805 hours for their first reconnaissance flight of about eight hours.

The only real problem with this part of the world was that the seabed appeared to be made up of solid rock, so smooth that an anchor could not get a grip, making it impossible to anchor off the usual mooring buoy for the aircraft. However the rocks along the coast provided enough foundations for the men to rig up their own effective system to make the BV138 fast. This worked well; although it was difficult to camouflage the aircraft because the men could not walk over it and they did not have cranes for lifting heavy netting. In the end the aircraft bows were attached to the stern of the U-boat with one member of the crew constantly on duty inside so that the engines could be started while it was pulled alongside for the rest of the crew to get on board. Later, when the weather worsened and a sharp wind started blowing the aircraft into the shore, it was pointed into the wind and the central engine started to help keep the boat in the right position. Unfortunately the weather was not cooperative and eventually became the decisive factor in breaking off the reconnaissance flights.

U601 under Kptlt. Peter-Ottmar Grau, the relief aircraft supply boat, had problems finding the well camouflaged supply base when coming to contribute to the undertaking by delivering more supplies. U255 had left Narvik on 19 July 1943 and had by this time been at sea for three weeks, so the provisions were most welcome. After this, things started going wrong. Waves became too choppy, meaning the BV138 could not gain enough speed for taking off and flights had to be suspended from 11 August until the 20th, when it was decided that the aircrew should commence their return to Norway. The waves had a settled a little by midday, but it was not long before U255 received a distress call from the BV138 saying it was in the process of making an emergency landing. Harms's first reaction was to jettison everything that was not required, get to top speed as fast as possible and make for Square AT 2288. This was not far away, but on the western side of Novaya Zemlya and it would take some time for him to reach the spot. Luckily for the airmen, U601 was considerably closer and also picked up the distress call. Heading immediately for the crash site, the men found the aircrew with what looked like their undamaged aircraft at 22.55 hours of 20 August 1943, just over eight hours after the distress call. It had been a long eight hours for the aircrew.

A moderate south-westerly of Force 4 with a moderate swell made the salvage operation awkward. Waves kept crashing over the top of the cockpit, despite the U-boat putting itself on the windward side of the somewhat flimsy bird. The first watch officer of U601, Lt.z.S. Walter-Bruno Koch, who later became commander of U1132, distinguished himself by falling overboard three times while attempting to tow it. The wind together with choppy water made it impossible to keep the towing rope taught, and at times it would slacken. Then, suddenly, without warning the U-boat and aircraft were pulled apart for the rope to jerk, snapping it with profound ease. Yet despite these most unfavourable conditions, there were no thoughts of evacuating the BV138 and the senior pilot Oblt.z.S.

Shallow waters near land, especially the sheltered bays would have made ideal landing places for aircraft except that these were often littered with enough ice to make to rule out such areas for aircraft operations. This clearly shows how easy it would have been for the ice to destroy an aircraft if it attempted landing in the wrong places. Surface support was more than urgently required if reconnaissance aircraft ventured into the Arctic realm. *Photo Michael and Brenda Lyons*

U255 under Kptlt. Reinhard Reche with a number of airmen on the top of the bridge in Norway. Four light machine guns have been mounted on the conning tower wall; there is a circular radar detector aerial to the right of the commander with the white cap and what looks like two single 20 mm anti-aircraft guns on the winter garden at the rear of the conning tower. The badge above the navigation light is the emblem of the 11th U-boat Flotilla in Bergen.

Polar bears, one of the largest carnivores one is likely to meet, could be a real danger in the Arctic, especially if they were marooned on lonely islands by melting ice. This made it necessary for men to carry arms to prevent them from accidentally becoming the lunch for one of these huge predators. U255 possibly with a bear shot as trophy, rather than in self-defence.

An iceberg photographed from U255.

Stieler managed to get aboard the submarine to discuss the situation with Peter-Ottmar Grau.

This fiasco with the towline breaking was in full swing when two Russian bombers of Type DB3 came into sight at a height of about 1,500 metres. It looked as if the aircraft were out searching for something because they were not following the usual straight course, but for some reason they did not seem to have noticed the pantomime below and eventually the Germans were left in peace again. Despite the lack of interference, it was quickly becoming obvious that the aircraft was going to sink. The men inside were already up to their waists in water while trying to salvage as much as possible and in the end there was no alternative other than to sink what remained of the wreck. The men on the upper (outside) deck of the U-boat did not fare much better and were also soaked to skin in near freezing temperatures with the steady breeze adding a good bite to the wind-chill factor. It was impractical to wear the usual Arctic gear donned on by lookouts because that made it almost impossible to move with the agility required to prevent oneself being washed over deck even during such a moderate sea that prevailed during this incident. This was, once again, very much a case of the boat's cook supplying hot necessities to keep the workers at it under those arduous conditions.

The end of the BV138 was not the end of the story because by that time there were a number of other U-boats in those challenging Arctic seas. Some formed patrol lines to search for illusive convoys while others were on their own mining operations. It was planned that U703 (Oblt.z.S. Joachim Brünner) should relieve U601 after bringing fresh supplies to U255, which was still in the original refuelling location on the north-east coast of Nova Zemlya at what was now known as 'Base One', to await a replacement aircraft from Norway. This period of calm was not without drama for U255. It was shortly after lunch, with the sun high in the sky when an incredible explosion shattered the men's nerves. Luckily no one was on the deck to be seriously injured. Following the usual procedure for such events, the men discovered that the aft torpedo storage container under the upper (outside) deck had burst by having had its screwed-on cover blown off. Someone back at base had come up with the bright idea of using this for storing a vast number of cans containing lubrication oil for the BV138 and it seemed as if these had been heated to a high enough temperature by the nearby exhaust pipe for the remaining petroleum gasses in the thin oil to have evaporated, creating enough pressure to blow the container apart. The engines of the U-boat were run for several hours each day for recharging the batteries, and this had caused the exhaust pipe to heat.

The next BV138, due to arrive around the 21 August 1943, returned to Norway when it ran into dense fog over large stretches of the northern

*Left:* U703's anti-aircraft gun.

*Below left:* U703 refuelling a Blohm & Voss BV 138.

*Below right:* U703's on duty lookout on Novaya Zemlya with a loaded rifle in case polar bears arrive looking for lunch.

U703 with aircraft adjacent to a Blohm & Voss BV 138.

U703 and another unidentified U-boat with a Blohm & Voss BV 138.

waters. It started again two days later on the 23rd. This day also saw the arrival of U703 (Oblt.z.S. Joachim Brünner) with fresh supplies and the experienced senior pilot, Oblt.z.S. Stieler, who had come on board from U601 after his earlier rescue. Once again the weather made watering (landing) impossible and the aircraft returned to base. Since conditions were so bad, it was suggested to use the alternative Base Three on the western side of Novaya Zemlya, where U255 met with U636 (Kptlt. Hans Hildebrandt) on 25 August. Both food and ammunition for the large 88 mm deck gun were handed over. but the swell was bad enough for U636 not to remain alongside U255 for long, and the boat moved further way before anchoring. Both heavy fog and an abundance of floating ice then kept U636 in place for a while before it could return to Norway. It had already been on a short, but successful mining operation, having left Narvik on 14 August.

U255 eventually returned to Base One on the north-east coast of Novaya Zemlya, but the weather remained offensive enough not to allow aircraft into the area until the end of the first week of September, and it was the evening of the 4th that the replacement BV138 arrived. This was immediately refuelled for a reconnaissance flight on the 5th and 6th September. Following this, the tricky swell made further take-offs impossible, but both U703 and a newcomer U629 (Oblt.z.S. Hans-Helmuth Bugs) called with spare provisions for the airmen and for U255. These two boats were both on their way back from separate mining operations further east. By this time the BV138 had already started back to northern Norway and another aircraft had arrived to take its place. The reason for this constant coming and going was that Base One was very much at the aircrafts' limit of operations and the operational headquarters required detailed information about sea conditions between Novaya Zemlya and Norway, whence this was deemed to be more important than flying further east.

The last aircraft to arrive did so only by curious chance. Radio communications had been bad enough for U255 not be aware that it was in the air and the plane's gyrocompass failed so that it ended up far too far to the north. The radio operator in U255 happened to hear to aircraft and managed to guide the incoming plane to the right location. The aircrew must have been exceedingly pleased with the hot meal they received after thinking that they might never get home again. The first reconnaissance flight was jinxed as well, and this time the aircraft ran out of fuel before reaching Base One, where U255 was still waiting. The U-boat up-anchored immediately and made off to search. On hearing this, the operations room in Norway ordered both U629 (Oblt.z.S. Hans-Helmuth Bugs) and U307 (Oblt.z.S. Friedrich-Georg Herrle) to help as well and it was the last mentioned that eventually took the BV138 in tow to bring it to U255. By this time the trio was far enough east and weather conditions in the west were not encouraging that the plan was changed to make for Franz-Joseph Land. Although the submarine had no problems here, the flimsiness of the aircraft did not allow for such strenuous operation and it was finally scuttled by gunfire. U255 was on its way back to Base One when a radio call came saying there would be no further aircraft operations in the area. There was nothing for it. U255 headed for home. Making fast next to the depot ship *Black Watch* in Hammerfest, U255 had been at sea in the Arctic for 63 days, which must be one, if not 'the' longest single U-boat voyage in those cold and icy waters.

The aircraft mentioned earlier operated with two U-boats. There were a further three U-boats of the Viking Pack waiting for news of possible targets, and in addition to this the pocket battleship *Lützow* (formerly *Deutschland*) was standing by in Altafjord, fuelled and ready to pounce on any ships sighted by the reconnaissance flights. So the expense was substantial, but the results remained poor. Operation *Wunderland II* did not contribute a great deal to the outcome of the war, although the men achieved a great deal in their own individual ways. The annoying point about the whole venture was that the ice conditions were considerably better than the Wunderland Operation of 1942. The men thought that it was the use of their radios and the search for survivors from the survey ship, which brought a considerable amount of traffic into those waters. The Germans were also of the opinion that the combination of these two factors was responsible for Russian freighters avoiding those cold seas. Whatever, the performance of individuals during Wunderland II was exemplary, but the overall results in terms of ships sunk and damage inflicted incredibly disappointing and the air reconnaissance did not bring the expected results. The operation did prove quite clearly that the aircraft were much too flimsy for the arduous role that they had been given.

# 11

# Svalbard—Spitzbergen
# The Double-Edged Centre Forward
# of the Arctic

(Spitzbergen is officially known as Svalbard in Norway and has the alternative spelling of Spitsbergen because the name came from the Dutch language meaning pointed mountains.)

Following several centuries of squabbling, the Svalbard archipelago eventually came under Norwegian sovereignty as a result of an international treaty signed early in 1920. This also stated that there should be free scientific and economic access for other nationalities, and the islands could not be fortified or be used for military purposes. West Spitzbergen, the largest of the Svalbard islands, with an area of almost 40,000 square kilometres, is also the biggest of all Norwegian islands and when added up entire archipelago covers an area of about 62,000 square kilometres, making it a substantial land mass. It was first discovered towards the end of the sixteenth Century when the Dutch explorer, Willem Barents was searching for a north-eastern sea passage to the Far East. The textbooks tell us that finding this set of lonely Arctic islands was not difficult since they are located at the end of a massive funnel-like feature of open water, where warm currents from the Gulf Stream prevent the sea from being frozen solid during the cold winter months. However, the adjective 'warm' is definitely an overstatement. The West Spitzbergen waters might be free from permanent ice, but the temperatures of a few degrees below zero are fierce enough to kill any human falling into them, even when wearing a modern survival suit. These, of course, were not invented until many years after the Second World War.

The multitude of wildlife supported by the islands attracted fur trappers and other European hunters, especially whalers who set up temporary camps on Spitzbergen for boiling blubber to extract whale oil. Other valuable resources, such as phosphates, iron and lead ore are still not the easiest to exploit, but coal did have a major influence on the local economy for more than a hundred years. The first mine was opened towards the end of the nineteenth

Spitzbergen seen from U307 while setting up weather station Schneehuhn.

century and by the time the Second World War started, several pits along the west coast had given rise to the main settlements of Barentsburg and the capital Longyearbyen, on the shores of the Icefjord. The most isolated mine was located at Ny Alesund about a hundred kilometres to the north. This small settlement, the most northerly in the world and with the world's most northerly hotel, became a hub for all manner of scientific and exploratory activities, especially those who were seeking to be the first to stand on the North Pole. The Spitzbergen settlements have the added advantage that the west coast is relatively mild when compared with the rest of the archipelago. Summer temperatures hardly ever get much higher than eight or nine degrees Celsius, but in winter they tend not to drop far below minus fifteen. This is comparatively mild if one considers that the east coast and north coast often drop to minus twenty, thirty or more for many days on end.

By the time the Second World War started there was already a tiny network of roads, railways and aerial cables for carrying coal within the settlements, but no communication system connecting the towns. Despite this, access by sea was relatively easy, with regular summer scheduled shipping services having been introduced as early as 1935. Mining has now shrunk and much of Spitzbergen has become a protected area with scientific research and tourism high in the list of important activities.

## The Battle for Spitzbergen

At the beginning of the Second World War there were three active mines on Spitzbergen, at Longyearbyen, Barentsburg and Grumantbyen. The first

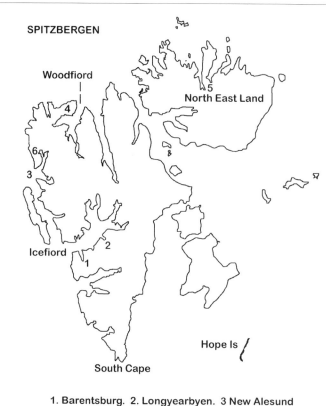

**SPITZBERGEN**

Woodfiord

North East Land

4

5

6

3

8

7

Icefiord

2

1

Hope Is

South Cape

1. Barentsburg. 2. Longyearbyen. 3 New Alesund
4. Kreuzritter Weather Station. 5. Haudegen Weather Station
6. Knospe and Nussbaum Weather Stations

*Left:* Spitzbergen has been used by hunters ever since it was first discovered and consequently many of the features have been named, but it is only necessary to know the locations of a few of these places.

*Below:* Spitzbergen or sharp mountains had a charming side dominated by impressive glaziers and tantalising seas under a brilliant blue sky.

mentioned exported about 270,000 tons to Norway while the other two Russian mines produced a total of almost 300,000 tons. In 1939, when the shipping routes of the North Atlantic were becoming more precarious, the Norwegians took steps to increase production and later to re-open the idle mine at Ny Alesund. Although some miners returned home at the outbreak of war, the exports continued to supply Norway until the German invasion of March 1940, when colliers already at sea sailed to the United Kingdom. The Germans showed very little interest in this mining activity, other than send a team of experts to find whether it might be possible to increase production. This inquiry showed that there was enough potential to double the exports for 1941 and these quantities could still be increased further for the following year, if sufficient resources were provided for the mining companies. The population shortly after the outbreak of war was about 2,200, meaning the coal output remained at a reasonable level and did not drop off significantly as a result of the war.

All this changed in June 1941, when Germany invaded the Soviet Union and military concepts were added to the economic equation. It would seem that Germany still showed no immediate interest in this new theatre of war and Britain was not clear about what to do with it either. Bearing in mind that Spitzbergen hardly featured in atlases, it could well be that these isolated Arctic islands did not come within range of thought of the high-ranking officials in London. It would seem that their first step was to find out what was going on up there. As a result a powerful expeditionary force under Rear Admiral Philip L. Vian, consisting of the cruisers *Nigeria* and *Aurora* and escorted by the destroyers *Punjabi* and *Tartar*, set sail from Scapa Flow during July 1941. Once within sight of the pointed mountains, a Norwegian officer was sent on ahead to assure that the normal radio traffic continued without mentioning the arrival of the British force. Despite some limited military action, what followed was without problems and the squadron was back at Scapa Flow early in August. Vian then flew to report to the Chiefs of Staff in London before heading north once more. On this occasion he left behind heated arguments and bitter recriminations. The Chiefs of Staff were in favour of removing Spitzbergen from the face of the earth by destroying everything there, but this produced so many protests from the exiled Norwegian Government and other Norwegian leaders that they were forced to soften their demands.

After his return to Scapa Flow, Vian set sail with his two cruisers, this time escorted by destroyers *Antelope* and *Anthony* and the troopship *Empress of Canada*, capable of carrying several thousand passengers. Once more he sailed into protests, with the Norwegian and Russian authorities on Spitzbergen vehemently objecting to the proposal to set the coal stocks on fire and to destroy the mines, power plants and loading installations. The British force did give them the assurance that everything would be demolished in such a manner that the damage could be repaired quickly, and gave the miners time to insert more pit props to prevent the underground workings from collapsing due to prolonged neglect. Arriving with large guns made it impossible for the local authorities to protest, but the Russians referred to this act of destruction with crude language.

In addition to the destruction, and despite objections, the British force ordered the evacuation of the entire population. Apparently only one man refused to obey the command by hiding among the wilderness, and was consequently left behind. The place was not completely deserted as Rear Admiral Vian left a radio crew to ensure that the normal transmissions continued so as not to give the Germans any clues that Spitzbergen had been evacuated. The *Empress of Canada* first sailed to Archangel with over 2,000 Russians, where she picked up more than a hundred prisoners of war who had escaped from German camps by heading east towards the Soviet Union. A destroyer was also sent north to Ny Alesund to ensure that the newly re-opened mine there and its accompanying power supplies were demolished before forcibly removing the work force. It was also necessary to go even further north to collect a number of fur hunters who were known to be in the area.

The tasks of destroying the mines, the means of delivering coal to the jetties, radio stations and power plants, and then setting fire to the coal stocks was completed by the end of August 1941. Three colliers that were being loaded when the task force arrived then set sail for Iceland with volunteer crews, and the *Empress of Canada* was back in Greenock on 8 September. All of this was accomplished with the Germans remaining totally unaware that anything untoward had occurred. Even the fake radio signals that continued for many weeks did not provide them with any positive clues, although some people guessed something must have been amiss when the colliers failed to return according to their usual schedule.

The German invasion of Russia changed the country's requirements for weather forecasting and instead of focusing mainly on the west, it was deemed necessary to also obtain data from places further east. To that end the Luftwaffe Weather Flights were moved far north to Lakselv Airfield on the Banak Peninsula; to the east of Altafjord and not too far away from North Cape and Hammerfest. These weather flights were first attracted by excessive smoke rising above the mountains of Spitzbergen and then a closer inspection indicated that the main settlements around the Icefjord appeared deserted. As a result a reconnaissance aircraft landed on what looked like smooth ground in Adventdalen near Longyearbyen and soon afterwards another two flights landed there on the firm ground. This activity led to a weather team being quickly installed under the leadership of Erich Etienne. This was hurriedly enlarged before severe winter weather was likely to curtail further flights and the undertaking became known as Operation *Banso*. It remained active until the summer of the following year. These initial stages were by no means easy. Britain had by this time discovered the presence of the Germans, and four minesweepers on their way back from Archangel were diverted to explore the Icefjord area. HMS *Britomart*, HMS *Halcyon*, HMS *Harrier* and HMS *Salamander* were spotted by an aircraft that then landed on the improvised strip, warning the Germans, and then helping the other two planes there to evacuate the entire team. Finding the nest empty, the British force had to satisfy itself with finding a few codebooks and some material of interest before heading home. This time it did not take long for the Germans to discover that the coast was clear again. They quickly re-installed the weathermen back in their base, much of which had not been touched. Accommodation was no great problem for the team because the British task force only destroyed industrially important installations and left the houses intact.

Having arrived in Britain the Norwegians from Spitzbergen and the exiled Norwegian Chiefs of Staff continued with their protests about having to abandon their livelihood in such a state that the mines could quickly decay into ruin. By this time things had also changed in Britain, where more people were prepared to listen to the Norwegian side of the argument. Apparently no one had seriously considered the prospects that Spitzbergen could now become a German base for easy interference of the Arctic convoys running to Russia. At the same time, British convoys needed oilers to refuel the escorts on their long run through the icy seas. As a result several voices started calling for the establishment of fuel depots on Spitzbergen. The other problem was that there was not enough information about the weather *en route* to Russia, and Spitzbergen would make an ideal location for a British meteorological station.

Having forced the people off Spitzbergen, it was now decided to reinstate some as mining maintenance workers, and also to report meteorological data. As a result Britain launched Operation *Fritham* where the two sealers SS *Isbjorn* and SS *Selis* were due to take some eighty people back to Spitzbergen. Very long range Catalina aircraft had already been sent north to establish that there was no German activity on Spitzbergen. This was no mean achievement, and flying from Lerwick in Scotland, each flight took the planes beyond the limit they had been designed for and lasted for more than twenty-four hours. As a result of this reconnaissance, both boats arrived without enemy interference. This also was no mean achievement because heavy ice had forced the pair further east than planned and into the area covered by German aircraft. The Germans, however, had observed the ships, and sent four Focke Wulf Kondor bombers to sink them while they were cutting a channel through the ice of Icefjord in order to reach Barentsburg. A dozen or so men were killed and another dozen injured, but the rest managed to reach the old Russian settlement where they found

Spitzbergen with coal dumps and railway at New Alesund on Spitzbergen.

Kingsfjord with Ny Alesund in the distance showing the splendid Arctic panorama on a clear day. *Photo: Mike and Brenda Lyons*

plenty of food preserved by the cold temperatures and enough clothing not to freeze.

The survivors had enough energy to send a reconnaissance expedition inland, where they discovered the German centre of occupation. Leaving a small group behind to spy on the Germans, the rest of the group returned, convinced there were anything up to about fifty men in the secret camp, but in reality there were not much more than about half a dozen.

The absence of radio signals from the two sealers led to concern with the authorities back home, and a Catalina was sent north for reconnaissance. This eventually led to the evacuation of the wounded. At the same time the team leader, Lieutenant Commander Alexander Glen, was ordered to report to his higher authorities. Having assessed the situation, the cruiser *Manchester* escorted by the destroyer *Eclipse*, and both under the leadership of Vice Admiral S. S. Bonham-Carter, arrived on 2 July 1942 to land reinforcements of about one hundred Norwegians. This intervention was followed by two more flights to bring in more essential supplies and about two weeks later the cruisers *Cumberland* and *Sheffield* delivered still more provisions. By this time the fully functioning weather station that had been set up was provided with additional defences supplied by the cruiser *Argonaut*, which had arrived with the destroyers *Intrepid* and *Obdurate*. This intense British activity did not go unnoticed in Germany. One reconnaissance plane that approached too low while a gun crew was ready and waiting crashed as a result of fire from a comparatively small machine gun. This made another aircraft remain at a respectful distance while observing and reporting the events in the fjord by Barentsburg. Some accounts state that a nearby U-boat closed in shortly after the British ships had left and bombarded shore installations with its 88 mm deck gun. So far it has not been possible to trace the boat or the incident in German records.

Small-scale activities continued throughout the winter, but it was June 1943 before the next major force, consisting of the cruisers *Bermuda* and *Cumberland*, were sent to Spitzbergen with more supplies. At this stage the Germans also started taking a greater interest in the Allied activities. Sending the battleships *Tirpitz* and *Scharnhorst* to remove the by now 200 men strong allied occupation of the Icefjord. However, this was not as easy as had been anticipated. Unable to move out of range of the land-based inferior guns due to the proximity of rocks, the destroyer Z29 was hit so badly that several men were killed when one of its guns was put out of action and it took a while before Z33 retaliated to silence the offensive opposition.

Radio connections were good enough for Britain to be aware what was going on while the action was still unfolding, and later ordered HM Submarine *Tantalus* to explore the Icefjord. There were no signs of life at first but later it became apparent that earlier signals had been correct and some men did succeed in escaping from the German onslaught by hiding in the hills. As a result HM Submarine *Seadog* was immediately dispatched with several doctors to help the injured. Not willing to leave the Icefjord unoccupied the United States cruiser *Tuscaloosa* and four destroyers (USS *Fitch* and HMS *Onslaught*, HMS *Oribi* and HMS *Orwell*) were sent north to land a large reconnaissance party. This resulted in the accompanying destroyer HMS *Onslaught* ramming a U-boat, which managed to escape and has not yet been identified. This is indeed most remarkable because *Onslaught* suffered considerable damage to experience such a hazardous return voyage that *Orwell* was detached from the main force to assist the destroyer.

The general situation report about the state of affairs on Spitzbergen was not good. The burning coal dumps, still smouldering under a blanket of ash that was thick enough for snow to settle on top, had spread into some of the mine shafts leading sideways into the hills and urgent action was required to prevent a large scale disaster that might take years to extinguish. This scenario led to the cruiser *Jamaica* and two destroyers landing a sizable party to extinguish this irritation before it could creep deep underground and destroy the entire mine. By this time it was the late autumn of 1943. Germany had suffered considerable defeats; most of them created by Hitler's strict orders that commanding officers were not to take any risks. They had to break off any action at the slightest sign of danger. Things were not going well for German ships in northern Norway. Battleship *Tirpitz*, which had led the attack on Spitzbergen early in September 1943, was attacked in her anchorage in the heavily guarded Altafjord by British midget submarines, X-craft, putting the battleship out of action, and requiring major repairs.

Battleship *Scharnhorst*, often classed as battle cruiser in Britain, left her anchorage in northern Norway with five destroyers, Z29, Z30, Z33, Z34 and Z38 over the Christmas holidays of 1943 to attack convoy JW55B. Instead of meeting the merchant ships, the squadron ran into incredible action which ended with the sinking of the *Scharnhorst* on 26 December 1943 and has since gone down in history under the name of the Battle of North Cape. It is interesting to note that a similar battle had taken place a year earlier, over the Christmas period of 1942 when an inferior British force succeeded in driving away much more powerful German heavy units from Convoy JW51B. That action had been so embarrassing to Hitler that he ordered all heavy naval units to be scrapped. At the same time the Supreme Commander-in-Chief of the Navy, Grand Admiral Erich Raeder was replaced by the U-boat Chief, Admiral Karl Dönitz. A year later the famous Battle of North Cape of December 1943 marked the end of big ship activities in the Arctic. However, small highly secret naval operations continued until September 1945, five months after the official end of the war.

# 12

# Weather Ships

It is rather confusing that the identification numbers for Weather Observation Boats, prefixed with the letters WBS from Wetter-beobachtungs-schiff (without hyphens in the original) were often used for more than one ship during different periods of the war. Therefore the original name of the fishing boat has been added to the following text.

Despite having spent more than twenty years studying weather activities in the Arctic, Franz Selinger never found any clear details about how weather ships came into being. Information about their early origins is sufficiently obscure to hide even the name of the authority which first came up with the idea. The initial moves were probably not naval because there were no members of the Kriegsmarine on board, so it could well have been the brainchild of either the Abwehr (Military Security) or the civilian National Weather Service. This appears strange as from the very beginning of the war the navy was anxious for up-to-date information about the weather conditions in the Denmark Strait between Iceland and Greenland. We do know that the many 'neutral' weather stations around the North Atlantic did not immediately stop broadcasting their valuable data the moment the war began; instead these were faded out slowly. It is possible that the collection of weather data was not deemed as crucial in 1939 as it later became.

Franz Selinger was under the impression that the first weather ship was the sealer *Sachsen*, which later received the military identification of WBS 3. This almost 23-metre long, 106 GRT ship left Hamburg on 25 February 1940 under Kapitän E. Völker. The absence of the 'zur See' part in his title indicates that he was a civilian. Going first to Norway to pick up specialist seal hunters, the boat sailed into controversy and excitement, ending up in Russia because it was not allowed back through still turbulent Norwegian waters. Political pressure had already curtailed the reporting of weather information on 9 April. The crew was made up entirely of civilian sealers, all well acquainted with the weather, but none of them qualified as meteorologists and Selinger questioned whether the data they sent back was actually processed by anyone in Germany.

Planning for the first purely naval weather reporting operation started shortly after the beginning of the war, when the already prepared mobilisation plans went into operation. These included converting merchant ships into auxiliary cruisers and also modifying fishing boats for meteorological purposes so that they were ready for the sole purpose of helping warships break out from Germany. The favoured procedure was for warships to sail north, wait for bad weather and then break out past the British fleet by sailing through the Denmark Strait. The admirals responsible for this planning were all impressionable youngsters when the 'unsinkable' *Titanic* went down. Therefore they knew full well that even if this route was likely to be free from British warships, there were high chances of meeting rather hard icebergs. So, it was essential to obtain information about the state of the ice before auxiliary cruisers attempted to dash through at high speed. At this stage of the planning, secrecy added a curious dimension to the proceedings. Auxiliary cruiser *Orion* that left a few days after auxiliary cruiser *Atlantis*, towards the end of March 1940, did not know about the planned invasion of Norway. So, it is likely that the authorities fitting out the first weather ships were not informed either. Perhaps this massive undertaking, with so much activity along the Norwegian coast, was responsible for the Royal Navy losing sight of the goings-on further west, to leave the weather ships free of trouble.

The navy had a list of deep-sea fishing boats suitable for conversion as mobile floating weather stations and in the end chose *Fritz Homann* (WBS 3), *Hinrich Freese* (WBS 4) and *Adolf Vinnen* (WBS 5) to assist with the first auxiliary cruiser breakout. These were ordinary-looking fishing boats that could have belonged to any nationality. Built around 1930 they were about 45 metres long, displaced in the region of 380 tons and carried a crew of fifteen. All three had enough room to also accommodate up to five meteorologists. WBS 4 and WBS 5 left Wilhelmshaven during the night of 21/21 March 1940 and WBS 3 followed before the end of the day. Whether these three actually contributed much to proceedings is now difficult to assess as luck was on the German side. *Atlantis*, the first auxiliary cruiser, reached the Denmark Strait while a storm was brewing, and a gale of Force eight whipped up the seas to make life most unpleasant. The ship headed south at a time when heavy rain helped to further reduce visibility.

The weather ships reached the western Atlantic without even spotting *Atlantis* or *Orion* and were later re-called to be back home by the middle of April. It would seem that this was the end of weather observation activities for the time and it was not until after the fall of France that the navy poured more energy into proposing new ventures.

The next breakout attempt by *Admiral Scheer* and *Admiral Hipper* with their supply ship *Uckermark* never took place because both heavy cruisers remained in port with mechanical problems and *Uckermark* ran onto a mine. The weather ship, WBS 5 *Adolf Vinnen*, sent out to help them through the Denmark Strait, was lost on its way back when the British destroyers *Matabele*, *Punjabi* and *Somali* attacked it during the night of 23/24 October 1940. By this time WBS 1 *Sachsen* had been handed over to the Luftwaffe for helping with the setting up of weather stations on the Greenland side of the Atlantic and in consequence 1940 ended without much naval meteorological activity on the high seas. Despite this, there had been some Abwehr activity around Jan Mayen and along the Greenland coast that resulted in an attempt to set up the first manned weather station.

Plans for this Greenland venture began during the summer of 1940 when political connections made it possible for the Germans to charter a Danish crew for this exacting task through connections in Norway. It was thought to have been too risky to organise this direct from Germany as it would have been impossible to have kept it secret. Even working through Norway was not easy and some well-thought-out cover stories had to be concocted to get foreign nationals to volunteer for such a precarious venture. The crew was rather on naïve side as far international relations were concerned and they believed the story that this operation was necessary because Denmark had to provide evidence for maintaining its sovereignty of Greenland for the International Court in Den Haag (Holland). In the end the 140 GRT sealer *Furenak* and the 296 GRT *Vaslekari* were chartered for setting up what was going to be the first manned German weather station in Greenland. Unfortunately for the Germans, they were not the only ones showing an interest in this rather isolated coast and the detachment was eventually captured.

The lull in weather activities towards the end of 1940 did not last long, and the first fishing boat for the New Year (WBS 5 *Ostmark*), left on 8 January 1941, to be followed by WBS 2 *Coburg* a month later and following on from that, WBS 6 *München*, set out for the Iceland area. The boats were still unarmed, but by this time had at least a couple of trained meteorologists on board for sending up to five reports per day. Nothing much happened during this thrust. The ships operated without interference, almost as if they had been swallowed up by the long Arctic night. The second phase of 1941 was also launched without too much interference. First WBS 1 *Sachsen* was sent out on 17 March for the main purpose of preparing the plans for the next breakout by heavy units. This was going to be the operation by the battleship *Bismarck* and the heavy cruiser *Prinz Eugen*, both destined to reach the convoy routes of the North Atlantic by sailing through the Denmark Strait from Norway. WBS 1 ran out of provisions before the surface ships were ready and was replaced by WBS 3 *Lauenburg*, which had in the meantime returned to base, refuelled and had set out for another operational tour. WBS 6 *München* had left Trondheim in Norway at around the same time when there was little activity in the northern waters around Iceland.

Despite the Germans feeling relatively safe, there were rumblings in Britain, where Harry Hinsley at Bletchley Park was studying messages coming from somewhere in the Arctic Seas. He was unable to read the text and was not even certain where they came from, but guessed they were being sent from some kind of weather trawler. The curious thing about these messages was that it looked as if an Enigma machine rather than the usual type of signal pad had coded them. Things were becoming rather critical at Bletchley Park where Hinsley worked. The cryptanalysts there had a lot of information about the German Enigma machine and now urgently needed a working model with the necessary codebooks so that their work could progress. Trying to convince the naval authorities that one set of jumbled letters contained a pattern generated by a machine was not easy, but eventually sufficient pressure was put on the admirals to agree for a special hunt for capturing at least one of these machines from one of the weather stations known to be operating around Iceland. The *München* or WBS 6 had actually been captured, brought to Scapa Flow and was inspected by high level intelligence officers, who found enough interesting material aboard to have made the effort worthwhile. The German radio operator had thrown the Enigma machine and the codebooks overboard in a lead weighted sack and destroyed much of his secret radio equipment. The crew had also made some attempt to sink their ship, but there were so many provisions on board that the seacocks, for allowing water to flood into the interior, could not be reached because they were hidden behind masses of heavy cargo.

WBS 3 *Lauenburg* (under Steuermann (S) Gewald) left Trondheim in Norway during the night of 27/28 May 1941 to relieve WBS 1 *Sachsen* near Greenland. This went reasonably well except that the initial reports were being intercepted by radio direction finders in Britain, giving the Royal Navy fairly accurate information about the ship's position. It seemed like an excellent opportunity to capture a weather ship and perhaps get the Enigma machine as well. A powerful force, consisting of the cruiser HMS *Nigeria* and destroyers HMS *Tartar*, HMS *Bedouin* and HMS *Jupiter* left Scapa Flow on 25 June 1941, sailed towards the last known position of the *Lauenburg* and then formed a line abreast to search for the illusive ship. This became quite a

The weather trawler *Externsteine* that was captured off Greenland. *Photo: Franz Selinger*

hazardous undertaking. On the one hand it was necessary to go in at a fairly fast speed, but on the other there was fog with varying intensity and enough icebergs to be worrying. Despite these obstacles, *Tartar* sighted the trawler towards late afternoon and the group immediately went in at fast speed, with each ship firing training shells once it was within range. These were similar to fireworks inasmuch that they exploded with an impressive detonation, but did not do much damage. The ruse worked. The crew evacuated the *Lauenburg* at a fast speed but not before the Enigma machine and vital codebooks were thrown overboard. Two men also remained behind to burn papers in the galley stove so the vital pieces that the Royal Navy had come for were already missing. This time no attempt was made to bring the ship back to Britain. Instead it was searched, the men in the lifeboats were picked up and then the trawler was scuttled.

The events of 1941 made it clear to the Germans that there was no point in sending out any more floating weather stations and operations were curtailed. Yet, that was not the end of weather ship operations in the Arctic. Converted fishing boats that maintained strict radio silence remained active right up to the end of the war, supporting all manner of naval operations. The other fishing boats that were used to support naval operations were not given the official title with the prefix WBS.

The following Weather Observation Ships were operational:

| | |
|---|---|
| WBS 1 | *Sachsen* |
| WBS 1 | *Wuppertal* |
| WBS 2 | *Coburg* |
| WBS 3 | *Carl J. Busch* |
| WBS 3 | *Lauenburg* |
| WBS 4 | *Hinrich Freese* |
| WBS 5 | *Ostmark* |
| WBS 6 | *Kehdingen* |
| WBS 6 | *München* |
| WBS 7 | *Sachsenwald* |
| WBS 8 | *Hessen* |
| WBS 11 | *Externsteine* |

# 13

# Weather Stations

Around the beginning of the Second World War, two different authorities within Germany produced automatic weather recording equipment for remote locations where it would be difficult to establish manned meteorological stations. The civilian National Meteorological Office (Reichsamt für Wetterdienst) developed a device known as *Kröte* (Toad) for setting up on land and the navy built its own version for floating on water, called Wetter-funk-gerät (Weather Radio Apparatus—without hyphens in the original). The WFS (Wetterfunkgerät–See or Weather Radio Apparatus–Sea) worked exceedingly well when it was tested on Tegeler Lake in Berlin, but failed miserably when an experimental model was ejected through a torpedo tube of U29 (Kptlt. Georg Lassen) off Memel in the eastern Baltic. Unlike a torpedo, one end of the device was considerably heavier than the other so that the cylinder would float upright, with its periscopic aerial extended above the surface of the water. This meant that instead of gliding out of the torpedo tube as expected, the buoy tilted and jammed, making it clear that more time had to be spent on modifications. The problem was overcome by placing the buoys inside the upper deck torpedo storage tubes—in the space between the pressure hull and the upper (outside) deck of Arctic U-boats. This was just high enough for a person to crawl through on all fours. The U-boat's upper deck torpedo storage tubes each contained two of these and each boat was also equipped with a simple crane arrangement for loading these into the bow or stern compartments. The anchors for the buoys were lashed in this space close to the tube as well, while the aerials with the more delicate instruments were stored inside the bow and stern compartments. The box containing these sections was too long to pass through the conning tower hatches. They reached the floor of the central room without difficulty, but there was not enough space to tilt them from the vertical to the horizontal position. This meant it was necessary to open the torpedo hatches at sea.

With these hatches being so close to the sea, made this a highly dangerous operation that could only be performed during exceptionally calm seas. Assembling the gear by screwing the various parts together on the upper deck was easy and straightforward except that the rear jumping wires had to be dismantled so that a special slide that had been screwed to the upper deck could be rotated to allow the heavy buoy to slip into the water.

The two-metre long aerial had a thermometer, barometer and hygrometer (for measuring humidity) attached and later models also contained an anemometer for determining the force of the wind. A clock switched the device on twice a day and many of these buoys worked well for periods of up to six months, after which the battery became too weak. The humidity indicator, being less than two metres above the water did not produce accurate results and radio problems resulted in some transmissions not being picked up. The other problem of drifting with strong currents was later overcome by attaching a steel cable and anchor to the bottom of the buoy.

The dangers of approaching close to Arctic coasts. Note the black rocks in the foreground looking something like the Loch Ness Monster lurching through the water. Such rocks are quite common in some areas and many of them do not break through the surface of the water, making them incredibly dangerous for any ship that attempts to get too close. Known as 'skerries' they often look like harmless sand banks, ideal for beaching small boats, but they are made up of hard and often rather slippery rock. Ideal for wrecking all manner of boats and some of them even caught large ocean-going ships, holding them fast long enough for them to rot.
*Photo: Mike and Brenda Lyons*

The first operational trials took place on 28 September 1940 when U103 (Korvkpt. Viktor Schütze) ejected an automatic floating weather buoy near Rockall to the west of Scotland. This time everything went well until the radio operator tried checking its signal. It obviously did not work. Even patience did not help. The buoy remained dumb and was eventually sunk because the U-boat did not have any means of hauling it back on board. These devices were designed to sink rapidly once the battery power got too low or if anyone tried fishing them out of the water by tilting them more than 45 degrees. The second weather buoy, launched by U103 near Porcupine Bank (to the west of southern Ireland) shortly after this fiasco appeared to have worked well. As a result of these early experiments it was possible for U156 (Kptlt. Werner Hartenstein) to launch the first operational buoy to the west of Scotland on 29 December 1941 and several more followed from April 1942 onwards.

Launching these torpedo-like canisters was easy enough for the U-boat crew to carry out without help from specialist engineers, although such technicians often accompanied the U-boat. Setting up an automatic land-based weather station (WFL—Wetterfunkgerät-Land) was more difficult and Heinz Fritsch has left an interesting report about how U-boat crews viewed this contraption. U355 was on its way back from Arctic waters when a radio signal ordered the commander, Kptlt. Günter La Baume, to meet the outward-bound U360 (Kptlt. Klaus Becker) to take a seriously ill man home for medical treatment. He was transferred by rubber dinghy without too many difficulties other than putting up with the extreme cold and wet and U355 arrived in Hammerfest at 0930 hours of 5 September 1943.

After having made fast to the side of the depot ship *Black Watch*, the men enjoyed a hot bath, the sauna, comfortably soft beds, and some took advantage of watching a film show, when suddenly and most unexpectedly all hands were ordered on deck. This came as a bit of a shock because the ill man was running such a high temperature that everybody was hoping they might get some time off in quarantine until it was certain none of them had caught whatever had brought him down.

Coming back on board U355, the men could see that a crane had deposited a number of large pots on the upper (outside) deck, where there was also what looked like a large-scale construction kit of spars and bars. A number of boxes and two large collapsible sledges, designed to fit through the torpedo-loading hatch, were still waiting to be lowered. Each pot, weighing somewhere in the region of 100 kilograms and only marginally smaller than the U-boat hatches, required two to four people to move it and with there being ten of them, plus all manner of other clutter, meant the task took a while. Sweat and specialised naval language was

*Above and opposite page:* Some examples of Arctic coasts showing how difficult it was to find suitable places for establishing land-based activities. *Photos: Mike and Brenda Lyons*

obviously required to stow everything below. There were also two Silver Fish (Silberlinge) from the naval administration branch, who normally did not fit into ships at sea. They turned out to be engineers, Dietrich Kuckuck (Cuckoo) and Edwin Stöbe, who were not shy about the task in hand. As soon as they were at sea, at 0800 hours of the following day, less than twenty hours after U355 had arrived, they explained that they were going to set up an automatic weather station on Bear Island. The men had hardly digested this when they were already there, searching for a good landing site. Their guests had obviously done their homework from aerial photographs and it did not take them long to point out the exact spot. Having gone close to the shore before, La Baume and his men had enough experience not to be caught out by the unexpected on this occasion. The boat was trimmed bows down so that there was ample room to raise the front higher if it touched the ground and electric motors were then used to approach the beach. Beach is somewhat of an understatement. It was a wrecker's and ankle twister's paradise with so many loose boulders that the majority of tourists would have avoided the spot and would never have allowed their children anywhere near it, but there was not much choice. Bear Island is not much more than a large torturous rock, inhabited by masses of seabirds and avoided by almost everybody else. Landing there is more than just difficult.

U737 under Friedrich-August Greus on 30 April 1944 while launching the floating weather station WFL33 in North-East Spitzbergen.

A detailed look at the coast close to where automatic weather stations were set up.
*Photo: Mike and Brenda Lyons*

The type of transport U-boats carried for manoeuvring in extremely freezing Arctic waters. Climbing into such inflatable's from a U-boat demanded considerable will power and there was no way anyone doing so could avoid getting wet and cold.

Once close in, luggage and the cumbersome pots were unloaded quite rapidly. The ten heavy cylinders, each one about a metre in length and rather cumbersome were slowly hauled ashore. Then there followed a variety of poles and lattices for holding the entire contraption together. One of the cylinders contained the automatic radio gear, another had a wind speed and direction indicator screwed onto the top and there was the ten metre high main aerial mast with thermometer and other detectors, all with an accuracy tolerance equivalent of half a degree Celsius. Assembling the whole contraption was not difficult, if you knew how all bits fitted together. Yet this would have been a little beyond the U-boat men had the two engineers not told them where each component had to go. The various bits looked like part of an impossible puzzle at first and it was not until they were connected in right order that is was possible to work out the shape of the station.

The men were exceedingly lucky; the weather gods were definitely on their side. Not long after the last man was back on board, the wind increased in strength until it developed into such a gale that Seaman Heinemann had his shoulder dislocated by the force of the water hitting him. Trying to make headway back to Hammerfest, with the bows pointing directly into this Force six, shattered the entire boat every time a wave crashed against the conning tower. It was 07.30 of 9 September when U355 was back alongside the *Black Watch* and the passengers vanished as quickly as they had arrived, as if they had never been on board.

Such automatic weather stations were set up by U-boats, aircraft and perhaps fishing boats in a number of locations and the majority worked well until ice jammed them solid, preventing the moving parts from functioning. The longest operating station was Landjäger (WFL 35) set up on an island in the Baltic between Sweden and Finland on 22 November 1944 and still working when Finish forces discovered it shortly before the end of the war. The data sent back to was so valuable that all manner of other projects were tried out to obtain essential meteorological information.

Towards the beginning of the war Germany used converted fishing boats and seal hunter smacks, but these became easy targets for British forces focused on capturing Enigma machines and the majority did not survive for long. Yet, the need for meteorological data kept increasing and became so pressing that the highest authorities ordered manned weather stations to be established in remote Arctic locations. Since these used radios to broadcast weather details twice a day, it was not going to be difficult for British direction finders to determine their locations and to put an end to their activities. To prevent possible intrusions the stations were usually established late in the season, when natural ice prevented the Royal Navy from getting anywhere close until the thaw of the following summer had set in.

Once again Heinz Fritsch's diary provides a fascinating insight into how these manned weather stations were established. In this case technical details have been added from papers by Franz Selinger, whose fantastic study of Arctic weather activities will probably never be surpassed.

Heinz Fritsch's boat, U355 (Kptlt. Günter La Baume), had undergone an overhaul and was fully provisioned when it was ordered to anchor in Altafjord, close to battleship *Tirpitz*. It was not uncommon to move U-boats away from main piers to isolated parking areas until escort and pilots for the coastal waters could be organised. Usually they remained there only for a few hours or a few days, so it became rather worrying when the men still found themselves there after almost two full weeks of doing nothing, other than using up their fresh provisions. An official visit to the battleship added to their misery inasmuch that they met many unhappy and disillusioned men who had been only once at their action stations and were now spending all their time loafing about, doing nothing other polishing underused equipment. For the men from U355 this visit felt like going back to their early days in barracks where naval drill and strict discipline ruled each day. None of them had the slightest notion of wanting to return to this rigidity and felt pleased that they were part of a considerably less formal setup.

Doing nothing in Altafjord during the beginning of October 1943 was rather unsettling and only the commander knew why they were not yet at

Men from U668 climbed this incredible cliff near Norway's North Cape to set up an automatic weather station on the top.

U377 while establishing the manned weather station at Cape Mitra, to the north of
New Alesund in 1942.

sea. U355 was waiting for another ship with the innocuous identification
of WBS 3. Some people at the time might have known that this stood for
Wetter-beobachtungs-schiff 3 (Weather Observation Ship 3—without
hyphens in the original) but no one had the slightest inkling of what sort
of ship that might be. WBS 3 had set out from Kiel on 15 September 1943
with a full load of cargo and a dozen or more men. Unable to travel at
night, having to wait for coastal convoys and having to pass through the
most atrocious weather meant it was the 26th before the boat put into
Narvik to meet an aircraft carrying the last essential pieces of equipment,
such as some especial sleeping bags made from reindeer skins.

Progress was slow. Something as simple as maintaining the correct
course was not easy as WBS 3 did not have a gyrocompass and the
magnetic needle often looked irritated, pointing some ten degrees away
from the correct position, possibly due to the masses of magnetic iron ore
in the rocks. Moving on from Narvik was so difficult that it looked as if
WBS 3 was going to be stuck there for some time. Unable to find a pilot,
the commander, Steuermann Fritz Sittig, a peacetime fishing boat captain
without much military training, made his own way along Norway's
treacherous coast to Tromsö and from there on to Hammerfest to meet
U355. The waters there were narrow and rocky with strong currents,
making this a noteworthy achievement.

*Above, left and following pages:* Finding themselves frozen in the ice shocked the men of U377 at first until they discovered this was an ideal aid for unloading the many tons of cargo to set up a manned weather station to the north of New Alesund on Spitzbergen.

After two weeks of loafing, U355 moved out of Altafjord to lie alongside a pier that already had a number of crates and packages lined up on it. The setting up of the unmanned weather station 'Dietrich' on the north coast of Bear Island had taken place only four weeks or so earlier, so loading a lot of heavy gear was still fresh in everybody's memory. Yet, moving all these packages looked considerably worse. Instead of the ten missionary sized *cooking pots* with a few spars and boxes, some eight tons of various bits pieces appeared. Many boxes had been soldered shut, suggesting there was something extraordinarily special inside. Almost all of it fitted through the hatches, yet stowing the packages below decks became a major problem, with bundles blocking the corridor so that men had to squeeze past sideways. With so much on the floor, there were many places where there was not even enough headroom to stand upright. It was all rather problematical. Without any accompanying bodies, the men were none the wiser as to what this was all about and some more time passed before they were told that this was part of the provisions for Operation *Kreuzritter* (Crusading Knight); a manned weather station to be established in North Spitzbergen.

Four men from this team had been driven out of Spitzbergen by armed raiders from the Royal Norwegian Navy earlier in the year when they were part of Nussbaum Weather Station in Kings Fjord to the north of New Alesund. Now they were on their way back with a new leader, Hans-Robert Knoespel, and six other men. Operation *Nussbaum* came to a dramatic end shortly after the group had evacuated its winter quarters near the water's edge to occupy a summer camp further up in the hills. The attackers killed Heinz Köhler, despite him having been unarmed, but their gunfire gave the others enough warning to report the matter to base in Norway before making their way along one of the prepared escape routes. They were picked up by U302 (Herbert Sickel) on the west coast and the U-boat then sailed into Kings Fjord to destroy the Norwegian boat and rake nearby tents with gunfire so that the opposition could not make use of the German facilities. To complicate matters, the men from Operation *Nussbaum* were handed over to U625 (Hans Benker) in mid ocean, which then took them back to Norway. This rather nerve-tingling experience made it quite plain that any locations along easy to reach shores were no longer viable and *Kreuzritter* would have to be established in an even more remote area than the west coast above New Alesund.

When U355 was seemingly loaded to beyond bursting point and ready to depart, five men with two large dogs and heaps of personal luggage turned up to join the U-boat. They were going to spend many months up in the long Arctic night, and had therefore packed a little more than pyjamas and toothbrush. They also brought along two huge, collapsible sledges that were so long that they could only be loaded into the bow torpedo room where they occupied a couple of bunks, and additional hammocks had to be strung up for the men. Despite the squash, the newcomers were cheerful, the dogs were friendly and all accepted the exceedingly cramped conditions without complaining. The dogs took full advantage of the many hands that made a fuss of them. Following the customary trim dive, U355 was joined by a 305 ton, 43 metre long fishing boat *Carl J. Busch* from 'Nordsee'—Deutsche Hochsee Fischerei in Cuxhaven (North Sea—German Deep Sea Fishing Industry) that had been given the new identification of WBS 3. Rather confusingly, WBS 3 was also used to identify two other fishing boats, *Fritz Homann* and *Lauenburg*.

The flotilla of two did not get far before a healthy Force six gale started blowing with such intensity that the little WBS 3 could no longer maintain the prearranged speed. Waves crashing against the wheelhouse were threatening to destroy the large pile of pre-fabricated timber sections for the main hut lashed to the bows, and this storm was also fierce enough to wash away sacks of coal and other gear that were tied to the open deck. In addition to this, the almost twenty-year-old fishing boat was leaking so badly that bedding had to be sacrificed to block holes. It may not have been a happy passage north, but the storm did not get much worse and

U625 (Oblt.z.S. Karl-Heinz Sammler) with a wooden Biscay Cross in the bottom of the picture. This was a makeshift aerial for a radar detector.

both boats eventually caught sight of Spitzbergen at a range of over sixty kilometres, indicating that the earlier storm with its accompanying fog had changed into exceptionally clear and calm conditions. This eased life on board and due to the clear conditions both boats gave the land a wide berth, to avoid any possible observers concealed among the barren rocks.

The rugged mountains appeared to float on the water as U355 closed in and men peered at an impressive mirage spectacle. Navigation was perfect, despite some interference causing the compasses to wobble away from magnetic north. Eventually the two crept close to Woodfjord on the north coast, where steep, black, snowcapped mountains gave the impression of swallowing up the comparatively tiny craft. WBS 3 was sent on ahead to find a good unloading spot near the destination while U355 moved to the eastern side of the fjord to explore a hut that dominated the entrance. This was the building that had been occupied by Hermann and Christiane Ritter with their friend long before the war and features in the book *Eine Frau erlebt die Polarnacht* (translated as *A Woman in the Polar Night*). When the men from U355 saw it, it definitely looked deserted and the natural conditions prevented them from getting anywhere near it. The water was too shallow to get any closer than about half a kilometre and the wind, blowing heavily against the shore, would have made any return journey in the rubber dinghy most difficult. As a result it was decided not to go any further and another hut that might have been in use was also not investigated because it looked unoccupied from the distance. Reaching it would have been too risky. In any case the weather detachment had far superior firepower to any guns carried by hunters and they could have dealt with any opposition if such an incident had arisen.

Earlier, when the officer commanding the tiny WBS 3 had come to the U-boat in a rubber dinghy for making the final plans, it was decided that he should go in first to find a suitable location for unloading as close to their destination as possible. Since no one had any idea of the water depths in the fjord and with this being much too shallow for the echo sounder, a man had to swing the old fashioned lead from the bows. This worked well, although hauling the wet rope back out of the freezing cold water became rather painful on the fingers and more strong naval language was necessary to make good progress.

In the end there was not much choice of landing areas. WBS 3 ran aground on a fairly high tide and would obviously not re-float until some weight had been taken out. Since there was a good beach close at hand, this became the unloading port for Weather Station Kreuzritter. Although it looked good, landing was most uncomfortable. The water near the beach was so shallow that the rubber dinghy stopped some distance from dry land and men had to walk through icy cold water to get ashore. The

*Above:* According to the original caption, this is supposed to show U737, but the deck and the gun suggest this is a Type II with an early type of conning tower, rather than a Type VIIC. However, it does show exceedingly well the results when fiercely cold winds manage to cool steel structures to well below freezing point.

*Left:* Hans-Robert Knoespel, leader of the Kreuzritter Weather Detachment, who died so tragically as a result of thinking about others who might come after him.

Obersteuermann Martin Weidmann and Dieselobermaschinist Jak Mallmann helping to set up a weather station on Spitzbergen, showing the type of clothing worn by landing parties.

Men on the top of the conning tower of U377 in northern Norway.

first task in hand, before anything could be unloaded was to explore a hut not far away. From the sea it was impossible to determine whether this was occupied or not, so a machine-gun and as many people as the dinghy could carry were taken ashore to approach the building from the rear. Then the gun was set up and made ready before two others approached the building. They were relieved to find it empty. Climbing up without proper mountaineering gear and without having walked anywhere far during recent weeks meant the men were ill-prepared for such energetic infantry manoeuvres. To make matters worse they came across a number of holes under the drifting snow that were large enough to fall into, and then require a hand for getting out of again.

A lot remained to be done in addition to setting up the main winter base. This was bound to be the first spot that any raiding party might discover, and there was always the possibility that some determined opposition would arrive before the thaw of the following summer. An aircraft, flying overhead might spot the proceedings and thus help to put an early end to the *Kreuzritter* undertaking. To cope with such an eventuality another hidden summer location was established, and a couple of escape routes were planned as well. Each of these contained survival gear, provisions and essential radio transmitters and some were a considerable distance of several kilometres from the main base. This meant that the U-boat had to take a couple of men around the other side of the mountains, unload everything they required and then leave them to establish their depot before testing the overland route by making their own way back on skis.

The other major problem was that there were a good number of old fur hunter huts along this part of the north coast and Knoespel thought it important enough to investigate everyone in case the opposition was making use of them. Superior warring groups could well have been established in the area. So U355 and a group of meteorologists went off to explore while the tedious unloading of WBS 3 continued. This was made considerably more difficult by the boat's motor cutter having broken down early during the proceedings and everything had to be hand-handled to the beach over a distance of about 400 metres. These delays meant it was the 20 October before the weathermen could sleep in the hut for the first time, despite La Baume having allowed all spare men on land to help with the building work.

The weathermen were delighted with their new accommodation. Considerable friction and ill feelings had grown up between them and WBS 3's small crew. This became so bad that the commander of the submarine, Günter La Baume, had to have serious words of reprimand with the commander of the WBS 3. At one stage WBS 3's crew disappeared by rigging a sail on their dinghy with a view of exploring a nearby hut.

They got there without too much difficulty, but the wind was against them on the way back and they were punished by a hefty spell of rowing that was necessary before they were available again to help with the erection of the winter station. The meteorologists were convinced that this escapade was merely a strong desire to look for some possible loot, rather than serve any possible military purpose. In the end Knoespel wrote in his diary that he and his men were pleased when WBS 3 left them.

The departure did not go quite as smoothly as planned. First U737 (Paul Brasack) reported a squadron of five destroyers in Icefjord, on the west coast near the main settlements of Barentsburg and Longyearbyen and a short time later U956 (Hans-Dieter Mohs) spotted a freighter with two destroyers close to South Spitzbergen. As a result U355 was ordered to investigate and WBS 3 had to evacuate the weather station as well because the presence of a ship would have been a too obvious giveaway for any passing investigator. As it happened neither made contact with enemy forces. U355 returned to the landing beach where its appearance resulted in great jubilation. A number of deep friendships had been forged between the weathermen and the crew, both of whom who had similar characteristics of being able to live in close harmony with others without going on each other's nerves. The return of U355 also confirmed that the camp was exceedingly well hidden and would disappear completely during the next snowfall.

Although it was now almost the end of October, the sea remained free of ice, meaning it was not possible to make use of the radio because broadcasts could still attract enemy forces before ice would prevent ships from approaching close to the coast. The two men from the escape base on the north coast, Emil Laurenz and Helmut Köhler were back on 16 October and the other two from the end of the Raudfjord or Klinckowströmfjord, Fritz Kraus and Anton Pohoschaly returned four days later on the 20th. Since everything was going quite well, Knoespel took the opportunity of asking La Baume to help with establishing further depots along the coast. No one knew exactly how far the raiding party that had found the Nussbaum Weather Station earlier in year had penetrated. So this exercise was going to serve two purposes, one of depositing supplies in a few vital spots in case Kreuzritter had to be evacuated, and at the same time establish how far the opposition had penetrated into these remote highlands. Knoespel and part of his team were made up of pre-war hunters, bird watchers, naturalists and adventurers rather than men from a pure military background. They knew full well that before the war all manner of nationalities had been hunting for furs on Spitzbergen and these activities continued during the first years of the conflict. This meant that there was a chain of established huts along the desolate coast, and any of them could now be serving the enemy by sending back essential intelligence information. Knowing a little more about the depths of water around the north coast, U355 eventually left Kreuzritter at a much faster speed than when arriving. Having met WBS 3 for their joint return to Norway the men discovered that some dark corners of the U-boat still contained bits and pieces belonging to the weathermen, making a turn-round essential.

Eventually, when the weathermen were left on their own, there was still a lot of work to be done to make the setup fully operational and at the same time it was necessary to start with the main task in hand; that of recording the weather. Knoespel had enough experience to know that it was all too easy to lose control of the general situation and allow the crew to drop into such depression that the men literally lost their normal senses to develop anything from mild rages to severe mental disorders. The military of that period got over the problem by engaging men in numerous pointless activities, but this was not going to work with a small group in the Arctic where everybody was an essential member of the team. To overcome possible boredom he had drawn up a list of about fifty meaningful studies and projects in addition to their main duties of weather reporting and eavesdropping on radio messages that might not reach German radio stations in Norway. This varied from mapping their surroundings, making biological collections to measuring the thickness of the ice and so forth.

Having established themselves in a hidden location on the coast, it was also necessary to establish another base some twelve or more kilometres higher up in the mountains and to do this a total of some hundred trips were going to be necessary for carrying provisions and other equipment into the interior. The steep climb and the distance alone made this quite a challenge and the need to cross avalanche areas made it even more hazardous. Yet the Ice Camp was eventually manned to be fully operational and even had a telephone connection to the main base. It is interesting to read Knoespel's diary about how this rather difficult task was accomplished. Rather than sit out the cold winter storms where temperatures often dropped to minus twenty to minus thirty degrees Celsius, he used these conditions to best advantage by carrying the heavy loads so that a strong tail wind helped by blowing the men along.

In addition to reporting the weather at ground level, the men were equipped with balloons for carrying measuring equipment that would broadcast the details back to the Kreuzritter base. Thirty-six of these hydrogen filled balloons were launched in December 1943 alone and the men consumed 25 bottles of hydrogen to fill them. It might be interesting to add that someone in the supplies department made rather a significant mistake. Seven of the steel bottles were found to be empty.

The thaw of 1944 came much later than expected and by the end of May there was still rather a lot of ice in the north-facing fjord by the main Kreuzritter base. It was as late as 18 June that a radio signal from Tromsö told the men to be ready for evacuation during the next eight days or so. Everything was in good enough condition and there had been no interference from the opposition that the base was going to be left so that it could be occupied again during the following winter. Making a detailed list of how many provisions were still in stock and what required urgent replacement, the men discovered that some thirty per cent of their provisions remained, meaning it would have been possible for them to stay there for some time to come without any great problems.

Knoespel was faced with one rather pressing problem that he couldn't delegate to other members of his team because he was the only person trained in the use of explosives. Some two to three kilometres to the south of the main base was an old hunter's hut by the water's edge and any in-coming force set to attack Kreuzritter was far more likely to spot this than the well camouflaged main base. So, as extra security measure, Knoespel had set a mine inside it that would explode when anyone entered the place. This now gave him two concerns, first it would be possible for the in-coming U-boat crew to spot the hut without any of the Kreuzritter men noticing their presence, and even if the U-boat men came straight to the main base, it was likely that a hunter might make use of the hut in the future and then kill himself when he opened the door. In view of this, Knoespel wandered over with the surviving dog and set a fifteen-minute charge to detonate the explosives. He waited for another half hour after the fuse should have gone off before returning to the hut to see why nothing had happened. He was still some distance away when the explosion struck him. The men in the main base not only heard the blast but they also saw the dog running around the fallen figure, suggesting something serious had happened. Hurrying over they found their leader so seriously injured that he died some three hours later. In the meantime U737 (Kptlt. Paul Brasack) had arrived and the crew helped with the making of a stone grave for Hans-Robert Knoespel.

The return journey did not go as smoothly as the men had anticipated from their incident-free arrival. Some of the weather crew were at the escape base on the other side of the mountains to the main hut. Therefore it was necessary to first load U737 with valuable equipment that had to be taken back, supplement the boat with leftover provisions, set up an automatic weather station (Edwin III) brought along by the U-boat and finally arrange a funeral with full military honours. Getting out of the fjord by the main base was easy and the great problem occurred when U737 nosed into Raudfjord. Thirty kilometres long and about three wide at its narrowest this looked easy, but it was largely uncharted with a natural U-boat trap in the form of an underwater ridge where the water was so awkward that it grabbed the boat to hold it tight. Brasack reacted immediately but could not find a way of pulling the boat free and he had already resigned himself to having to abandon it when after a few hours it re-floated itself without help from any of the men. At one stage it was lying at a most precarious angle of 45 degrees or more. The remaining men were picked up and eventually taken back to Norway. Arriving first in Hammerfest on 7 July, U737 went on to land the weathermen in Tromsö.

Operation *Kreuzritter* made a significant impression on the U-boat men and their success can be gauged by the fact that they established an efficient base that sent back 608 messages with surface weather data and another 201 reports with high altitude readings from the hydrogen filled balloons. To put this into context, one must remember that the Allied landings in Normandy, D-Day took place on 6 June 1944, the U-boat offensive had totally collapsed on all fronts and other fronts were also all in retreat.

In July 1943 U703 (Kptlt. Heinz Bielfeld) rescued four survivors from the Russian freighter *Dekabrist* who had survived for several months in old hunter's huts on Hopen Island. This story is mentioned briefly in the chapter on Arctic Survival. Finding the huts in reasonable condition and remembering that the survivors had been marooned there for several months, it was decided to make use of the facilities by installing a manned

U737 while on the way to bring the *Kreuzritter* Weather Corps back to Norway.

*Above and below:* Men from U703 landing on Bear Island to set up weather station WFL 34 'Hermann'.

*Above:* U737 closing in on Spitzbergen while on their way to collect the Weather Corps during Operation *Kreuzritter.*

*Below:* Setting up action on U737 during Operation *Kreuzritter.*

Luftwaffe weather base in the now empty accommodation. As a result the Svatisen Weather Station was taken aboard U354 (Kptlt. Karl-Heinz Herbschleb) towards the end of October 1943 and installed on the island. Kptlt. Herbschleb added a résumé to his logbook that gives an interesting insight into the problems encountered while landing and carrying goods across shallow waters. The astonishing point about this is that he made those comments to his superiors in December 1943, more than a year after the first landings had taken place. It would appear that despite a good number of operations in shallow water the Naval High Command had not yet learned what sort of equipment was required for this most difficult work.

Herbschleb wrote that his boat was supplied with one eight-man rubber dinghy and two different four-man dinghies of similar construction. The

U354, which took on board a weather station towards the end of October 1943.

large inflatable became useless after a couple of trips back and forth due to the soft bottom scraping over rough ground and one of the smaller boats was already so well worn through by rubbing against its container that it could not be used at all. A boat with a solid metal bottom to slide over any obstacles in the water would be necessary for this type of activity and progress would have been much quicker if outboard engines had been provided. These were more than essential for any distances longer than 300 metres. The soft rubber bottoms of the inflatables were so unsuitable for carrying heavy boxes that the majority only managed four trips before the base was torn out. This made the carrying of heavy equipment, especially things like radios, which needed protection from water, most difficult. Had the men not found a leaking boat on land and temporarily repaired it, it would have been virtually impossible to unload some of the heavier crates.

Delicate machinery such as radios and weather recording equipment was stowed on board without adequate packaging and some form of protection would have been a great help when unloading. So would some additional handholds for the more bulky items, some of which were difficult to lift and almost impossible to carry any distance. Some men ended up having fallen into the ice-cold water several times. Others were marooned on land where a storm prevented them from returning to the boat and they had to spend several nights squeezed into a cold hut with very little food. Despite having suffered from cold hands, wet feet and numerous cuts and bruises, there were no serious injuries and the men worked very well without complaining and without slacking in their efforts.

# 14

# The Uncharted North-East Spitzbergen Weather Station Haudegen

The decision to continue with the Kreuzritter Weather Station in North Spitzbergen was made so early in 1944 that the replacement crew could start training at the Goldhöhe Mountain Centre in the Riesengebirge to the north-east of Prague while winter conditions still prevailed there. By the early summer of 1944 these were no longer severe enough for Arctic conditions and the men moved high into the Austrian Alps where they could get better acquainted with ice and snow. By this time all fronts were in retreat, Allied forces were advancing north through Italy, D-Day was already history and German cities were being reduced to rubble by intensive bombing campaigns. As a result, this specialists' course had to be curtailed because the instructors were called up for front line duty. The weathermen were luckier. Instead of training they were given home leave; the last that they were likely to get for some time to come. Dr Wilhelm Dege, a scientist who had worked on Spitzbergen before the war, was appointed as team leader for the twelve or so men. Since there was no one in Germany who knew more about Spitzbergen and the Arctic, he was given a free hand in planning and organising the expedition. All the cumbersome naval administration contributed was to provide a list of orders of what was to be done.

When this continuation of the Kreuzritter undertaking had to come up with an official name, someone suggested Haudegen, which should not be confused with the famous U-boat Commander Reinhard Hardegen. Translated into English the play on the leader's name means broadsword or swordsman and can also be used to describe an experienced fighter or fire-eater. The group had not yet been named when Dr Dege decided it would be better if they were to avoid the successful Kreuzritter location and set up a base in a more remote spot. His reasoning was that even if the site had not been molested, the opposition was almost certainly aware of its presence and the way that the Allies were hitting hard at German cities showed that they almost certainly also had the determination to shut down any activity on Spitzbergen. The remoteness of his chosen site can be appreciated when looking at the naval chart of Spitzbergen. The German naval issue for the Second World War with water depths having been added in 1901 shows that even the fjord to the north of New Alesund, where U377 (Kptlt. Otto Köhler) set up the first automatic weather station, was well charted compared with the North-East Land which appeared as a blob of land with hardly any water depths marked around it.

There was no one to argue with Dr Dege when he suggested an isolated spot on the north coast of North-East Spitzbergen as an alternative. This separate island had the advantage that it could only be approached from the north and there was no way that any warring expedition could easily find it by following the coast from the main centres at Barentsburg and Longyearbyen on the Icefjord. The other suggestion he made was to set up the station so late in the year that the U-boat and supply boat would only just get out before they were locked in by the ice. This might have sounded logical to him, but it sparked off strong protests elsewhere. The supply ship crew was so alarmed that they put in for enough provisions to last for one year so that they would be well provided for if they had to overwinter in the ice. In addition to this the boat was overhauled and the hull strengthened to cope with the possible additional stress due to having to cut a path through ice.

The waters around New Alesund on Spitzbergen.

This support ship was the same old WBS 3 (*Carl J. Busch*) commanded by the same fishing boat skipper, Fritz Sittig, who had installed Kreuzritter during the autumn of 1943. However, the basic infrastructure for fitting out the boat had changed dramatically. With the Allied air forces intent on destroying ports, homes and killing civilians without hitting at vital targets such as U-boat building yards, it was thought too dangerous to get the boat ready in Kiel. So the small fishing port Wismar, to the east of Lübeck was chosen instead. The 1,800 crates adding up to some eighty tons was too much for WBS 3, so WBS 8, the fishing boat *Hessen*, which had originally been called *Sachsen*, was brought in to help ferry some of the cargo as far as North Norway. Leaving Wismar on 2 August 1944, WBS 3 ran into immediate trouble. It was obvious that the ship was far deeper in the water than the Plimsoll line allowed. Therefore much of the fuel had to be pumped into a tanker and arrangements made to fill up again in southern Norway. It had not got that far when the naval authorities ordered it to remain in port until a special, heavily protected convoy could be organised. The departure had coincided with a dramatic increase in air attacks against shipping in Norwegian waters and extra strong defences had to be assembled before proceeding further. All this happened quickly, making it possible for WBS 3 to reach Narvik on the 16th to meet the U-boat.

So far this had been identified only as 'the U-boat' because no one was sure who would be available for the rather exacting task of helping to establish the Haudegen Weather Station. As it turned out, U354 was chosen to carry the provisions and equipment for the escape routes. It was also made quite plain, in writing, that the boat's commander, Oblt.z.S. Hans-Jürgen Sthamer, was going to be in overall control of the operation and he could be overruled only by Dr Dege as far as matters for the weather station were concerned.

WBS 6 (the fishing boat *Kehdingen*) on its way to Greenland with the Edelweiss Weather Corps under command of Dr Weiss arrived one day later, making it possible for the two teams to exchange news, views and experiences. Despite the smooth running of transferring goods from WBS 3 to the U-boat, things were not running too well and Operation *Haudegen* was held up in Norway because the well-guarded Convoy JW59 had been reported in the Arctic seas.

Every available U-boat, including U354, put to sea to intercept this heavily laden group running from Loch Ewe in Scotland to the north Russian ports. U354 headed into action with much of the gear for Haudegen's escape routes on board and by luck ran into a separate British force of aircraft carriers sent north to attack battleship *Tirpitz* in Altafjord. This group was in the process of withdrawing when U354 attacked by firing a spread of anti-convoy torpedoes of Type FAT (known as 'Curly' in Britain). Having slowed down the target without sinking it, U354 fired a T5 or acoustic torpedo of Type Zaunkönig, which missed its intended target to hit another carrier, HMS *Bickerton* instead. The ship did not go down either but was so badly damaged that it was later sunk by the destroyer HMS *Aylmer*, after the crew had been taken off. U354's first target, the escort carrier HMS *Nabob*, was towed back to Britain and survived the war to be converted back into a freighter. While this drama was still being enacted, U354 headed off on the surface to find Convoy JW59 that was now known to be not too far away. U354 got close enough to be forced under several times by aircraft that finally sunk the boat with all hands and with the valuable stores for the Haudegen expedition on board. All of this happened during an incredibly short period of time; only a couple of days passed between leaving port and being sunk and with several U-boats milling about, many sending contradictory information back. As a result it was difficult for the German High Command to work out exactly what was happening. A few more days passed before the Admiral for the Polar Seas realised that one of the key elements for Operation *Haudegen* was not going to come back, and hurried efforts had to be made to find substitutes for the missing provisions. By this time it was almost September. Wintry weather with harsh winds was blowing such cold currents over the water that even the sea freezing over was already becoming a regular feature at night. This meant that there was no time to wait for replacements to be sent from Germany.

The loss of U354 was a considerable blow to Dr Dege and his team. Although U354's commander had been a relative newcomer to the Arctic, the boat had a startlingly unusual number of twenty voyages to its credit and it had both installed and evacuated the weather station Schatzgräber on Hopen Island, making this a serious loss for the Haudegen operation. Around this time there also came a radio message from the Edelweiss Weather Station saying it had met strong opposition forces while crossing over to Greenland. Following that there was an ominous silence suggesting that this undertaking had come to an end. Things were becoming most depressing for the Haudegen team, still waiting for permission to set sail.

The new U-boat support came from U307 (Oblt.z.S. Friedrich-Georg Herrle). This boat had some eleven operational tours to its credit and Herrle was the type of chap who was not going to be put off by the intense enemy activity of the recent days. Instead of commiserating, he suggested that the Haudegen team should be divided into two autonomous groups, each one capable of fulfilling the objectives if the other was lost. One team would obviously travel in the U-boat while the other was accommodated in WBS 3. No one was quite sure, but rumours had started filtering through to the Norwegian bases that two Allied destroyers appeared to be lurking near Spitzbergen's west coast, waiting for something to happen. Being the key area where any expedition would have to pass through, this suggested that running into trouble was high on the list probabilities. It was even suggested that Haudegen had been compromised, perhaps by spies in the German bases. Again, Herrle was not unduly perturbed and proposed that they avoided the possible hot spots by sailing anti-clockwise around Spitzbergen, to make it look as if they were heading towards the Russian ports rather than making for the wild north. Dr Dege agreed, but such drastic changes of selecting a more dangerous route as far as the ice and uncharted waters were concerned, had to be approved by the Supreme Naval Command in Berlin. So there was not much that could be done until the men received a reply. Between them Herrle and Dege also worked out that they could lighten the loads by leaving behind some of the provisions and the U-boat could go to the Kreuzritter hut to bring over any leftovers that were going to be of use to the Haudegen team.

The new plan sounded good and the Supreme Naval Command did not have a great deal of alternatives as far as the two waiting weather contingents were concerned. No one in Berlin could offer better solutions. The authorities did make one positive contribution in ordering a large reconnaissance Kondor bomber to fly over the proposed routes and this produced far better results than expected. Neither a great deal of ice nor enemy activity was spotted, making it possible for both Haudegen and Schatzgräber to sail without too many worries. Haudegen left on 8 September 1944 and arrived at the designated location without too many mishaps. There were slight hitches, such as WBS 3 trailing behind U307, unable to go much faster than about nine knots. The two boats encountered a few impressive icebergs, but no damaging pack ice and no interference from the opposition.

The men felt relatively safe when they arrived without having been spotted. Despite this, every precaution was taken against a possible surprise attack and a lookout, complete with signal pistol and machine gun was established on a good vantage point. This remained manned for some time until the weather made it difficult for shipping to come close to the shore. Dr Dege had taken along a plentiful supply of pistols, one for each man working on land, to prevent him from becoming lunch for a hungry polar bear. Many of the men had not handled sidearms before, could not shoot properly and a single bullet was unlikely to stop such a large animal. As a result some became careless about carrying their gun and one man almost paid with his life for leaving it lying near his workplace. Hannes Semkrat, one of the radio operators, was attacked while taking bearings, without having noticed the creature stalk up on him. Luckily a lookout a long way away on the boat saw what was happening and took a rifle to shoot the bear, but that did not stop the animal. It was not until the Oblt. z.S. Friedrich-Georg Herrle delivered the *coup de grace* that the frightened weatherman stopped running away. It was an unpleasant lesson that never occurred again. From then on all men carried their guns without cursing the additional weight.

Unloading the 1,800 crates was a painfully slow procedure, made worse by the twenty centimetres of snow not being deep enough for the large sledges. Luckily Dr Dege took the advice of the earlier Nussbaum weathermen and brought a couple of wheeled barrows for carrying heavy items such as electricity generators and fuel tanks. These were fitted with large inflatable tyres to ride over rough terrain. Once again, a German friendly weather god was on duty to assure that everything ran smoothly. In many ways, it was still a little too warm for the Arctic and the hut suffered rather badly. There had been some misunderstanding with the firm that built the individual sections. It was specified that some small parts should be made from wood fibreboard and the firm understood that all of the hut, including the walls, should be composed of this material. Since it had all been bundled up for easy transport and to prevent individual sections from being damaged at sea, this discrepancy was not noticed until it was too late. Now the men had to pay the price by watching water slowly soak up the walls and, at the same time, the ground underneath the foundations was soft enough for everything to slowly compress into it. Luckily the warm weather did not last and it was not long before the walls froze solid.

Dr Dege first stepped ashore on 14 September 1944 and WBS 3 and U307 finally weighed anchor on the 27th to leave the weathermen to their own devices. Bearing in mind that Oblt.z.S. Herrle spared as many as thirty or more people each day to help with the labour-intensive work on land; the setting up of the Haudegen Station was indeed a most incredible achievement under conditions, which were not of the easiest. To make matters worse, the good weather for the initial landings turned into such an intensive storm that one man was almost killed when the rubber dinghy capsized and packages threatened to drown him.

Although the next step—that of checking the coast for possible enemy activity—may have sounded exciting, it was indeed a most challenging task, demanding a high level of seamanship. So far the U-boat had not needed to cope with shallow water, narrow channels or uncharted underwater rocks. The problems these presented was emphasised to Herrle by the high command before he left port, when he was warned about the incident of U737 running aground while evacuating the Kreuzritter contingent only a few months earlier. The chart that U307 was using, dated 1901, was not going to help a great deal as the men scoured exceedingly close to the coast. To make matters worse the fact that North-East Spitzbergen was a separate island had been discovered as late as 1863 and since then no other ship was known to have sailed all the way around this barren clump of mountains. So, U307 became the second ship to circumnavigate the island. Ironically it was the British explorer Alexander Glen, who had set up a major exploration camp along this stretch of coast during the 1935/36 winter, who supplied some of the navigational information and it was his camp that became U307's first port of call. It was considered essential to check whether this was still in use. A few remnants of this expedition were found, but most of the base had deteriorated so badly that it could not be spotted under the already fairly thick snow cover. Sir Alexander or 'Sandy' Glen was indeed a major protagonist in helping to secure information about these desolate coasts and it might be of interest to add that he met Christiane Ritter when she came to Spitzbergen to overwinter there with her husband during that same season when Glen's Oxford University Expedition was there.

U307 continued after having investigated the British camp, rode out several storms while at anchor in sheltered fjords, and thereby circumnavigated North-East Spitzbergen before starting on the perilous voyage back home. The main problem with sailing south through possible heavy storms was that WBS 3 was now bouncing about mercilessly on top of waves because the boat was much too light. Since there was a noticeable shortage of provisions back in Norway, it was decided to raid the old Kreuzritter Station, to take back whatever could be loaded. It was also thought that the opposition was more likely to make use of the rich supplies than the Germans, so removing the provisions was thought to be a good military decision. As it happened, the Naval Command in Norway decided that there was so much enemy activity in the Arctic waters that they told U307 and WBS 3 to remain where they were until conditions improved. This gave the men ample opportunity to find the now deserted weather station, yet that was not as easy as they had imagined. Several hours were spent in finding it, despite having had an accurate description of its location. Later, the men also searched for one of the escape depots, but never found it. Both U307 and WBS 3 eventually made fast in by the side of the *Black Watch* depot ship in Hammerfest shortly after midday of 4 October 1944.

In the meantime weather station Haudegen was facing numerous difficulties while the men were slowly settling into their new routine. The eleven men all knew that a rigid timetable was going to be essential if everything was going to function properly and efficiently, but they were not quite ready for the inflexible military rules that were going to govern their lives. First, the group was split into two divisions, one under the leadership of Dr Dege and the other under command of Obermaat Heinrich Ehrich. One of these had to be constantly ready to fend off an attack and therefore slept fully clothed. Although the outside lookout was eventually withdrawn, it was essential to keep one man awake when the others were sleeping to check on various parts of the station and to make sure everything functioned well, the men devised a route that had to be checked at regular intervals. The other imposition was that none of them were allowed to show lights outside the hut. This was so strict that every possible opening was covered to make the outside of the station totally lightless.

At first these measures were partly necessary to cope with a possible invasion from the sea because, annoyingly, the fjord did not freeze over until November. The very real danger came from polar bears rather than soldiers with guns and these creatures made it quite plain that these rather draconian watch-keeping duties were more than necessary. One such huge furry brute tried to get into the kitchen at one stage, probably attracted by the smell of food and later a hungry mother came along with two cubs to also run havoc with the station. Luckily nothing essential to operations was destroyed, although she seemed to have liked the rubber dinghy and the three managed to rip it into small shreds. Bears were likely to creep up on the station and lurk silently without making the slightest noise that even going out to the loo could spell so much danger that men were not allowed out at night, when everybody else was asleep. The men saw the sun for the last time on 18 October and shortly after that the permanent Arctic blackness set in, so that talking about day and night became a little pointless. Anyone wanting to go to the heads 'at night' had to use the relief facility inside the building, rather than the main loo in the colder storeroom. The bear attacks also made it more than obvious that the standard military weapons were not much use against the huge white monsters and a volley had to be fired to stop them in their tracks.

The mild weather that had been helpful for setting up the station quickly gave way to severe conditions, making it obvious to the men that they were not on a camping trip. Siegfried Czapka and Sepp Reyer were both caught out by such extreme weather that they had to set up a bivouac to ride out a storm and to prevent them from getting lost in a blizzard blazing through the darkness. With temperatures dropping many degrees below freezing they were lucky to have got away without serious frostbite.

Having adapted to the new way of life the men slowly discovered that the authority that had calculated their rations had not done its arithmetic very well. Despite having ample food, there appeared obvious shortages in certain areas such as fruit and vegetables. Even meat was not in such great supply as the men had hoped. Despite the dangers from bears, Dr Dege gave permission to hunt reindeer, which were plentiful enough in that part of the world during the winter and made a welcome supplement. In fact these added so much meat to the menu that he put the men's good health down to the fresh nourishment obtained from this source. Each day two to three men scoured the coast for driftwood while another two were responsible for sawing and chopping it into usable chunks. Although a chore at home, the men looked upon such activities as contributing vital physical exercise and the supply was so plentiful that by the end of November the station had not yet started using its store of coal.

The Austrian-born engineer, Franz Selinger, who must rank as 'the' leading authority on weather activities in the Arctic, stated that Haudegen was 'the' most successful and the longest of all German weather undertakings. In view of that it should be unnecessary to outline its achievements throughout the long dark winter of 1944/45. The most startling part of this setup came on 3 March 1945, shortly after the men had changed their daily schedule to fit in with the coming of daylight. A radio call from the German Naval Command in Norway asked whether the men had sufficient resources to remain on Spitzbergen for another winter. Of course, this came as a shattering blow, but Dr Dege and his crew were well prepared for such an alternative. They had left civilisation, if that is what one can call the slaughter and destruction of the Second World War, at a time when all fronts were in full retreat and the possibility of being cut off by an end of the war had been taken into account when collecting provisions. In addition to this, Dr Dege knew enough about ice conditions around northern Spitzbergen not to make the same mistake as previous expeditions where men starved because they were cut off by ice and did not have sufficient provisions to see them through. Although he did not admit it to the authorities, Dr Dege thought the men had sufficient provisions for a third overwintering. What was more, he knew full well that the men were healthy enough and the comradeship between them was strong enough for the group to make its own way to the major settlements around the Icefjord in West Spitzbergen, if conditions demanded it.

The fact that there was a great deal of open hostility in Europe was made clear on 26 April when an obviously Allied radio station tried not only to interfere with the weather reports, but also sent the message in German saying, 'We'll get you pigs as well in time.' The German High Command had sent a warning two days earlier that Haudegen had to make preparations for possibly spending a third winter on Spitzbergen. It was not long after this that the men heard about the death of Adolf Hitler and that news was followed by masses of bureaucratic messages of how they were to surrender and what they had to do with their equipment and other material in the weather station. An especially laid mine belt for protecting the station from attack was blown up on 9 May and the stock of over fifty hand grenades were blown up as well, but ammunition for the guns remained while scientific studies continued throughout the summer of 1945. Launching a number of mini expeditions, Dr Dege's team added considerably to the wealth of Arctic knowledge. Again they were determined that this was not going to be handed over unconditionally to anyone and therefore much of it was well packed and hidden away from the main base. This hidden cache of notes and materials was not recovered until some forty years later.

The expected onslaught of Allied naval forces never materialised and the end came rather quickly and without much warning. On 3 September 1945, four months after the end of the war, the sealer *Blaasel* under a civilian seal hunter Ludwig Albertsen and a crew of seven arrived and the surrender was officially signed the following day. Firing off every available gun then marked this event. The Norwegian seal hunters had come from a similar mould to the German explorers and an immediate friendship developed between the two teams. It was not until the Germans returned to Norway that things started to turn sour. There the Haudegen team was locked in the local jail while their personal belongings were looted, certainly not by the men who had evacuated them. It was not a happy homecoming. Instead of having their achievements recognised, the Germans were accused of having committed war crimes and were at times treated rather badly. These recriminations were not unique to northern Norway; they happened to many who surrendered. The war might have been over, but the recriminations, ill treatment and killing continued for some time to come. To make the homecoming even worse, some of the men's homes had been destroyed or overrun by Russian forces, making it difficult or even impossible for them to return to their families.

# 15

# Arctic Survival

## Merchant Ship Survivors

The call sign UOML belonged to the Russian 7,363 GRT freighter *Dekabrist* that sailed from Iceland without the benefit of a convoy. This occurred during the fateful crisis when the Allied navies could not spare escorts for the Polar seas as every available destroyer was required to help with Operation *Torch*—the North African landings. Being without protection, *Dekabrist* was sunk on 4 November 1942 by Ju88 aircraft from Kampfgeschwader 30 (not by a U-boat as has been claimed in some sources) and vanished from the records until the name surfaced again unexpectedly some nine months later. This re-surfacing part of the story started on 23 July 1943 while the men of U703 (Oblt.z.S. Joachim Brünner) were expending some choice naval vocabulary to launch one of those awkward weather buoys mentioned above in Chapter 13. At that moment when nerves were frayed, the radio operator handed the commander a signal that had just arrived. All it said was, 'When the launching of the buoy has been completed make for the southern tip of Hopen Island at fast cruising speed.' There was no further explanation.

Launching the cumbersome object was not easy. The brisk west-north-westerly of Force three was blowing enough spray from the wave tops to make working on the outside deck rather unpleasant, especially as the various bits did not appear to fit together very well and the deep sea anchor was not functioning at all. Later, after having completed the task, the commander received another signal saying that a reconnaissance plane had spotted people on Hopen Island near Spitzbergen and U703 was told to find out what they were doing there. If shipwrecked, they were to be brought home and if it was an Allied radio station, it was to be destroyed.

It would appear that details of what happened to the survivors from the freighter *Dekabrist* between the sinking and the rescue have got lost in the murk of time. Although the rescue boat, U703 went down with all hands, the second watch officer, Heinz Schlott, was replaced in March 1944 shortly before the last voyage so that he could train to become a commander before going on to U2329, a brand new electro Type XXIII. After the war he took the trouble to illuminate the events of this incredibly emotive event. Despite the absence of information about how the survivors from *Dekabrist* reached Hopen Island, one can get a general impression of what these survival artists achieved because the men from the freighter *Chulmleigh* (call sign GJGM), which ran aground off the southern tip of Spitzbergen at around the same time as the *Dekabrist* was sunk, have left a record of their ordeal.

Although self-righting lifeboats with enclosed accommodation had already been invented, not many ocean-going ships of the Second World War carried this type. Open cutters with oars and sails still predominated. Modern survival suits did not exist either. They were not invented until after the war and the majority of people who ended up in lifeboats wore their usual clothing which did not differ a great deal from their everyday wear back home. One of the four lifeboats launched from the *Chulmleigh* dropped at such an acute angle that two men fell into the water. Their cries for help were heard and another boat came alongside to fish them

Photos of Hope Island taken when men from U703 rescued the survivors from the Russian freighter *Dekabrist*.

out again. Despite this quick reaction one man was already dead and the rescuers were exhausted to the point of being unable to do anything else—the extreme cold had taken an early toll. The cliffs of southern Spitzbergen which could be seen from the lifeboats were no great comfort. One did not need a master mariner's certificate to work out that landing there would result in certain death. Even if one did get ashore without crashing on the rocks, there would be no food and there were more than 150 miles of steep mountains between this lonely coastal tip and the settlements on the shores of the Icefjord. Therefore, setting sail the men ignored the coast, to make for Barentsburg. It quickly became apparent that the smallest of three boats could not cope with the heavy seas, leaving no alternative other than to distribute its occupants in the two bigger cutters. This meant twenty-eight and twenty-nine bodies were cramped in the totally inadequate supply of lifeboats. This precarious situation was made worse a day later when the wind dropped to almost zero, making progress with sails virtually impossible.

The long Arctic night that had set in during the beginning of November changed to a vague grey for a few hours each day as the southern horizon became slightly lighter. After having endured a few of these daily cycles in wet and frozen clothing with little food, the men in the master's boat were horrified when the morning dullness revealed that they had drifted away from the coast. This was definitely a case of making use of the engine. There was not enough fuel for covering any significant distance, but on this occasion it did help to bring the men back to the Spitzbergen shore and to spot the other boat, which did not have any mechanical means of propulsion. Realising that these men were in even worse condition than those in the master's boat, it was decided to use the remaining fuel and the sail to go on ahead, to hopefully get help from the mining settlements along the southern shores of the Icefjord. Progress was still painfully slow, with spray on the sail, boat and clothes freezing solid rather quickly. Only the water that spilled into the bilges remained liquid long enough to bale it out again. Possibly it was the movement and the mass of bodies that prevented this from freezing solid as well. The situation was far beyond desperate. There was hardly any food, breath was freezing on the men's beards, everybody acquired at least a few frostbite injuries and the boat was making only painfully slow progress. Many men must have wondered whether there was any hope at all of surviving this harsh punishment.

Things got even worse when the master fell into unconsciousness and the chief steward died, leaving the third mate to take control. It was a pitiful sight, yet the men did manage to reach the entrance of Icefjord and see lights in the far distance, but too far away for them to reach. Spotting huts on the shore close by, they turned towards them. The men had now been in

Rough seas that sailors have to get used to.

The north-west coast of Spitzbergen.

the boat for several days with little food and surrounded by temperatures well below freezing. The men were lucky. Instead of snow-covered cliffs dropping into the sea, there was a small beach, strewn with boulders, a significant amount of timber and even the remains from some ships. On approaching this, the men were literally tipped out of their boat by the surf and those still capable of moving pulled their unconscious mates out of the water before clambering into the huts and dropping into deep sleep. It was still cold, but at least they were out of the incessant wind and excruciatingly cold salt water was no longer being sprayed over them.

On waking up again the men discovered some tinned food and coffee that was heated on a driftwood fire in the hut's rusty stove. With a considerably raised morale the men then faced their next hurdle of severe pain as the frostbitten areas thawed. The frostbite or flesh that had frozen solid was not only restricted to toes and fingers. Arms and legs of some men had also frozen solid so that twelve died of gangrene, an awful experience. The characteristically unpleasant smell dominated the air inside the hut for a long time after the bodies had been buried by covering them with stones. The ground was frozen, making it difficult to dig holes without tools.

. Strangely the master, Captain D. M. Williams, regained consciousness, to resume a leading role and he agreed to two of the fittest men, setting out to walk to Barentsburg. They did not get far before finding that the inhospitable mountains were too much of a challenge. They did not have the clothing, footwear, food or the equipment such as snowshoes or skis for negotiating the deep snow over the steep terrain. Yet the men were not put off and a second and even a third attempt was made to reach the settlement they had seen earlier by different routes. Again the men were driven back by the natural elements. Only the third route took them past another hut containing small quantities of corned beef and beans. The food did not last long and things got so bad that by Christmas the survivors were living off water that was heated by burning timber from the walls of another nearby hut.

The small expeditions sent into the Arctic by Germany and Britain had a great advantage over these shipwrecked men inasmuch as they took with them enough fuel to heat and to light their accommodation and they had considerable amounts of luxury foods in addition to their basic rations. This meant they were well equipped to find their way through the eternal darkness of the cold Arctic night. For the shipwrecked survivors the huts provided only the basic shelter during the intensely cold winter storms. There was no light, food or adequate heating for the survivors.

Having reached almost the end of their tether the survivors were discovered by two Norwegian soldiers out on patrol and eventually taken back to Barentsburg, where they waited for several months until two

Scree slopes near Longyearbyen on the side of Icefjord (Spitzbergen). The mountains of many Arctic islands can be intimidatingly high, difficult to climb for non-mountaineers and nowhere near ideal for setting up a camp that requires a reasonable supply of fresh water.

A hunter's hut photographed around the war years, probably on Spitzbergen. Such huts were nothing more than wooden boxes made from timber washed up on the beaches and waterproofed with canvass with a bit of tar added if that was available.

British cruisers appeared with provisions for the radio station, to take nine men back to the United Kingdom, where they arrived during the middle of June 1943.

The survivors from the sinking of Russian freighter *Dekabrist* found themselves in a similar situation to the men from SS *Chulmleigh*, only that they were out of sight of land when they took to the boats. Yet, despite this the possibility of being marooned had occurred to them and they had taken some precautions against such an eventuality. Unfortunately communication between the Russian survivors and their German rescuers was not ideal, meaning they could exchange only a few essentials by using the international navigation language of English and many details of their incredible experience have been lost. It is just possible that snippets of their interrogation by Russian speaking intelligence officers and possibly post-war Russian reports are still hidden somewhere in dust-covered archive files. If anyone finds them, please send copies or details to the Russian Arctic Convoys Museum at Loch Ewe in Scotland or to the German U-boat Museum. If the records of the sinking are correct, then one can assume that the survivors were driven towards Hopen Island by the natural elements, they would have headed in the opposite direction if the weather had permitted it.

Hopen Island is a long narrow mountainous ridge, about twenty miles (35 km) long and much of it less than two miles (3.5 km) wide with steep inhospitable peaks rising to about five hundred metres above the surrounding sea. The angles of these slopes tend to be a little too steep for hill walkers and there is too much scree and with no firm vertical angles to attract rock climbers. The plus point was that there are a good number of beach-like boulder areas with coarse sand or pebbles for gaining a reasonable foothold when landing there. As U703 approached this barren hell, the Germans were impressed by a vast number of stark gullies running down the bare rocky slopes. These were partly covered with snow, so they could not see the sparse vegetation underneath. In any case only a few plants survive along those rocky, scree covered slopes. Sighting the island at 06.15 hours of 25 July 1943, the officers of U703 concentrated far more on a massive ice field that had settled along the coast. This had to be avoided at all cost to prevent the boat from being disabled if the constantly moving thick sheets were to surround it. There was not enough water under the keel to dive under it. U703 was kitted out for a long voyage along the Siberian Seaway and could not risk being put out of action during this early stage of operations by this unscheduled obstruction.

Keeping the ice in sight, all available weapons were made ready while the landing crew, consisting of the second watch officer, Leutnant zur See Heinz Schlott and three men, inflated a rubber dinghy on the foredeck.

It is rather difficult to interpret this photo without some more 'inside' knowledge. The original caption stated that it shows U307 in Sassenfjord of Spitzbergen in August 1944 and it looks as if there is a rubber dinghy in the foreground. The submarine is difficult to make out because almost all the hull is submerged and the rather large black structure around the conning tower is difficult to explain. The mountains in the background are of special interest because they look similar to the coast of Hopen Island where survivors from the freighter *Dekabrist* ended up for several months to be rescued by U703.

While heading towards the hut mentioned in the radio signal, the lookouts had spotted another shed further towards the south. The four men were back pretty quickly; having established that it contained nothing much more than a load of water soaked quarrying explosives and a ten-year-old Norwegian newspaper.

The next hut, still not the one reported by the aircraft, was tackled slightly differently. Instead of paddling over to it, the gun crew fired a couple of 88 mm shells over the top. This produced a solitary figure with waving arms, meaning it was necessary to launch the rubber dinghy once more while the landing party got very wet again. This time Heinz Schlott approached the hut with pistol in hand. Finding the man with his hands up and also very frightened, Schlott defused the situation by offering him a cigarette and tucking his gun away. Schlott and his landing team had good reasons for being scared. The lone characters one met in the Arctic wastes were a law unto themselves and could turn exceedingly aggressive when challenged by interfering outsiders in what they considered to be their territory. Some also suffered from severe mental problems due to the hardships of the isolation. As it happened there was no hostility on this occasion and it was not difficult to establish that the Germans had found Captain S. P. Beliaev of the Russian *Dekabrist*, who explained with clumsy English what had happened. Although dressed in nothing more than rags with a face reflecting many months of extreme hardships, Captain Beliaev was reasonably well equipped with methylated spirit for his primus stove, matches, dry timber for an old oven and even some guns with which he had shot a number of bears to supplement his meagre rations. The hut was made comfortable with skins and blankets; although hardly adequate for the cold winter they did allow him to survive on this inhospitable and uninhabited island for more than half a year. He told his rescuers that there were more people in a hut further north, so it was a case of packing his bags and then setting off for another wet paddling experience. It would appear that one of the three was a woman, whom Beliaev referred to as 'Miss Doctor.'

Finding the next hut was not difficult. Again a few shots, this time with the 20 mm anti-aircraft gun, produced signs of life, in the form of three waving figures to whom Captain Beliaev shouted in Russian through the German megaphone. Launching a boat that had been hauled up on a tiny beach, the three rowed over to the U-boat and had hardly reached it when strong currents washed the U-boat onto a sandbank. It did not take too long to extract it again and luckily there was no serious damage. At the debriefing after the voyage the U-boat Command in Northern Norway agreed that running aground could not have been the commander's fault because Hopen Island had hardly been charted, the commander could therefore have had little knowledge of water depths along its shores.

The sad point about this emotional episode was that things were rather tense in U703. This was Brünner's first voyage as commander, and three of his key officers were new as well. The first watch officer, the engineer officer and the navigator or Obersteuermann plus twelve other men had joined the boat for the first time only a few days before setting out on this momentous voyage to the far side of the Barents Sea. This meant that a third of the crew were inexperienced greenhorns and the boat urgently needed some time for training before setting out on an operational voyage. Standing instructions allowed the U-boat to take ship captains and key officers on board as prisoners, but there were no rules for allowing the other foreign nationals on board, despite one of the men being obviously seriously ill. Military operations usually took priority over the well-being of people and continued even when members of the crew were seriously ill. It was a difficult decision to make, but the boat's commander, Oblt.z.S. Joachim Brünner had his orders. It would have been difficult to carry out the planned operation with three more healthy prisoners on board and these three wrecks would have made the forth-coming long voyage next to impossible. The three Russians, Dr Nadezda M. Natalic, Matrose V. N. Borodin and J. Lobanov,

Part of the Spitzbergen coast that looks similar to the hills of Hopen or Hope Island where the survivors from the freighter *Dekabrist* found refuge in old hunters' huts. The men from U703 were most impressed by the deep gullies running down the cliffs and the masses of scree that had collected along the bottoms to make this a rather precarious coastline. Hopen Island is more exposed and lacks the protective lowland that can be seen in this photo. *Photo: Mike and Brenda Lyons*

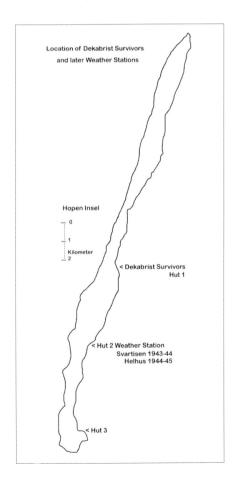

Location of Dekabrist Survivors
and later Weather Stations

Hopen Insel

0

1

Kilometer

2

< Dekabrist Survivors
Hut 1

< Hut 2 Weather Station
Svartisen 1943-44
Helhus 1944-45

< Hut 3

Hopen Island to the south-east of
Spitzbergen.

did not show many emotions when they were told of his decision not to rescue them, and the Germans did their best to soften the harsh situation by providing as many provisions as could be spared. Rum, first aid materials, food, sewing materials and other things were left behind. Yet, no one, not even his crew, believed the commander when he said that he would make a point of picking them up on his way back.

It was obvious that some form of tension existed between the Russian captain and three members of his crew. Beliaev did not communicate easily and remained somewhat reserved, answering questions politely with his limited English. This made it difficult to establish the reasons for the group separating. Bearing in mind that they were the last from a group of thirty that had taken to the lifeboats, they must have had a horrendous survival experience where they had to watch many of their friends die under the most harrowing conditions. Beliaev recovered quickly. After an improvised shower in the engine room, a shave and some new U-boat clothing he started looking much better, although the men did not trust him and kept him under close guard the whole time. He adjusted well to the unnatural life in the U-boat and even put up with a depth charge attack without flinching. U703 did not get orders to pick up the other three from Hopen Island. Instead it was recalled to Narvik, where Beliaev officially became a prisoner of war.

U703 set out for another mission on 14 August 1943, sailing this time as far as the eastern edges of the Kara Sea near Port Dikson. On 2 October, on the 50th day at sea in most difficult conditions, the boat received orders to return home and to bring all the people left on Hopen Island. Two days later another signal arrived confirming that air reconnaissance had spotted two people on the island and nobody was to be left behind this time. Things had not been easy in U703 with constant threats from the air and on the surface having made Brünner cautious enough not to be caught out in unfavourable lighting conditions. So, sighting the northern tip of the island while it was still dark, he laid the boat onto the seabed to wait for dawn, when there would be a little light to see both approaching radar-equipped aircraft and to make it easier for the three survivors to row over to the U-boat.

Two of them waved frantically in response of being woken up by shots from the gun, but none of them made any effort to launch the boat with which they had come alongside during the first meeting many weeks earlier. In the end Schlott and Matrosengefreiter Helmut Wapniarz paddled ashore in the rubber dinghy. Once on the beach they noticed that the boat had been smashed into little pieces to be used as firewood for heating the hut. Things were obviously getting more than just desperate with a dire shortage of reasonably dry washed up timber. The man who was ill the last time U703 called, J. Lobanov, could hardly be moved and could only be brought to the U-boat with the most strenuous of efforts. He died a few days later, despite a considerable endeavour to get some life back into him and was given a sea funeral with full nautical honours. None of three was in good shape and getting them through the horrendous surf was most difficult. This little manoeuvre of moving three people a few hundred metres from the shore to the U-boat took the best part of the day and had not been completed by the time it got dark. In the end it was 19.00 hours when U703 turned to head back to Norway.

The huts that the Germans found on Hopen or Hope Island were in such good condition that it was decided to man them again with a Luftwaffe weather station from the end of 1943 onwards. The argument was that if the Russians had remained there undetected for such a long time, then a radio station might survive on the island as well. Some brief details of this undertaking are mentioned in the chapter on Weather Stations.

Despite this pitiful ordeal, Captain Beliaev went to sea again after the war and Dr Natalic was known to have lived until at least 1979, but making contact with them during the harsh Cold War era, when the impenetrable Iron Curtain divided the world into east and west, made it impossible for ordinary people like Heinz Schlott to contact the people whom he had met so briefly during the war. To make things worse, both the propaganda organisations and the newspapers used the stories of the *Dekabrist* and the *Chulmleigh* survivals to their end, distorting the humanity of those difficult times into hateful fantasy. It is a pity that even government departments and the purveyors of news from so-called civilised nations cannot tell the truth or recognise the goodwill that abounded among so many 'ordinary' people who were forced to lead extraordinary lives.

Ships sailing in convoy had the advantage that rescue ships often accompanied them. Unfortunately by 1942 U-boats were finding it difficult to approach close to convoys and therefore often attacked from such long ranges that they could not see what these ships were doing. Rescue ships were usually small easily manoeuvrable vessels but without any form of distinctive markings and they looked like every other ship in the convoy. By international law they did not qualify to bear a red cross and many were sunk as sitting ducks. In any case, the courtesies exhibited by both sides towards the beginning of the war had faded by the time the Arctic convoys had started running. Post war interviews also suggested that some merchant ships, especially those carrying passengers, sailed without anyone on board having practised lifeboat drill. Such action was considered to have been counterproductive inasmuch that it created unnecessary anxiety. It is also interesting to add that the monthly secret anti-submarine reports circulated by the Admiralty to officers hunting U-boats stated that by the end of 1940 (after one year of war) the high losses of personnel was partly due to ships not having been supplied with adequate life-saving aids.

## The German Side

When looking at the problem of survival from the German angle one finds an even worse scenario with very few survivals from sinking U-boats. This was largely due to the absence of rescue ships and men having no option other than to jump into freezing water which killed them in a matter of minutes. Even those who managed to clamber into a life raft could not have done so without getting wet and they would not have survived long in the cold Arctic, where temperatures were often well below freezing. Of over forty U-boats that went down in Polar or cold Norwegian seas, there were only nine of which survivors were definitely rescued. These were, in chronological order of sinking:

| | | | |
|---|---|---|---|
| U472 | (KL Wolfgang Friedrich Freiherr von Forstner) | 22/27 | 4 March 1944 |
| U973 | (OL Klaus Paepenmöller) | 49/2 | 6 March 1944 |
| U476 | (OL Otto Niethmann) | 33/18 | 25 May 1944 |
| U990 | (KL Hubert Nordheimer) | 20/31 | 25 May 1944 |
| U957 | (OL Gerd Schaar) | 0/49 | 19 October 1944 |
| U1060 | (OL Herbert Brammer) | 61/13 | 27 October 1944 |
| U737 | (OL Friedrich-August Greus) | 31/20 | 19 December 44 |
| U425 | (KL Heinz Bentzien) | 48/1 | 17 February 45 |
| U307 | (OL Erich Krüger) | 37/14 | 29 April 1945 |

The above columns are:
Boat number, name of last commander, casualties/survivors, date of sinking.

Crews for Type VII U-boats were originally about 4 officers and 40–44 men, but by 1944 many U-boats carried heavier anti-aircraft armament and therefore required additional gunners. U1060 was a special torpedo transporter of Type VIIF, slightly longer than a standard VIIC boat. The others were ordinary Type VIIC boats.

# U472

U472 was sunk on 4 March 1944 by a Swordfish aircraft piloted by Sub-lieutenant P. J. Beresford from HMS *Chaser* using recently introduced rockets. These were neither heavy nor large, but hit with enough punch to crack open the pressure hull of a submarine. They had the great advantage over depth charges that they streaked ahead of the aircraft, meaning they reached their target before bombs would have been dropped. Two of the rockets were seen to hit and at least one of them created a serious leak immediately behind the diesel engine where there was insufficient room for men to get in to shore up the hole. Water flooding in faster than the ballast pumps could pump it out left little choice other than to abandon ship. The anti-aircraft guns were fully manned when this happened and the Swordfish was seen to approach, but there was so much ice on the top of the conning tower and the gun platform that at the critical moment the guns would not fire. The interesting point was that no one on the bridge realised that the rocket had created so much havoc. Even the blast was hardly noticed and the commander, who was looking in a different direction at the time, was not aware of any possible damage until the engineering officer reported the matter by calling through the speaking tube.

Unfortunately for the U-boat, the destroyer HMS *Onslaught* under Commander the Hon. A. Pleydell-Bouverie was also close at hand to assure that there would be no escape for the stricken boat. The reports of the sinking are somewhat contradictory with the Kptlt. von Forstner mentioning two escorts. Whatever happened, as far as the survival was concerned the destroyer now became the saviour, with the Royal Navy rigging up scrambling nets on the side nearest to the U-boat for the Germans to climb on board and those who no longer had the strength were helped up. Von Forstner was among the lucky ones, with considerable energy left when his boat dropped way under him. First, he was not inside when the explosion occurred and secondly the engineer officer Leutnant zur See Damm was killed by gunfire while standing next to him. So, Forstner was indeed exceptionally lucky. Arriving on *Onslaught*'s deck he still had the presence of mind to follow naval etiquette, as he would have done before the war when stepping aboard a foreign ship. He stood to attention as he saluted both the White Ensign and then the officer supervising the rescue effort. Had it not been for *Onslaught*'s presence there would probably not have been any survivors at all and the seriousness of the leak would not have allowed the U-boat to reach land either.

What was rather unexpected with these few hectic minutes was that von Forstner was only aware of the engineer officer having been killed because both men were standing next to each other when he came up to report that everybody had vacated the boat. The water temperature was about one degree Celsius and is seems likely that a good number of men fell foul to the freezing conditions. This was a case where life jackets did not help and those who had donned them on to rely on their added buoyancy found themselves cooled down so quickly that the body ceased functioning in the low temperatures. Men who jumped overboard without life jackets knew that they should discard their boots and loosen any scarves around the neck and then the rigorous action of struggling in the water prevented them from cooling down so quickly.

# U973

U973 can be recognised on some photographs by its most unusual conning tower with an additional 37 mm anti-aircraft gun forward of it. There were very few boats with such a modification and the majority were employed as aircraft traps in the Bay of Biscay. Unfortunately the additional weight high above the pressure hull caused a number of stability problems, making it so difficult to control that the commander, Oblt.z.S. Klaus Paepenmöller, reported the matter by radio to the U-boat Command in Norway. During the boat's second cruise the U-boat surfaced close to a Swordfish from HMS *Chaser*, the same aircraft carrier that was instrumental in sinking U472. The usual procedure after surfacing was for the commander to climb up to the top of the conning tower for a cursory look around to check that nothing offensive was lurking nearby. Following this he would order the boat to either dive again or to blow the tanks with exhaust gases from the diesel engines. This saved compressed air and was less likely to assist a fire if one was to break out during any subsequent action. On this occasion, on 6 March 1944, while the engineer officer was waiting for the order to blow the tanks and the lookouts were ready to come up, the boat was hit fair and square by a single rocket from a salvo of six. The result was so damaging that the boat could not remain afloat for any length of time. Instead of ordering the tanks to be blown, Paepenmöller ordered everybody out while he watched a white cloud erupt with great fury. The engineer officer, Leutnant zur See Franz Rudolph, the last to leave, reported that everybody had left except for one man, who refused. Then, seeing the futile situation Rudolph jumped into the cold water as well. Neither he nor the action helmsman, Obergefreiter Bergmann, were wearing life jackets and therefore struggled for some four hours to remain afloat before the Canadian corvette *Queen Budgega* picked them up. It would seem that the rest of the crew, many of them wearing their escape apparatus succumbed to the cold water that had a temperature of only four degrees Celsius.

# U476 and U990

No one with the right qualifications has ever offered an explanation as to how and why the sinking of U476 under Oblt.z.S. Otto Niethmann came about and both the report from survivors and from the aircraft that sunk it differ sufficiently to make one think they refer to two different incidents. It would appear that Captain F. W. Maxwell flying in Catalina V from Squadron 210 attacked with such accuracy that much of the boat flew into the air before dropping from view. When it surfaced again, a few minutes later, the aircraft no longer had any depth charges and could only rake the boat with gunfire. Captain Maxwell reported heavy gunfire from the U-boat as well; although he could not have known that the 37 mm anti-aircraft gun had broken down after only a few shots and all that was coming up were small 20 mm shells. It may have been 24 May 1944, but being close to the Lofoten Islands of Norway meant that the natural elements were going to make a major contribution and a heavy snow squall eventually turned the aircraft away from its target. Yet the damage it had inflicted was indeed fatal. In addition to water seeping into the interior, one of the diesels had been hit so violently that it had dropped out of its seating, to sit at a precarious angle. The men did not notice this at first because the lighting had also failed and the second, gunfire, attack had resulted in more damage as well as noisy casualties on the upper (outside) deck.

There was no way that the boat would ever come back to the surface if it dived, so there was no alternative other than to carry the injured to the life rafts while attempting some emergency repairs. The sea and the wind were so uncooperative that the life rafts quickly drifted apart, making it difficult to keep the floating mass together and there was a real danger of exhausted men being swept under by the waves. They were sitting up to their stomachs in water with a temperature of only three degrees Celsius, resulting in a rapid loss of body heat, draining out whatever energy remained after the exhausting abandoning of the boat. Despite this frantic activity and things looking so gloomy, the engineer officer managed to keep the boat on the surface for another seventeen hours and it was around midnight of 24/25 May that U990 appeared to take on board twenty-one survivors before sinking U476 with a torpedo.

The amazing and most significant point about this rescue is the length of time the men remained alive in such incredibly cold conditions. They almost certainly owe their lives to the air temperature having been cold, but not freezing, so there was no danger of frostbite or other hazards associated with parts of the body freezing solid, as would have been the case if it had been winter. The men were also lucky that they were not hampered by darkness and although the weather may not have been calm, the men of U990 described it as extreme, it was not fatally punishing either.

U990 was on its 6th war voyage when the radio operator intercepted the distress call from U476. The commander (Kptlt. Hubert Nordheimer) immediately asked for signals for the radio direction finder. The weather had been so appalling for some time that it had been difficult to establish accurate positions and finding a U-boat floundering in heavy seas was going to be extremely difficult. The turbulent water was such a problem that Nordheimer ordered there to be eight instead of the usual four lookouts. Four were to continue with their normal duties of looking for approaching enemy units and the other four were to concentrate on survivors in the water. Depressingly, all they found at first were a number of empty life rafts, some of them upside down, making it look as if the weather had been too rough for the inflatables. Unknown to them though, during the earlier chaos on the upper deck, when a number of men were launched in one-man life rafts, the first watch officer, Wolf-Dietrich Kornrumpf, managed to get a large inflatable into the water and with it collect a number of single rafts so that the men could transfer to what appeared to be a more stable rescue platform.

By the time U990 spotted a red star shot into the air from U476, a full scale storm of Force six to seven was sweeping over the sea and rescue activities had to be suspended when this was interrupted for short periods by gusts of Force ten. The stern of U476 was now lying deep in the water while the bows were sticking high up in the air. The interior had filled with poisonous gases produced when seawater mixes with battery acid, and with there being no power to run ventilators it was impossible for anyone to remain inside, even in the comparative dry bow section. All the remaining men were either outside on the bows or on the top of the conning tower, cooling rapidly in exposed positions while holding on for dear life. There was no hope of attaching a towrope and, in any case, both commanders thought that any salvage attempt was bound to end in disaster as soon as the reinforcements from the opposition turned up with more depth charges; something that was bound to happen as soon as the weather calmed. The only positive news during this fatefully chaotic situation was a message from Trondheim saying patrol boat (Vorpostenboot) V5901 was on its way to help. This may have caused the morale to rise, but no one would have put any value on this information, if they had known what was going on aboard this tiny fishing boat.

V5901 under Kapitän C. A. Klaassen, a converted trawler, had been at sea for too long. The machinery was protesting by constantly blowing out gaskets to spray the engine room with a fine mist of black oil that condensed into the most offending grease. Even green soap did not wash it off the crew. Yet, despite this mechanical disaster and being entitled to some longer leave, the men volunteered to set out once more to help U990 and U476 some 300 kilometres northwest of Trondheim. It would have taken a good day's worth of hard sailing to have reached the two boats under the best of conditions and the storm that was blowing meant that progress was considerably slower. U476 had been sunk by the time V5901 got there and U990 was lying under low snow clouds that were also hiding a number of aircraft. These attacked with such great accuracy that it was all too obvious the U-boat was not going much further. U990's 37 mm anti-aircraft gun failed at the critical moment, after having fired only seven shots, leaving the gunners no alternative other than to jump into the water when they saw their boat was sinking under them. Failures with the 37 mm anti-aircraft gun were not unique to the Arctic; many boats made similar complaints.

At least one life raft was launched amidst this confusion to accommodate the wounded and up to eight men in the water were allowed to hold on to it at any one time for a rest from swimming. Trying to reach this spectacle was exceedingly difficult for V5901 as the wind, now at good gale force, kept blowing the ship away from the men in the water at an alarmingly fast rate and unconscious or dead men in lifejackets added to the difficulties. Apparently German fighters drove away the aircraft that had sunk U990, which contradicts the statement about the gale force winds. Or would fighters have managed to remain in the air under such extreme conditions? Having pulled fifty-two people out of the water, V5901 was faced with the next problem of not having enough accommodation for so many. Had an author described this incredible chain of events in a work of fiction, readers would have claimed the story to be too far-fetched. No one would have believed that the acts of heroism could be true. The war has produced a vast number of such events that are hard to believe and sadly many have never seen the light of day in any publication. So, it is good that there are centres like the German U-boat Museum and the Russian Convoys Museum at Loch Ewe that make a point of recording such extraordinary happenings.

In the end V5901 brought home the survivors from the two U-boats. What is so astonishing is that it was left to this old, worn out ship with a tired crew to go out into gale force winds to the rescue and a large centre like Trondheim, with a major German naval base, could not provide any better rescue ships. The survivors were lucky that this happened in

May when only a few snow showers added to the unpleasantness of the occasion. Had this happened in winter, it is probable that everybody would have been killed by the natural elements.

# U957 and U1060

There are times when research ends in complex riddles, especially when records were compiled shortly after the war when many of the official documents remained classified and people had to rely on their memory. The details from various quarters relating to the last voyage of U957 differ considerably, and a lengthy study of the available accounts would be necessary to obtain an accurate picture. The following narrative includes only those aspects that appear to be undisputed.

U957 under the command of Oblt.z.S. Gerd Schaar had been far enough along the Siberian Seaway to see Cape Chelyuskin, about 95 degrees east on the Taimir Peninsula. This is the most northerly point of the continent, considered to be the westernmost part of the north coast that is recognised as being Asia rather than Europe. Together with a chain of islands to the north, this cape also forms the barrier between the Kara and Laptev Seas.

There the boat received such punishment from ice floes that the torpedo doors could not be moved in any direction and the engineer officer, Leutnant zur See Paul Naujokat, took advantage of the ice to inspect the damage from close quarters. Flooding the stern tanks and blowing those in the bows made the front lurch upwards at a precarious angle enabling him to stand on the ice to look at the damage from close quarters. This was so severe that he ordered all four doors to be removed, and they were simply cut off with a welding torch.

Everything went well until the boat was travelling through Norwegian coastal waters where it was either attacked by aircraft or had a collision with a merchant ship. Since the engineer officer described a depth charge attack that pressed in parts of the hull by buckling it by some thirty centimetres, one can assume that the first mentioned is the more likely. Whatever the cause, the damage incurred was so bad that the boat had to be decommissioned after it arrived in Narvik. (Some reliable reports also mention Trondheim, but Narvik is more likely. It would seem that only a small 'skeleton' crew was on board when the boat was transferred from Narvik to the German Naval Dockyard in Trondheim.) The end sum of the contradicting reports adds up to the crew having brought their boat back to port, and after that the machinery was cannibalised for spare parts required by other boats.

Following this there is another gap in the records and the next definite point was that majority of the crew ended up on board U1060 under Oblt. z.S. Herbert Brammer. This was one of the unusual Type VIIF, a special variation of the more common Type VIIC with an additional section fitted immediately aft of the bow torpedo compartment to carry just over twenty torpedoes as cargo.

Having delivered a consignment of torpedoes to northern Norway, U1060 was an ideal vessel for taking most of the crew from U957 back to Germany. U1060 had carried out sixteen shuttle voyages between Germany and northern Norway, but had hardly been involved in any serious aggressive action. On this occasion, with the additional bodies on board, Fairey Fireflies from the aircraft carrier HMS *Implacable* bombed the boat, which resulted in it being driven aground between two skerries to prevent it from sinking. (Skerries are low smooth hard rocks that may look like sandbanks.) The attack was so ferocious that all the lookouts and officers on the bridge had been killed and the next set of men to go up there, to take over were also killed before they could make any impact on the chain of events. In the end the men had only one choice, to get off the boat or die with it. With large numbers of men on board chaos was to be expected, but luckily the weather was not at an extreme and many managed to clamber onto the rocky shores, where they were neither warm nor comfortable. It was the type of situation one would not have volunteered for, but at least it was not so extreme that low temperatures killed anyone. Norwegian fishermen later collected the survivors and took them to a local hospital where they received friendly and excellent treatment, with the staff doing their utmost to ease the pain.

# U425 and U737

The men of U425 (Kptlt. Heinz Bentzien) were not lucky when they jumped into the darkness of a February night in 1945, less than three months before the end of the war. Fifty-three men died in the cold water while only one, Matrosengefreiter Lochner, was picked up alive. Incidentally, at around the same time U711 (Kptlt. Hans-Günther Lange) torpedoed the corvette HMS *Bluebell* from which there was also only one survivor, showing that Arctic winters hit indiscriminately with great force. It would seem that nature hit especially hard at well-organised and calm crews, while the chaos of the more unruly was rewarded with them surviving for longer. This was due to the fact that anyone remaining calm with life jackets keeping them afloat was likely to be killed much faster by low temperatures than men who were actively thrashing about. The poor swimmers who struggled hard did better than those who used their superior swimming skills to expend the minimum of effort in remaining on the surface. This was demonstrated by the sinking of U737 under Oblt.z.S. Friedrich-August Greus, from where the first watch officer, Oblt.z.S. Hans-Joachim Kleffel left a detailed account in the German U-boat Museum. Being deadly tired he dropped into deep sleep immediately he came off duty to be awakened sometime later when the engines stopped unexpectedly. Lying in semi-consciousness he was aware that there had also been a loud thump, suggesting the boat had hit something. Still dazed by semi-consciousness he found himself being washed out of his bunk by water squirting through the panelling. Thinking first that he was experiencing a bad dream it took a few seconds before he realised that this was real and everyone had to get out fast before they were drowned by the torrents pouring in.

The general situation was one of panic. U-boat men were used to obeying orders, thinking for oneself was not part of the daily routine, but now, in the absence of orders, everybody seemed to be trying to solve the problem their own way. Only the men squeezing into the central control room from the front appeared to be aware that the precarious angle was due to water pouring in, others were under the impression they could correct the tilt by adjusting the levels in the diving tanks. The petty officers were organising a queue, but this was made difficult by injured men near the hatch, blocking the people behind. All of this took time and matters were made worse by an absence of orders. By the time Kleffel reached the top of the conning tower he found no one there to give any instructions. Seeing a large ship nearby, Kleffel realised that the duty watch together with the commander must have been swept to their deaths and it was obvious from the wash that the engines were still running in reverse. The diesels could only do this by halting them and then restarting them in the opposite direction; meaning that when Kleffel was woken by the sudden absence of noise, the commander must have rung down for the almost silent electric motors to be set full speed in reverse to stop the boat. Despite being cold and soaked to skin Kleffel could see that the front of the boat was flooding fast. He concluded that the pressure-resisting hatch to the rear must have been closed because when he rang the telegraph to stop engines it was obeyed at once and even acknowledged. The engineers were obviously still at their post. It could well have been that the men in rear of the boat were not even aware of the seriousness of the chaos in the bows.

The boat was obviously sinking fast and it was not long before everybody on the outside deck found themselves in the freezing cold February water, surrounded by darkness. Some of the men weakened so quickly that they needed help just holding on to the side of a life raft. The majority of rafts remained locked in their foredeck containers because the acute angle made it impossible to reach them, they were located so far forward that on this occasion they were submerged rapidly as the bows vanished below the surface of the water. Shortly after that everybody on the outside found himself being tipped into the water.

Despite making a concerted effort to remain on the surface Kleffel was so stiff that he could no longer grasp the life raft or the two men that he was supporting and had a cutter from the large ship not appeared he would not have survived. He also remarked in his report that he was struggling hard in the water, especially as there were a large number men in a small space. At times these men appeared to float on top of him and he had to make a great effort to push them aside when he needed a mouthful of air.

# U307

U307 under Oblt.z.S. Erich Krüger went down in the Barents Sea on 29 April 1945, just five days before the Instrument of Surrender was signed at 18.30 hours of 4 May. The third watch officer, Hans Georg Hembd, described how the men were sitting in the mess enjoying the end of their evening meal and feeding the ship's cat with sardines when the quietness of the early evening was suddenly smashed by a metallic crash. Other than creating this disturbing noise nothing else happened. The light continued to burn and it was just as silent afterwards as it had been before, only the commander sprang up to dash into the central room and then the others realised that the stern had started going downhill. Scrambling up into the conning tower a few minutes later, Hembd looked up through the already open hatch to see a number of bright tracer lines shooting at various angles across the night sky. Getting up to the top of the conning tower became a difficult due to wounded men getting stuck in the opening. Once up the top, it was possible to see five ships surrounding the hapless U-boat and in the far distance he could make out the snow-covered Murmansk coast. By that time there were so many shells of varying calibre bouncing around the top of the conning tower that it was advisable to keep a low profile.

It would seem that the Royal Navy was using its capturing tactics to get a boarding party onto the U-boat by frightening the Germans so much that they abandoned ship. The detonation that had brought U307 to the surface had been so accurate and ferocious that there was no chance of anyone getting aboard the already fast sinking U-boat. Fourteen men made it aboard the frigate HMS *Loch Insh* of Escort Group 19. The reason they survived has got to be put down first to the Royal Navy having made a momentous effort to save the Germans and then providing the wounded with excellent medical treatment. The reason why so many died has got to be put down to intensely cold water and to the incredible firepower put up while men were jumping overboard. However, this was not due to callous reaction of the gunners on the surface ships, but to the orders they had from the British Admiralty, which stated in the monthly Anti-Submarine Reports that anyone who appeared to be surrendering should be machine-gunned to prevent them from manning their guns.

The questions that Hans Hembd found difficult to answer were why did their sound detectors not pick up the noise of the surface ships, and how it was possible to hit the submerged U-boat so accurately with a single depth charge? Normally it was possible for everybody to hear ships passing overhead without the aid of any amplification equipment. In view of the reports it would seem likely that it was not a depth charge, but a projectile fired from the so-called Squid. Had *Loch Insh* under command of Lieutenant Commander E. W. C. Dempster, run over the top of the submerged U-boat, it would have been heard in the mess without the sensitive sound detection gear. The Squid was a large mortar located on the stern and was fired high over the bridge to land in the water a long distance ahead of the ship. Although all records have put the sinking down to a depth charge attack, it would seem more likely that the recently-introduced Squid was the real cause. Again this action shows that the men who struggled fiercely through the water by swimming the short distance to *Loch Insh* were the ones who survived the cold water and those that relied on their life jackets or inflated escape apparatus were the ones who succumbed to the natural elements.

## Basic Arctic Survival

Some Arctic tragedies occurred without jumping into the water, instead the seas just sucked men off ships for them to disappear and never be heard of again. Throughout the Second World War U-boats lost over a thousand men that way and it would not be difficult to guess that the casualty rate on small surface ships must have been similar. Many of these incidents have not been documented, but U354 under Kptlt. Karl-Heinz Herbschleb did record the loss of Fähnrich zur See (Midshipman) Horst Meyn. This happened on 11 November 1942 during the boat's third operational voyage. A few days earlier, on the 6th, when the boat reached the edge of the pack ice, the men were having considerable problems with the hatch on the top of the conning tower. It was possible to close it with the teeth of the locking mechanism between the lid and its frame, meaning extra care was always necessary, something the men did not have time for during an alarm dive. Having reached the ice, it was necessary for the boat to extract itself from what could become a serious trap, but this did not worry the men a great deal as long as they had enough power in the batteries to dive under any offending ice sheets. At this stage the lookouts were astonished. They spotted a lone sailing ship in the far distance. Focusing on it, it took a while before they realised this yacht was nothing more than iceberg with a rather curious shape.

Following this, the wind increased and the sea changed from being mildly uncomfortable to an irritating rollercoaster ride. Despite the conditions, and the danger of bumping into some offensive ice, the boat had to remain on the surface to charge the batteries. This was still in progress when, without any form of warning, Horst Meyn was just washed off his feet and pulled overboard into the raging gale to vanish into the darkness of the Arctic night. The securing clips of his safety harness were still in place on the conning tower wall. What was so astonishing was that the brand new leather safety harness that he was wearing had snapped like a sheet of soggy paper. There was nothing the men could do, and realising that the batteries were full enough, Herbschleb decided it was time to dive and to ride out the storm in the safety of the depths. It was a horrific experience for all concerned. Despite a concerted effort, there was no way they managed to find the man among the turbulence of the crashing waves and the darkness of the night.

Safety harnesses were quite troublesome at times. They were designed in such a way that they could be worn comfortably and once attached to special loops on the conning tower wall the men could lie back without needing their hands to hold themselves in place. This meant that they could use both hands to grip the binoculars. Many of these did not need constant focusing once they had been adjusted for the lookout's eyes. The two hands were still necessary to use them because the lenses had to be cleaned every ten minutes or so and during storms they needed wiping more often.

The two belts of this safety harness had a carabiner type of mountaineering hook for attaching to the conning tower and this almost resulted in the loss of U377 under Kptlt. Otto Köhler. This happened during one of those not too critical alarm dives where an approaching aircraft had been spotted while still a long way away, and U377 dropped into the depths only as a precaution in case it came closer. The last person down was usually the most senior officer who would also twist the locking mechanism of the hatch to assure it was properly locked and would not jump open if a depth charge detonated close by. On this occasion the carabiner clip at the end of the safety harness dropped between two slats of the floor. These were there for water to flow out easily again when waves washed over the top of the conning tower. Having dropped between two slats the clip twisted and could not be pulled free because it was now much wider than the gap it had dropped through. At first the officer could not figure out why the hatch would not close and tried to solve the problem by twisting the locking mechanism harder. When he noticed that the chain connecting the clip with the body straps was in the way, the diving process was already under way, and not having experienced this before the officer tried pulling at the chain without comprehending why the harness had got stuck. Although this took only a few seconds, it was long enough for water to start gushing through the still open hatch.

The engineer officer, Oblt.z.S. Karl-Heinz Nitschke, usually stood at the bottom of the ladder during such alarm dives, keeping his eyes on the depth gauges and also on what was going on above him. When the shower of salt water told him that all was not well, the boat had reached such a stage that it was no longer possible abort the dive. Therefore he jumped up to close the hatch above his head leading from the central room to the commander's attack position inside the conning tower and hoped the boat would return to the surface without killing the unfortunate officer dangling helplessly above him. The men were lucky; U377 surfaced again quickly and the duty officer was extracted from his rather awkward predicament.

# 16

# Arctic Meteorological Operations

(Information originally from Reinhard Reche. Supplemented later by Franz Selinger and with additions by Kpt.z.S. a.D. Peter Monte at the German U-boat Museum.)

Abwehr = Military Security Service
Kröte = codename of an unmanned weather station for setting up on land, developed by the civilian National Weather Service.
L = Luftwaffe
M = Marine the German navy called itself Marine rather than Kriegsmarine and used the letter M instead of K.
WBS = Wetterbeobachtungsschiff (Weather Observation Ship), usually a converted fishing boat.
WFL = Wetterfunkgerät – Land (Weather Radio Apparatus - Land), unmanned weather station for setting up on land developed by the navy.
WFS = Wetterfunkgerät – See (Weather Radio Apparatus – Sea), unmanned weather station for floating on water developed by the navy.

| Location and name of weather station | Dates: setup and evacuated | Notes |
|---|---|---|
| Spitzbergen - L | | |
| Bansö | 25.09.41 – 09.07.42 | |
| Kröte Bansö | 15.05.42 – 15.07.24 | |
| Kröte Sorkapp | 24.07 43 | |
| Kröte Edgeoya | 04.08.42 | |
| Landvik | 15.10.44 – 06.08.45 | Out with U365. Supplied by U636. |
| Spitzbergen - M | | |

| Location and name of weather station | Dates: setup and evacuated | Notes |
|---|---|---|
| Knospe | 15.10.41 – 23.08.42 | Out with WBS 1 *Sachsen* and WBS 3 *Fritz Homann*. Back with U435. |
| WFL 21 *Gustav* | 09.09.42 | Set up by U377. The station was later captured and taken to Britain. |
| Nussbaum | 13.10.42 – 22.06.43 | Out with U377. Back with U302 and U625. |
| Kreuzritter | 06.10.43 – 01.07.44 | Out with U355. Back with U737. |
| WFL 33 *Edwin III* | 01.07.44 | Set up by U737 |
| Haudegen | 13.09.44 – 03.09.45 | Originally out with U355, which was lost with the weather station's equipment on board. Replaced by U307 and WBS 3 *Carl Busch*. |
| **Hopen Island - L** | | |
| Svartisen | 27.10.43 – 21.07.44 | Out with U354. Home with U354 |
| Helhus | 09.10.44 – 05.08.45 | Supported by U636 |
| **Bear Island - L** | | |
| Kröte *Bjornoya* | 29.10.42 | |
| Kröte *Bjornoya II* | 20.08.43 | |
| Taaget | 16.11.44 – 10.04.45 | Out with U1163. Supplied by U992. Back with U668. |
| **Bear Island - M** | | |
| WFL 22 *Edwin I* | 02.12.42 | Set up by U657. |
| WFL 23 *Edwin II* | 18.03.43 | Set up by U378. |
| WFL 24 *Robert* | 09.07.43 | Set up by U629. |
| WFL 27 *Dietrich* | 07.09.43 | Set up by U355. |
| WFL 29 *Christian* | 06.12.43 | Set up by U713. |
| WFL 34 *Hermann* | 17.06.44 | Set up by U737, which later checked the station as well. |
| **Jan Mayen - L** | | |
| WBS 4 *Hinrich Freese* | 17.11.40 | Lost |

| Location and name of weather station | Dates: setup and evacuated | Notes |
|---|---|---|
| **Jan Mayen – M** | | |
| WFL 31 *Walter* | 25.09.44 | Set up by U992. |
| **Nowaja Zemlya – L** | | |
| Kröte *Meshduscharski* | 13.10.42 | Abandoned due to enemy interference |
| **Nowaja Zemlya – M** | | |
| WFL 25 *Gerhard* | 22.08 43 | Set up by U703. |
| WFL 32 *Erich* | 15.10.44 | Set up by U387. |
| **Franz-Josef-Land – M** | | |
| *Schatzgräber* | 08.09.43 – 09.07.44 | Out with U387. |
| WFL 32 *Erich* | 14.10.44 | Abandoned due to too much ice |
| **Labrador – Canada – M** | | |
| WFL 26 *Kurt* | 22.10.43 | Set up by U537. |
| WFL 30 *Herbert* | 18.09.44 | Due to have been set up by U867 but lost on way out |
| **Greenland – Abwehr** | | |
| *Nanok* | 07.09.40 | with sealer *Furenak*. Weather detachment captured |
| *Busko* | 12.09.41 | Weather detachment captured |
| **Greenland – L** | | |
| *Schwager* | 26.11.44 | Abandoned due to technical problems |
| **Greenland – M** | | |
| *Holzauge* | 28.08.42 – 17.06.43 | |
| *Bassgeiger* | 13.09.43 – 03.06.44 | Out with U355 and WBS *Coburg*. Back by aircraft. |
| *Edelweiss I* | 01.09.44 | Supported by U703 but captured. |
| *Edelweiss II* | 04.10.44 | Out with U965. Captured |
| **Mainland Europe** North Cape Norway | | |
| WFL 36 *Wilhelm* | 22.11.44 | Set up by U1165 |

# Weather Buoys

| Date | U-boat | Notes |
|------|--------|-------|
| 29.12.41 | U156 | Rockall Bank |
| ??.04.42 | U159 | |
| 24.08.42 | U516 | Rockall Bank |
| 31.08.42 | | 48-27N 27-35W |
| 10.11.42 | U519 | 51-26N 30-13W |
| 01.12.42 | U167 | Left with weather buoy but abandoned the operation because the commander was seriously injured. |
| 29.04.43 | U531 | |
| 11.06.43 | U194 | Left with weather buoys on board. |
| 10.09.44 | U703 | Dropped weather buoy the north of Iceland. |
| 18.11.44 | ? | Dropped off weather buoy *Karin*. |
| 11.01.45 | U880 | Left with weather buoys on board. |

# 17

# Arctic Convoys

Place names:

HF = Hvalfjord, (Iceland north of Reykjavik)
LE = Loch Ewe (Scotland)
AA = Archangel (Russia)
SC = Scapa Flow (Orkneys)
MU = Murmansk (Russia)
MO = Molotovsk (White Sea coast near Archangel)
RV = Reykjavik (Iceland)
WS = White Sea
KI = Kola Inlet
CL = Clyde
BF = Belfast
SF = Seidisfjord (East Iceland)
UK = United Kingdom

Columns:

1 = Convoy. 2 = Departure port. 3 = Departure date. 4 = Number of ships sailed. 5 = Arrival port. 6 = Arrival date. 7 = Notes.

The numbers in column 5 (Number of ships) are most variable and it is difficult to determine the correct number. In view of this the minimum and maximum numbers from reliable sources have been given.

Based on information from the British Naval Staff History, Battle Summary No. 22 (Arctic Convoys 1941-1945) with some changes made by Bob Ruegg and Arnold Hague (World Ship Society) and data collected at the Russian Convoys Week by Loch Ewe (www.russianarcticconvoymuseum.co.uk).

| Convoy | 2 | 3 | 4 | 5 | 5 | Notes |
|---|---|---|---|---|---|---|
| Dervish | HF | 21.08.41 | 7 | AA | 31.08.41 | |
| PQ 1 | HF | 29.09.41 | 10/11 | AA | 11.10.41 | |
| PQ 2 | SC | 17.10.41 | 6 | AA | 30.10.41 | |
| PQ 3 | HF | 09.11.41 | 8 | AA | 28.11.41 | 1 ship returned due to ice damage |
| PQ 4 | HF | 17.11.41 | 8 | AA | 28.11.41 | |
| PQ 5 | HF | 27.11.41 | 7 | AA | 12.12.41 | |
| PQ 6 | HF | 08.12.41 | 7/8 | MU MO | 20.12.41 23.12.41 | 2 ships arrived 5 ships arrived |
| PQ 7 | HF | 26.12.41 | 2 | MU | 12.01.42 | 1 sunk by U-boat |
| PQ 7 B | HF | 31.12.41 | 9 | MU | 11.01.42 | |
| PQ 8 | HF | 08.01.42 | 8 | MU | 17.01.42 | 1 ship torpedoed – towed to Murmansk. HMS *Matabele* sunk by U-boat |
| PQ 9 | HF | 01.02.42 | 7 | MU | 10.02.42 | PQ9 & PQ10 merged and sailed as one from Reykjavik. |
| PQ 10 | HF | 01.02.42 | 3 | MU | 10.02.42 | |
| PQ 11 | LE | 06.02.42 | 13 | MU | 23.02.42 | |
| PQ 12 | RK | 01.03.42 | 16/17 | MU | 12.03.42 | HMS *Shera* capsized |
| PQ 13 | RK | 20.03.42 | 19/20 | MU | 31.03.42 | 2 ships bombed and sunk 2 ships sunk by U-boats 1 ship sunk by surface craft |
| PQ 14 | RK | 08.04.42 | 24/26 | MU | 19.04.42 | 16 ships returned to Iceland due to ice and weather. 1 ship sunk by U-boat. |
| PQ 15 | RK | 26.04.42 | 23/26 | MU | 05.05.42 | Plus 2 icebreakers sailed. 3 ships torpedoed and sunk by aircraft. |

| Convoy | 2 | 3 | 4 | 5 | 5 | Notes |
|--------|---|---|---|---|---|-------|
| PQ 16 | RK | 21.05.42 | 35/36 | MU AA | 30.05.42 01.06.42 | 1 ship damaged and returned to Iceland. 5 ships bombed 1 ship torpedoed by aircraft 1 ship torpedoed by U-boat |
| PQ 17 | RK | 27.06.42 | 35/39 | AA AA MO | 11.07.42 25.07.42 28.07.41 | 1 ship grounded. 1 ship returned to Iceland due to ice damage. 23 ships sunk. |
| PQ 18 | LE | 02.09.42 | 40/44 | AA | 17.09.42 | 3 ships sunk by U-boats 10 ships sunk by torpedo bombers. |
| JW 51 A | LE | 15.12.42 | 16 | KI MO | 25.12.42 27.12.42 | |
| JW 51 B | LE | 22.12.42 | 14/15 | KI WS | 03.01.43 06.01.43 | HMS *Achates* and *Bramble* and German destroyer *Friedrich Eckholdt* sunk. |
| JW 52 | LE | 17.01.43 | 14/15 | KI | 27.01.43 | 1 ship returned to Iceland because it could not keep up with the convoy's speed. |
| JW 53 | LE | 15.02.43 | 28 | KI WS | 27.02.43 02.03.43 | 6 ships returned to Iceland due to bad weather. |
| JW 54 | LE | 15.11.43 | 18/19 | KI WS | 24.11.43 28.11.43 | |
| JW 54 B | LE | 22.11.43 | 14 | KI WS | 02.12.43 04.12.43 | |
| JW 55 A | LE | 12.12.43 | 19 | KI WS | 20.12.43 22.12.43 | |
| JW 55 B | LE | 20.12.43 | 19 | KI WS | 29.12.43 31.12.43 | German battleship *Scharnhorst* sunk during the Battle of North Cape. |

| Convoy | 2 | 3 | 4 | 5 | 5 | Notes |
|--------|---|---|---|---|---|-------|
| JW 56 A | LE | 12.01.44 | 20 | KI | 28.01.44 | Convoy put in to port at Akureyri due to bad weather. 5 ships returned, 3 were sunk by U-boats and the escort HMS *Hardy* was sunk by U-boat. |
| JW 56 B | LE | 22.01.44 | 16/17 | KI | 01.02.44 | |
| JW 57 | LE | 20.02.44 | 42/45 | KI | 28.02.44 | HMS *Mahratta* sunk by U-boat |
| JW 58 | LE | 27.03.44 | 49 | KI | 05.04.44 | 1 ship returned to Iceland due to ice damage. |
| JW 59 | LE | 15.08.44 | 33/34 | KI WS | 25.08.44 27.08.44 | HMS *Kite* sunk by U-boat. |
| JW 60 | LE | 15.09.44 | 30/31 | KI WS | 23.09.44 25.09.44 | |
| JW 61 | LE | 20.10.44 | 29/30 | KI WS | 28.10.44 30.10.44 | |
| JW 62 | LE | 29.11.44 | 30 | KI WS | 07.12.44 09.12.44 | |
| JW 63 | LE | 30.12.44 | 35/38 | KI WS | 08.01.45 09.01.45 | |
| JW 64 | CD | 03.02.45 | 26/29 | KI WS | 13.02.45 15.02.45 | |
| JW 65 | CD | 11.03.45 | 24/26 | KI | 21.03.45 | 2 ships and HMS *Lapwing* sunk by U-boats. |
| JW 66 | CD | 16.04.45 | 22/27 | KI WS | 25.04.45 28.04.45 | |
| JW 67 | CD | 12.05.45 | 23 | KI WS | 20.05.45 22.05.45 | |
| QP 1 | AA | 28.09.41 | 14 | .SC | 09.10.41 | |
| QP 2 | AA | 02.11.41 | 12 | KW | 17.11.41 | |
| QP 3 | AA | 27.11.41 | 10 | SF | 07.12.41 | 2 ships returned due to bad weather |
| QP 4 | AA | 29.12.41 | 13 · | SF | 16.01.42 | 2 ships put into Murmansk |
| QP 5 | MU | 13.01.42 | 4 | RV | 24.01.42 | |

| Convoy | 2 | 3 | 4 | 5 | 5 | Notes |
|---|---|---|---|---|---|---|
| QP 6 | MU | 24.01.42 | 6 | UK | 02.02.42 | |
| QP 7 | MU | 12.02.42 | 8 | SF | 22.02.42 | |
| QP 8 | MU | 01.03.42 | 15 | RV | 11.03.42 | 1 straggler sunk by surface craft |
| QP 9 | MU | 21.03.42 | 18/19 | RV | 03.04.42 | |
| QP 10 | MU | 10.04.42 | 16 | RV | 21.04.42 | 1 ship returned to Murmansk, 2 ships bombed and sunk and 2 ships sunk by U-boats |
| QP 11 | MU | 28.0442 | 13 | RV | 07.05.42 | HMS *Edinburgh* sunk by U-boat and 1 straggler sunk by surface craft |
| QP 12 | MU | 21.05.42 | 15/17 | RV | 29.05.42 | 1 ship returned to Murmansk |
| QP 13 | AA<br>MU | 26.06.42<br>27.06.42 | 12<br>23 | LE<br>RV | 07.07.42<br>07.07.42 | 4 ships and HMS *Niger* sunk in a British minefield. 1 ship damaged and partly beached |
| QP 14 | AA | 13.09.42 | 15/20 | LE | 26.09.42 | 3 ships sunk by U-boats and HMS *Somali*, HMS *Leda* and RFA *Gray Ranger* (Force Q) sunk by U-boats |
| QP 15 | AA | 17.11.42 | 28/31 | LE | --.--. | Scattered by gales and appalling weather. 2 ships sunk by U-boats |
| RA 51 | KI | 30.12.42 | 14 | LE | 11.01.43 | |
| RA 52 | KI | 29.01.43 | 10/11 | LE | 08.02.43 | 1 ship sunk by U-boat |
| RA 53 | KI | 01.03.43 | 30 | LE | 14.03.43 | 3 ships sunk by U-boats and 1 ship foundered in a gale |
| RA 54 A | AA | 01.11.43 | 13 | LE | 14.11.43 | |
| RA 54 B | AA | 26.11.43 | 9 | LE | 09.12.43 | |
| RA 55 A | KI | 23.12.43 | 22/23 | LE | 01.01.44 | 1 ship returned to Kola Inlet |

| Convoy | 2 | 3 | 4 | 5 | 5 | Notes |
|--------|---|---|---|---|---|-------|
| RA 55 B | KI | 31.12.43 | 8 | LE | 08.01.44 | |
| RA 56 | KI | 03.02.44 | 37/39 | LE | 11.02.44 | |
| RA 57 | KI | 02.03.44 | 31 | LE | 10.03.44 | 1 ship sunk by U-boat |
| RA 58 | KI | 07.03.44 | 36/38 | LE | 14.04.44 | |
| RA 59 | KI | 28.04.44 | 45 | LE | 06.05.44 | 1 ship sunk by U-boat |
| RA 59 A | KI | 28.08.44 | 9 | LE | 06.09.44 | |
| RA 60 | KI | 28.09.44 | 30 | LE | 05.10.44 | 2 ships sunk by U-boats |
| RA 61 | WS KI | 30.10.44 02.11.44 | 33 | LE CL | 09.11.44 10.11.44 | |
| RA 62 | KI | 10.12.44 | 28 | LE CL | 19.12.44 20.12.44 | Torpedo bomber attacks re-commenced. |
| RA 63 | KI | 11.01.45 | 30/31 | LE CL | 21.01.45 23.01.45 | |
| RA 64 | KI | 17.02.45 | 33/36 | LE CL | 28.02.45 01.03.45 | 1 ship returned to Kola Inlet, 1 ship sunk by U-boat, 1 straggler sunk by torpedo aircraft, 2 ships sunk before joining the convoy off Kola Inlet and HMS *Bluebell* sunk by U-boat |
| RA 65 | KI | 23.03.45 | 25/26 | KW CL BF | 31.03.45 01.04.45 01.04.45 | |
| RA 66 | KI | 29.04.45 | 24/27 | CL | 08.05.45 | |
| RA 67 | KI | 23.05.45 | 23/25 | CL | 31.05.45 | |

# Bibliography

The Admiralty; *Arctic Convoys 1941–1945, Battle Summary No. 22*; Naval Staff History, London, 1954.

Beesly Patrick; *Very Special Intelligence*; Hamish Hamilton, London, 1977 and Doubleday, New York, 1978. (An interesting book dealing with Admiralty intelligence by an officer who served there as the Deputy Head of the Submarine Tracking Room.)

Brennecke, Jochen; *Jäger – Gejagte*; Koehlers Verlag, Jugendheim, 1956. (One of the early great classics about life in U-boats, written by an ex-war correspondent.)

Busch, Harald; *So war der Ubootskrieg (U-boats at War)*; Deutsche Heimat Verlag, Bielefeld, 1954 (Also one of great early classics about the U-boat war.)

German U-boat Museum; Various pages on the Internet at www.dubm.de

Hall, Ivan; *Christmas in Archangel*, A Memoir of Life in the Merchant Navy 1939–1946; Trafford Publishing, North America, 2009. (A most interesting account.)

Knudsen, Svei Aage; Deutsache U-boote vor Norwegen 1940-1945; Verlag E.S. Mittler, Hamburg, Berlin, Bonn, 2005. (A detailed and most comprehensive book. Most useful.)

Lees, David J.; *Operation Cabal*; The U-boat Archive Series, Military Press, Milton Keynes 2005. (Edited by Jak P. Mallmann Showell. Deals with the delivery of German U-boats from the United Kingdom to Russia, November 1945-January 1946.)

Niestle, Axel; *German U-boat Losses during World War II*; Frontline Books, London, 2014. (A fully revised edition of an earlier book with the same title, published by Greenhill, London, 1998.)

Nusser, Franz; *Die Arktisunternehmen des deutschen Marinewetterdienstes in den Jahren 1940-45*; Deutscher Wetterdienst, Seewetteramt, Hamburg, 1979.

Ritter, Christiane; *Eine Frau erlebt die Polarnacht*; Ullstein Verlag, Frankfurt, Berlin, Wien. Originally published in 1938 and re-printed after the war, translated as *A Woman in the Polar Night* and available through the Internet.

Röll, Hans-Joachim; U997 – Geleitzugschlachten im Eismeer; Flechsig Verlag, Würzburg, 2012. (An interesting and most detailed account.)

Rohwer, J.; *Axis Submarine Successes of World War II 1939–45*; Greenhill, London, 1998.

- and Hümmelchen, G.; *Chronology of the War at Sea 1939–1945*; Greenhill, London, 1992. (A good, solid and informative work. Well indexed and most useful for anyone studying the war at sea.)

Ruegg, Bob and Hague, Arnold; *Convoys to Russia*; World Ship Society, Kendal, 1992. (A small but excellent and most useful publication. One of the best on the subject.)

Selinger, Franz; *Von 'Nanok' bis 'Eismitte'*; Convent Verlag, Hamburg 2001.

(German meteorological activities in the Arctic 1940–1945. A brilliant book with excellent illustrations by *the* leading authority on the subject.)

Selinger, Franz; *Abriss der Unternehmungen des Marinewetterdienstes in der Arktis 1945-45 nach dem Erkenntnisstand von 1990*; Deutscher Wetterdienst, Seewetteramt, Hamburg 1991.

Showell, Jak P. Mallmann; *U-boats at War – Landings on Hostile Shores*; Ian Allan, London and Naval Institute Press, Annapolis, 2000.

-; *The German Navy in World War Two*; Arms and Armour Press, London, 1979; Naval Institute Press, Annapolis, 1979 and translated as *Das Buch der deutschen Kriegsmarine*; Motorbuch Verlag, Stuttgart, 1982. (Covers history; organisation, the ships, code-writers, naval charts and a section on ranks, uniforms, awards and insignias by Gordon Williamson. Named by the United States Naval Institute as 'One of the Outstanding Naval Books of the Year'.)

-; *Hitler's Navy*; Seaforth Publishing, Barnsley, 2009. (A revised version of *The German Navy in World War Two* with additional text and new photos.)

-; *U-boats under the Swastika*; Ian Allan, Shepperton, 1973; Arco, New York, 1973 and translated as *Uboote gegen England*; Motorbuch, Stuttgart, 1974. (A well illustrated introduction to the German U-boat Arm, which was one of the longest-selling naval books in Germany.)

-; *U-boats under the Swastika*; Ian Allan, Shepperton, 1987 and Naval Institute Press, Annapolis, 1987. (A second edition with different photos and new text of the above title.)

-; *Enigma U-boats—Breaking the Code*; Ian Allan, London, 2000. (Contains information about floating weather stations in the Arctic.)

Wegener, Alfred; *Institut für Polar und Meeresforschung—125 Jahre deutsche Polarforschung*; Bremerhaven, 1993. (An interesting book, well illustrated and useful.)

Wetzel, Eckard; *U-boote vor Murmansk*; Ullstein Verlag, Berlin, 2008. (About U995 in the Polar Seas, sadly there does not seem to be an English translation.)

Witthöft, Hans Jürgen; *Lexikon zur deutschen Marinegeschichte*; Koehler; Herford, 1977. (An excellent two-volume encyclopaedia.)

Woodman, Richard; *Arctic Convoys 1941–1945*; Pen and Sword Maritime, Barnsley, 2011. (Interesting, useful and most comprehensive. Probably 'the' definite account of the Arctic convoys with a gripping narrative.)

Wynn, Kenneth; *U-boat Operations of the Second World War*; Chatham, London, 1997. (A useful reference book.)

# Index

Names have been indexed only once for each chapter, even where they occur more frequently and references in tables and lists have not been included in this index.